HOW
MONEY
WORKS

THE FACTS
VISUALLY EXPLAINED

Senior editor	Kathryn Hennessy	**Publisher**	Liz Wheeler
Project editor	Sam Kennedy	**Publishing director**	Jonathan Metcalf
Senior art editor	Gadi Farfour	**Art director**	Karen Self
Project art editor	Saffron Stocker	**Senior jacket designer**	Mark Cavanagh
Editors	Alison Sturgeon, Allie Collins, Diane Pengelley, Georgina Palffy, Jemima Dunne, Tash Khan	**Jacket editor**	Clare Gell
Designers	Clare Joyce, Vanessa Hamilton, Renata Latipova	**Jacket design development manager**	Sophia MTT
Managing editor	Gareth Jones	**Pre-production producer**	Gillian Reid
Senior managing art editor	Lee Griffiths	**Senior producer**	Mandy Inness

———

HOW MONEY WORKS

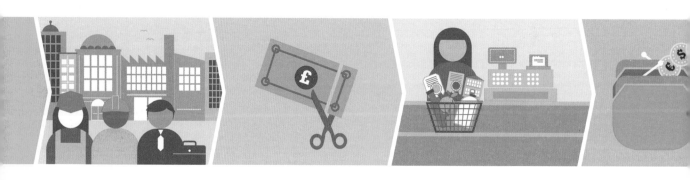

Contents

Introduction   8

MONEY BASICS   10

The evolution of money   12
Barter, IOUs, and money   14
Artefacts of money   16
The emergence of modern
  economics   20
Economic theories and money   22

PROFIT-MAKING AND FINANCIAL INSTITUTIONS   24

Corporate accounting   26
Net income   28
Expensing vs capitalizing   30
Depreciation, amortization, depletion   32
Smoothing earnings   34
Cash flow   36
Gearing ratio and risk   40
How companies use debt   42
Financial reporting   44

Financial instruments   46
Shares   48
Bonds   50
Derivatives   52

Financial markets   54
The money market   56
Foreign exchange and trading   58
Primary and secondary markets   60
Predicting market changes   62
Arbitrage   64
Manipulating the stock market   66
Day trading   68

Financial institutions   70
Commercial and mortgage banks   72
Investment banks   74
Brokerages   76
Insurance risk and regulation   78
Investment companies   80
Non-bank financial institutions   82

First published in Great Britain in 2017
by Dorling Kindersley Limited,
80 Strand, London, WC2R 0RL

A Penguin Random House Company

2 4 6 8 10 9 7 5 3 1
001–282964–March/2017

Copyright © 2017 Dorling Kindersley Limited

Printed in China

A CIP catalogue record for this book is
available from the British Library.

ISBN: 978-0-2412-2599-8

A WORLD OF IDEAS:
SEE ALL THERE IS TO KNOW

www.dk.com

GOVERNMENT FINANCE AND PUBLIC MONEY 84

The money supply 86
Increasing money circulation 88
Banking reserves 90
Recession and the money supply 92
Recession to depression 94

Managing state finance 96
Governments and money 98
The central bank 100
Budget constraint 104
How tax works 106
Government borrowing 108
Public debt 110
Accountability 112

Attempting control 114
Reading economic indicators 116
Deciding on economic policy 118
Interest rates 120
Quantitative easing 124
The level of taxation 126
Government spending 128
How governments provide for
  the future 130
Inflation 132
Balance of payments 136
International currency fluctuations 138
Managing state pensions 140

**Why governments fail
financially** 142
How governments fail: hyperinflation 144
How governments fail: debt default 146

Contributors

Dr Julian Sims (consultant editor) entered academia after a successful career in industry in the US and UK. He is a lecturer in the Department of Management at Birkbeck, University of London, UK; a Chartered Accountant (CPA Aus); and a Chartered Information Technology Practitioner (CITP). His work is widely published in academic journals.

Marianne Curphey is an award-winning financial writer, blogger, and columnist. She has worked as a writer and editor at *The Guardian*, *The Times*, and *The Telegraph*, and a wide range of financial websites and magazines.

Emma Lunn is an award-winning personal finance journalist whose work regularly appears in high profile newspapers such as *The Guardian*, *The Independent*, and *The Telegraph*, as well as a number of specialist publications and websites.

PERSONAL FINANCE 148

Worth, wealth, and income 150
Calculating and analysing net worth 152
Income and wealth 154
Converting income into wealth 156
Generating income 158
Generating wealth 160

Investments for income 162
Dividends from shares 164
Earning income from savings 166
Investing in managed funds 168
Rental income from property 170
Life assurance 172

Wealth-building investments 174
Investing in property 176
Home equity 180
Shares 182
Managed funds 184

Managing investments 186
Asset allocation and diversification 188
Dollar cost averaging 190
Risk tolerance 192
The optimal portfolio 194

Pensions and retirement 196
Saving and investing for a pension 198
Converting pensions into income 202

Debt 204
Why people use debt 206
Interest and compound interest 208
Loans 210
Mortgages 212
Credit unions 216
Credit cards 218

Money in the digital age 220
Cryptocurrency 222
Bitcoin 224
Crowdfunding 226
Peer-to-peer lending 228

Money in the UK 230
Index 248
Acknowledgments 256

James Meadway is an economist and policy adviser who has worked at the New Economics Foundation – an independent British think tank – the UK Treasury, the Royal Society, and for the Shadow Chancellor of the Exchequer.

Philip Parker is a historian and former British diplomat and publisher, who studied at the Johns Hopkins School of Advanced International Studies. A critically acclaimed author, he has written books that focus on the history of world trade.

Alexandra Black studied business communications before writing for financial newspaper group Nikkei Inc. in Japan and working as an editor at investment bank JP Morgan. She has written numerous books and articles on subjects as diverse as finance, business, technology, and fashion.

Introduction

Money is the oil that keeps the machinery of our world turning. By giving goods and services an easily measured value, money facilitates the billions of transactions that take place every day. Without it, the industry and trade that form the basis of modern economies would grind to a halt and the flow of wealth around the world would cease.

Money has fulfilled this vital role for thousands of years. Before its invention, people bartered, swapping goods they produced themselves for things they needed from others. Barter is sufficient for simple transactions, but not when the things traded are of differing values, or not available at the same time. Money, by contrast, has a recognized uniform value and is widely accepted. At heart a simple concept, over many thousands of years it has become very complex indeed.

At the start of the modern age, individuals and governments began to establish banks, and other financial institutions were formed. Eventually, ordinary people could deposit their money in a bank account and earn interest, borrow money and buy property, invest their wages in businesses, or start companies themselves. Banks could also insure against the sorts of calamities that might devastate families or traders, encouraging risk in the pursuit of profit.

Today it is a nation's government and central bank that control a country's economy. The central bank issues currency, determines how much of it is in circulation, and decides how much interest it will charge banks to borrow its money. While governments still print and guarantee money, in today's world it no longer needs to exist as physical coins or notes, but can be found solely in digital form.

This book examines every aspect of how money works, including its history, financial markets and institutions, government finance, profit-making, personal finance, wealth, shares, and pensions. Through visual explanations and practical examples that make even the most complex concept immediately accessible, *How Money Works* offers a clear understanding of what money is all about, and how it shapes modern society.

MONEY
BASICS

> The evolution of money

The evolution of money

People originally traded surplus commodities with each other in a process known as bartering. The value of each good traded could be debated, however, and money evolved as a practical solution to the complexities of bartering hundreds of different things. Over the centuries, money has appeared in many forms, but, whatever guise it takes, whether a physical coin or note, or as a digital currency, money always provides a fixed value against which any item can be compared.

The ascent of money

Money has become increasingly complex over time. What began as a means of recording trade exchanges, then appeared in the form of coins and notes, is now primarily digital.

Barter
(10,000–3000BCE)
In early forms of trading, specific items were exchanged for others agreed by the negotiating parties to be of similar value. *See pp.14–15*

Evidence of trade records
(from 7000BCE)
Pictures of items were used to record trade exchanges, becoming more complex as values were established and documented. *See pp.16–17*

Coinage
(600BCE–1100CE)
Defined weights of precious metals used by some merchants, were later formalized as coins that were usually issued by states. *See pp.16–17*

SUPPLY AND DEMAND

The law of supply and demand explains how the availability of a product (the quantity supplied) and the demand for that product affects its price. When supply is low and demand is high the price of a product tends to rise, whereas when a product is plentiful (there is high supply) but demand is low the price of a product tends to fall. In a free market the price of a product will only settle when the quantity demanded equals the quantity that is supplied and market equilibrium is reached. *See pp.20–21*

US$80.9 trillion

the estimated amount of money in existence today

Bank notes
(1100–2000)
States began to use bank notes, issuing paper IOUs that were traded as currency, and could be exchanged for coins at any time. *See pp.18–19*

Digital money
(2000 onwards)
Money can now exist "virtually", on computers, and large transactions can take place without any physical cash changing hands. *See pp.220–225*

Macro- versus Microeconomics

Macroeconomics studies the impact of changes in the economy as a whole. Microeconomics examines the behaviour of smaller groups.

Macroeconomics
This measures changes in indicators that affect the whole economy.

❯ **Money supply** The amount of money circulating in an economy.

❯ **Unemployment** The number of people who cannot find work.

❯ **Inflation** The amount by which prices rise each year.

Microeconomics

This examines the effects that decisions of firms and individuals have on the economy.

❯ **Industrial organization** The impact of monopolies and cartels on the economy.

❯ **Wages** The impact that salary levels, which are affected by labour and production costs, have on consumer spending.

Barter, IOUs, and money

Barter – the direct exchange of goods – formed the basis of trade for thousands of years. Adam Smith, 18th-century author of *The Wealth of Nations*, was one of the first to identify it as a precursor to money.

Barter in practice

Essentially barter involves the exchange of an item (such as a cow) for one or more items of a perceived equal "value" (for example a bushel of wheat). For the most part the two parties bring the goods with them and hand them over at the time of a transaction. Sometimes, one of the parties will accept an "I owe you" (IOU) or even a token, that it is agreed can be exchanged for the same goods or something else at a later date.

PROS AND CONS OF BARTER

Pros

> **Trading relationships** Fosters links between trading partners.

> **Physical goods are exchanged** Does not rely on trust that money will retain its value.

Cons

> **Market needed** Both parties must want what the other offers.

> **Hard to establish a set value to items** A goat may have a certain value to one party on one day, but less a week later.

> **Goods may not be easily divisible** A living animal cannot be divided, for example.

> **Large-scale transactions can be difficult** Transporting one goat is easy, moving a thousand is not.

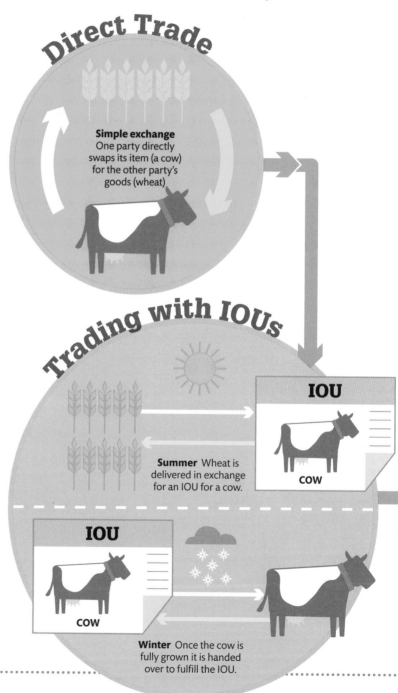

Direct Trade

Simple exchange
One party directly swaps its item (a cow) for the other party's goods (wheat)

Trading with IOUs

IOU
COW

Summer Wheat is delivered in exchange for an IOU for a cow.

IOU
COW

Winter Once the cow is fully grown it is handed over to fulfill the IOU.

How it works

In its simplest form, two parties to a barter transaction agree a price (such as a cow for wheat) and physically hand over the goods at the agreed time. However, this may not always be possible – for example, the wheat might not be ready to harvest, so one party may accept an IOU to be exchanged later for the physical goods. Eventually these IOUs acquire their own value and the IOU holder could exchange them for something else of the same value as the original commodity (perhaps apples instead of wheat). The IOUs are now performing the same function as actual money.

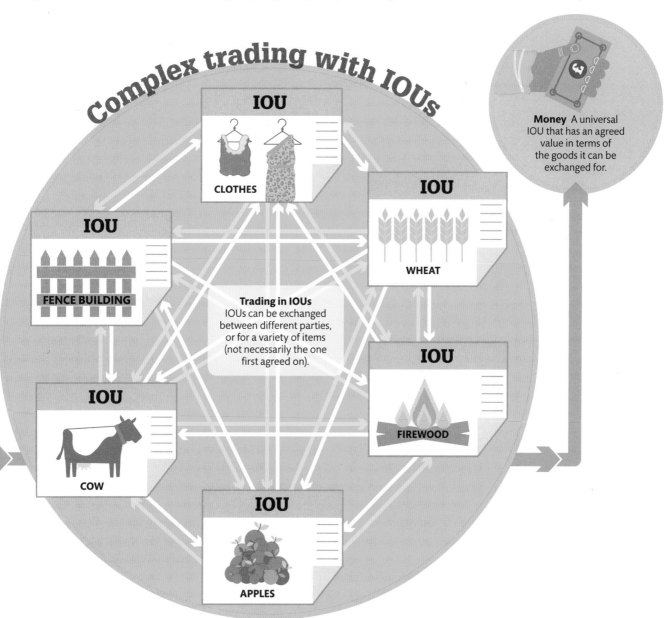

Complex trading with IOUs

IOU
CLOTHES

IOU
WHEAT

IOU
FENCE BUILDING

Trading in IOUs
IOUs can be exchanged between different parties, or for a variety of items (not necessarily the one first agreed on).

IOU
FIREWOOD

IOU
COW

IOU
APPLES

Money A universal IOU that has an agreed value in terms of the goods it can be exchanged for.

Artefacts of money

Since the early attempts at setting values for bartered goods, "money" has come in many forms, from IOUs to tokens. Cows, shells, and precious metals have all been used.

How it works

Bartering was a very immediate method of trading. Once writing was invented, records could be kept detailing the "value" of goods traded as well as of the "IOUs". Eventually tokens such as beads, coloured cowrie shells, or lumps of gold were assigned a specific value, which meant that they could be exchanged directly for goods. It was a small step from this to making tokens explicitly to represent value in the form of metal discs – the first coins – in Lydia, Asia Minor, around 650 BCE. For more than 2,000 years, coins made from precious metals such as gold, silver, and (for small transactions) copper formed the main medium of monetary exchange.

Characteristics of money

Money is not money unless it has all of the following defining characteristics: it must have value, be durable, portable, uniform, divisible, in limited supply, and be usable as a means of exchange. Underlying all of these characteristics is trust – people must be confident that if they accept money, they can use it to pay for goods.

Item of worth

Most money originally had an intrinsic value, such as that of the precious metal that was used to make the coin. This in itself acted as some guarantee that the coin would be accepted.

Timeline of artefacts

Sumerian cuneiform tablets
Scribes record transactions on clay tablets, which can also act as receipts.

Lydian gold coins
In Lydia, a mixture of gold and silver is formed into discs, or coins, stamped with inscriptions.

| · 5,000 BCE · | · 4,000 BCE · | · 1,000 BCE · | · 600 BCE · | · 600 BCE · |

Barter
Early trade involves directly exchanging items – often perishable ones such as a cow.

Cowrie shells
Used as currency across India and the South Pacific, they appear in many colours and sizes.

Athenian drachma
The Athenians use silver from Laurion to mint a currency used right across the Greek world.

Store of value

Money acts as a means by which people can store their wealth for future use. It must not, therefore, be perishable, and it helps if it is of a practical size that can be stored and transported easily.

GEORG SIMMEL AND *THE PHILOSOPHY OF MONEY*

Published in 1900, German sociologist Georg Simmel's book *The Philosophy of Money* looked at the meaning of value in relation to money. Simmel observed that in premodern societies, people made objects, but the value they attached to each of them was difficult to fix as it was assessed by incompatible systems (based on honour, time, and labour). Money made it easier to assign consistent values to objects, which Simmel believed made interactions between people more rational, as it freed them from personal ties, and provided greater freedom of choice.

Means of exchange

It must be possible to exchange money freely and widely for goods, and its value should be as stable as possible. It helps if that value is easily divisible and if there are sufficient denominations so that change can be given.

Unit of account

Money can be used to record wealth possessed, traded, or spent – personally and nationally. It helps if only one recognized authority issues money – if anybody could issue it, then trust in its value would disappear.

Han dynasty coin
Often made of bronze or copper, early Chinese coins have holes punched in their centre.

200BCE

Byzantine coin
Early Byzantine coins are pure gold; later ones also contain metals such as copper.

700CE

Arabic dirham
Many silver coins from the Islamic empire are carried to Scandinavia by Vikings.

900CE

27BCE

900CE

Roman coin
Bearing the head of the emperor, these coins circulate throughout the Roman Empire.

Anglo-Saxon coin
This 10th century silver penny has an inscription stating that Offa is King ("rex") of Mercia.

The economics of money

From the 16th century, understanding of the nature of money became more sophisticated. Economics as a discipline emerged, in part to help explain the inflation caused in Europe by the large-scale importation of silver from the newly discovered Americas. National banks were established in the late 17th century, with the duty of regulating the countries' money supplies.

By the early 20th century, money became separated from its direct relationship to precious metal. The Gold Standard collapsed altogether in the 1930s. By the mid-20th century, new ways of trading with money appeared such as credit cards, digital transactions, and even forms of money such as cryptocurrencies and financial derivatives. As a result, the amount of money in existence and in circulation increased enormously.

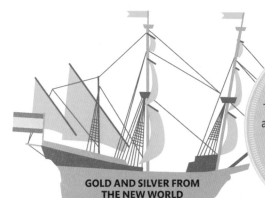

GOLD AND SILVER FROM THE NEW WORLD

1540–1640
Potosi inflation
The Spanish discover silver at Potosi, Bolivia, and cause a century of inflation by shipping 350 tons of the metal back to Europe annually.

COPPER

1542–1551
The great debasement
England's Henry VIII debases the silver penny, making it three-quarters copper. Inflation increases as trust drops.

EARLY 1970s
Great inflation
Rising oil prices and labour costs cause inflation to rise, especially in the UK, where it peaks at 25 per cent in 1975.

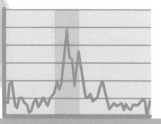

FROM 1844
Gold Standard
The British pound is tied to a defined equivalent amount of gold. Other countries adopt a similar "Gold Standard".

1970s
Credit cards
The creation of credit cards enables consumers to access short-term credit to make smaller purchases. This leads to a growth in personal debt.

1990s
Digital money
The easy transfer of funds and convenience of electronic payments becomes increasingly popular as internet use increases.

GRESHAM'S LAW

The monetary principle "bad money drives out good" was formulated by British financier Sir Thomas Gresham (1519-71). He observed that if a country debases its currency – reducing the precious metal in its coins – the coins are worth less than the metal they contain. As a result, people spend the "bad" coins and hoard the "good" undebased ones.

22 carat
gold has been used in all British gold sovereigns since 1816

JOINT-STOCK COMPANY

1553
Early joint-stock companies
Merchants in England begin to form companies in which investors buy shares (stock) and share its rewards.

1694
Bank of England
The Bank of England is created as a body that can raise funds at a low interest rate and manage national debt.

1775
US dollar
The Continental Congress authorizes the issue of United States dollars in 1775, but the first national currency is not minted by the US Treasury until 1794.

1696
The Royal Mint
Isaac Newton becomes Warden of the Mint. He argues that debasing undermines confidence and so new silver coins should be minted.

1999
Euro
Twelve EU countries join together to replace their national currencies with the Euro. Bank notes and coins are issued three years later.

2008
Bitcoin
Bitcoin – a form of electronic money that exists solely as encrypted data on servers – is announced. The first transaction takes place in January 2009.

The emergence of modern economics

By the 18th century, people had begun to study the economy more closely, as thinkers tried to understand how the trade and investment decisions of individuals could have an effect on prices and wages throughout a country.

How it works

With the massive expansion of trade that accompanied the discovery of the Americas and the growth of nation states in Europe in the 16th and 17th centuries, some individuals began to think in more detail about the idea of economics. They variously suggested that controlling the level of imports (mercantilism), trading only in the goods a country made best (comparative advantage), or choosing not to intervene in the markets (laissez-faire) might improve their people's economic well-being. In the 18th century, economist Adam Smith proposed that government intervention – controlling wages and prices – was unnecessary because the self-interested decisions of individuals, who all want to be better off, cumulatively ensure the prosperity of their society as a whole. In addition, he believed that in a freely competitive market, the impetus to make profit ensures that goods are valued at a fair price.

Adam Smith's "invisible hand"

In his book *The Wealth of Nations* (1776), the Scottish economist Adam Smith suggested that the sum of the decisions made by individuals, each of whom want to be better off, results in a country becoming more prosperous without those individuals ever having consciously desired that end. According to Smith, where there is demand for goods, sellers will enter the market. In the pursuit of profit they will increase the production of these goods, so supporting industry.

Furthermore, in a competitive market, the self-interest of sellers will limit the price rises they can demand: if they charge too much, buyers will stop purchasing their goods, or they will lose sales to competitors willing to charge less. This has a deflationary effect on prices and ensures that the economy remains in balance. Smith referred to this market mechanism, which turns individual self-interest into wider economic prosperity, as an "invisible hand" guiding the economy.

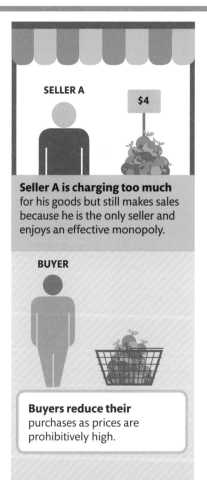

Seller A is charging too much for his goods but still makes sales because he is the only seller and enjoys an effective monopoly.

Buyers reduce their purchases as prices are prohibitively high.

Seller B sees an opportunity to enter the market and sets up her own stall, selling at a lower price in order to undercut A.

As Seller B's price is lower buyers begin to buy from her instead of Seller A.

PROTECTIONISM AND MERCANTILISM

Adam Smith's encouragement of free trade and competition was at odds with the dominant economic theories of his time. Most thinkers supported some form of protectionism – an economic policy in which a government imposes high trade tariffs in order to protect its industry from competition. In Europe at that time, this took the form of mercantilism, which held that to be strong, a country must increase its exports and do everything possible to decrease its imports, as exports brought money into a country, while imports enriched foreign merchants. This theory led to strict governmental controls on trade such as the Navigation Acts, which forbade any trade between Britain and its colonies in non-British ships.

Mercantilism began to go out of fashion during the late 18th century under the pressure of the new ideas about economic specialization put forward by Adam Smith and others.

> "By pursuing his own interests, he frequently promotes that of the society more effectually than when he really intends to promote it"
>
> **Adam Smith**, *The Wealth of Nations* (1776)

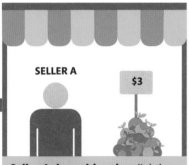

SELLER A

$3

Seller A drops his price slightly in order to regain customers and compete with Seller B.

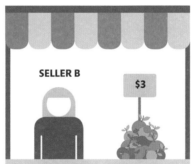

SELLER B

$3

Seller B sees she can raise her prices slightly and her goods will still be in demand.

The goods have found a price at which buyers are happy to continue to purchase. The "invisible hand" has worked and the market is now in equilibrium.

✓ NEED TO KNOW

❯ **Market equilibrium** When the amount of certain goods demanded by buyers matches the amount supplied by sellers – the point at which all parties are satisfied with a good's price.

❯ **Laissez-faire** An economic theory, which holds that the market will produce the best solutions in the absence of government interference. Trade, prices, and wages do not need to be regulated, as the market itself will correct imbalances in them.

❯ **Comparative advantage** The idea that countries should specialize in those goods they can produce at the lowest cost. By avoiding producing goods in which they do not have a comparative advantage, countries will become more efficient and therefore better off.

Economic theories and money

Since the birth of modern economic thought, people have tried to work out how the quantity of money in an economy affects prices and the behaviour of consumers and businesses.

Keynes' general theory of money

In his 1935 book *General Theory*, John Maynard Keynes argued that government spending and taxation levels affect prices more than the quantity of money in the economy. He proposed that in times of recession a government should increase spending to encourage employment, and reduce taxes to stimulate the economy.

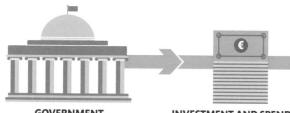

GOVERNMENT
When output is shrinking and unemployment rising, a government must decide how to react.

INVESTMENT AND SPENDING
As demand falls, firms reduce production, which raises unemployment and lowers demand.

STIMULATING DEMAND
The government increases its spending, for example on infrastructure. This reduces unemployment.

DEFENCE
WELFARE, HEALTHCARE, EDUCATION, AND POLICING
BUILDING: HOUSES, SCHOOLS, HOSPITALS
TRANSPORT INFRASTRUCTURE

Fisher's quantity theory of money

American economist Irvine Fisher's theory argued that there is a direct link between the amount of money in the economy and price level, with more money in circulation increasing prices.

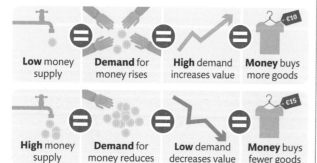

Low money supply = **Demand** for money rises = **High** demand increases value = **Money** buys more goods

High money supply = **Demand** for money reduces = **Low** demand decreases value = **Money** buys fewer goods

Marx's labour theory of value

The German economist Karl Marx argued that the real price (or economic value) of goods should be determined not by the demand for those goods, but by the value of the labour that went into producing them.

1 pair of shoes = **2 hours'** labour at €10 / hour = **€20**

1 dress = **10 hours'** labour at €10 / hour = **€100**

How it works

Scholars in the early 16th century were the first to note that the abundance of silver coming into Spain from the New World led to increased prices. Economists of the 18th-century Classical School believed that the market would correct for such events, reaching an equilibrium price by itself. By the early 20th century some economists believed that intervention by the government was necessary to maintain a balanced economy, arguing that government spending could boost employment by increasing overall demand.

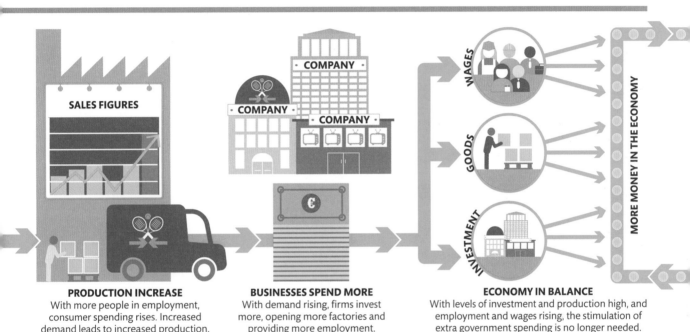

SALES FIGURES

COMPANY
COMPANY
COMPANY

WAGES
GOODS
INVESTMENT

MORE MONEY IN THE ECONOMY

PRODUCTION INCREASE
With more people in employment, consumer spending rises. Increased demand leads to increased production.

BUSINESSES SPEND MORE
With demand rising, firms invest more, opening more factories and providing more employment.

ECONOMY IN BALANCE
With levels of investment and production high, and employment and wages rising, the stimulation of extra government spending is no longer needed.

Hayek's business cycle

Austrian economist Friedrich Hayek noted a cycle in the economy, in which interest rates fall during a recession. This leads to an over-expansion of credit, necessitating a rise in interest rates to counter excess demand.

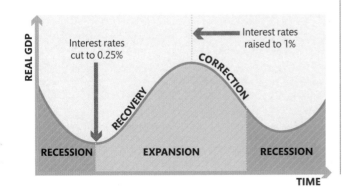

REAL GDP

Interest rates cut to 0.25%

Interest rates raised to 1%

CORRECTION

RECOVERY

RECESSION **EXPANSION** **RECESSION**

TIME

Friedman's monetarism

American economist Milton Friedman argued that governments could change interest rates to affect the money supply. Cuts would stimulate consumer spending; rises would restrict it and reduce the money supply.

LOW INTEREST
€100

Employee paid €100
Spends €100
Supermarket pays supplier €100
Supplier pays employees €100

HIGH INTEREST
€50

Employee paid €100
Saves €50 and spends €50
Supermarket pays supplier €50
Supplier pays employees €50

PROFIT-MAKING AND FINANCIAL INSTITUTIONS

> Corporate accounting > Financial instruments
> Financial markets > Financial institutions

Corporate accounting

Companies use money in different ways – some borrow to pay for investment to grow bigger, while others prefer to hold a lot of cash and to rely on income generation rather than borrowing in order to expand. Much depends on the type of business and management style. Start-ups and smaller companies tend to need a lot of cash in the early days, while larger, more established companies are better at growing their income internally and may hoard cash.

Cashflow

This indicates how much income a business is generating, and how this compares to its costs and the expenses that it has to pay out. A company is said to have a positive cashflow if its income exceeds its expenses. *See pp.36–39*

Smoothing earnings

This business practice, aimed at reducing volatility in income and reported profit, uses accounting techniques to limit fluctuations in company earnings. *See pp.34–35*

Net income

This is the income that a company reports at the end of the financial year after its costs and expenses have been deducted. It is calculated by starting with the total revenue earned and then taking away the total cost of tax, expenses, banking and interest charges, depreciation of assets, staff costs, and any other expenses involved in operating the business. *See pp.28–29*

Income = £10,000

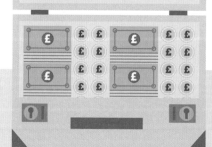

US$**1.7** trillion
the amount of cash, and cash equivalents, held by US non-financial companies in 2015

Expenses

These are the costs a business incurs on a regular basis. They might include staff wages, insurance premiums, utility bills, and other expenses involved in the running of the company.

Assets

These are the items that a company owns, some of which generate income, and many of which may also appreciate in value. Businesses often choose between buying assets that will fall in value, or leasing equipment.

Gearing ratio

Capital gearing is the balance between a company's capital (its available money or assets) and its funding by short- or long-term loans, expressed as a percentage. A company with relatively low gearing is regarded as being less risky and in a better position to cope with an economic downturn.
See pp.40–41

Debt = £2,000

Expensing vs Capitalizing

When a business incurs a cost or an expense it needs to record it in the company accounts, either by showing the full amount at the time it happens, or by spreading the cost over a number of years. *See pp.30–31*

Depreciation

This is a measure of how much the value of an asset falls over time, often due to use, or "wear and tear". Companies can record the reduction in the value of assets such as vehicles, machinery, or other equipment as depreciation in their accounts. This will then lower the company's tax liability and reduce their taxable profit. *See pp.32–33*

Net income

When a business reports how it has fared financially over the year, it provides investors with a figure for its net income. This is a good way to understand how much real profit a business is making.

How it works

If companies were simply to report the money they had earned, this would give an unrealistic picture of the underlying health of the business. For example, a business could be earning plenty of revenue, but also incurring a lot of expenses at the same time via investment in new markets, premises, or machinery.

In order for investors to work out whether a company is financially healthy, therefore, they need to be able to see how it is managing costs, and whether it is spending money in the right way.

Net income is a good way to understand how much real profit a business is making, and whether that profit is likely to be sustained in the future. It is also a way of calculating earnings per share (see right), which investors use to weigh up the value of the company and its shares.

Analysing the balance of revenue earned against the cost of tax, investment, and other expenses is one of a number of ways to assess how a company is faring compared with its competitors, and if it has a sound financial basis going forward.

Calculating net income

For investors trying to decide whether a particular company represents a good investment opportunity, net income provides a method of understanding the way the business is run and is a guide to the real profit the company is making, rather than just the revenues it is generating. Revenue earned is the starting point, and the cost of tax, banking and interest charges, depreciation of assets, staff costs, and any other expenses involved in operating the business are deducted from this figure.

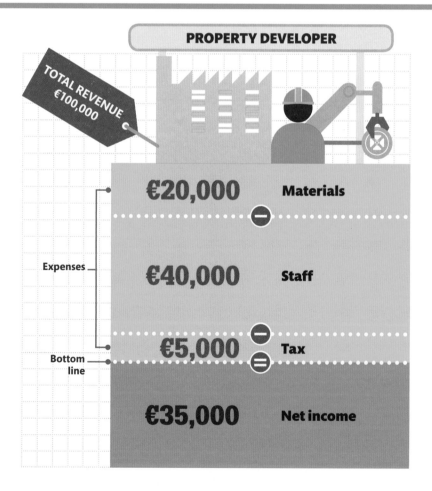

PROPERTY DEVELOPER

TOTAL REVENUE €100,000

Expenses

€20,000 — Materials

€40,000 — Staff

Bottom line

€5,000 — Tax

€35,000 — Net income

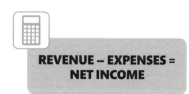

REVENUE – EXPENSES = NET INCOME

INFLATING EARNINGS

Some companies omit certain expenses from their calculations to make net income appear higher, while others inflate earnings to make profits appear higher, for example by including projected future earnings. In 2014, Tesco launched an investigation after discovering its first-half earnings estimate had been inflated by around £250 million due to alleged accounting errors. So, while net income is an important indicator of a company's financial health, it should not be used as the only means of assessment.

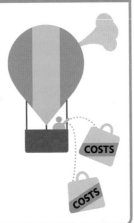

COSTS

COSTS

US$18.4 billion

Apple's first quarter net income **in 2016** – the highest quarterly profits in history

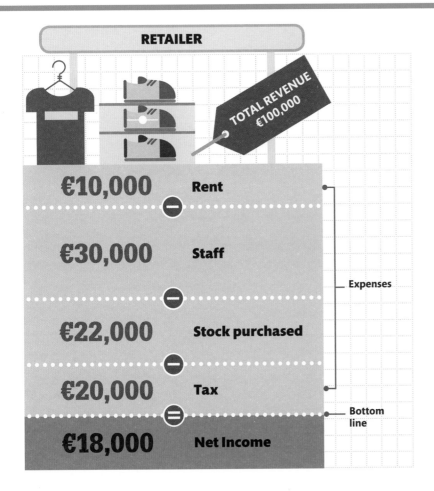

RETAILER

TOTAL REVENUE €100,000

€10,000	Rent
⊖	
€30,000	Staff
⊖	
€22,000	Stock purchased
⊖	
€20,000	Tax
⊜	
€18,000	Net Income

Expenses

Bottom line

✓ NEED TO KNOW

❯ **Bottom line** Refers to the bottom of the income statement, and is another expression for net income.

❯ **Earnings per share** Net income divided by the number of shares in issue; it is seen as an indicator of a company's profitability.

❯ **Expenses** The costs incurred in running a business that have to be settled immediately, rather than paid off gradually over a number of years.

❯ **Depreciation of assets** The decline in value of assets that the company has bought; this may be a plant for manufacturing processes, or specialist machinery.

❯ **Banking and interest charges** The cost of finance, including loans, debts, mortgages, and other amounts owing.

Expensing vs capitalizing

When a business incurs a cost it needs to record it in its company accounts. The company can do this for the full expense at the time it happens, or spread the cost over several years.

Capitalizing and expensing in practice

All companies have certain costs and expenses. Some such as electricity and other utilities, insurance, staff wages, and food need to be paid for upfront, so these are expensed. To qualify as capital expenditure an asset must be useful for more than one year. Businesses have to decide which option best fits their business model. This ski resort, for example, opts to capitalize the cost of a new ski lift, snow plough, bus, and furniture.

WARNING

Whether a cost incurred can legitimately be recorded as an asset is open to a degree of interpretation. Some recent financial scandals have involved companies recording one-off business expenses as investments in new markets that they projected would pay off in the future. In these cases, an order or an expense that had not yet been paid for was recorded as income earned, and as a result company earnings appeared higher than they actually were. The companies did this to inflate or "flatter" their profits rather than show the true figures.

Assets

SKI LIFT
The significant cost of building the lift is spread over a number of years.

SNOW PLOUGH
The snow plough is paid off over several years, as deductions from annual income.

FURNITURE
Furniture appears on the balance sheet as a cost spread over three years.

PASSENGER BUS
The passenger bus is recorded as a depreciating asset as its value will fall.

Capitalizing

A business may decide to capitalize a cost, and then spread it over a number of years. Capitalizing means recording an expense as an asset, and then allowing for its depreciation, or fall in value, over time. Accounting this way may be the difference between reporting a profit or a loss if the cost or expense is particularly large.

THE BALANCE SHEET

When to capitalize	*When to expense*
For businesses wanting to have a smoother flow of reported income and for start-up businesses, it can be attractive to capitalize purchases because by keeping costs down a business can report a higher income in its early years. However, there are tax implications if it is making a larger profit as a result.	If a firm expenses some of its costs, its profitability may be lower. This may be useful in order to reduce tax; lower profits mean lower taxation. A company may also choose to expense a cost if it has had a good year and wants to show high profitability in later years. Some costs, such as staff payments, must be expensed.

How it works

Business owners and managers have a choice. They can record an expense at the time of payment and reduce the annual profit accordingly. This practice, known as expensing, will show up immediately in the accounts. Alternatively, they can register an expense but record it as an asset, and then account for its depreciation over a number of years. Known as capitalizing, this practice has the advantage of taking costs out of the business gradually, rather than in one lump sum. The profit-and-loss account is not as dramatically affected in this case.

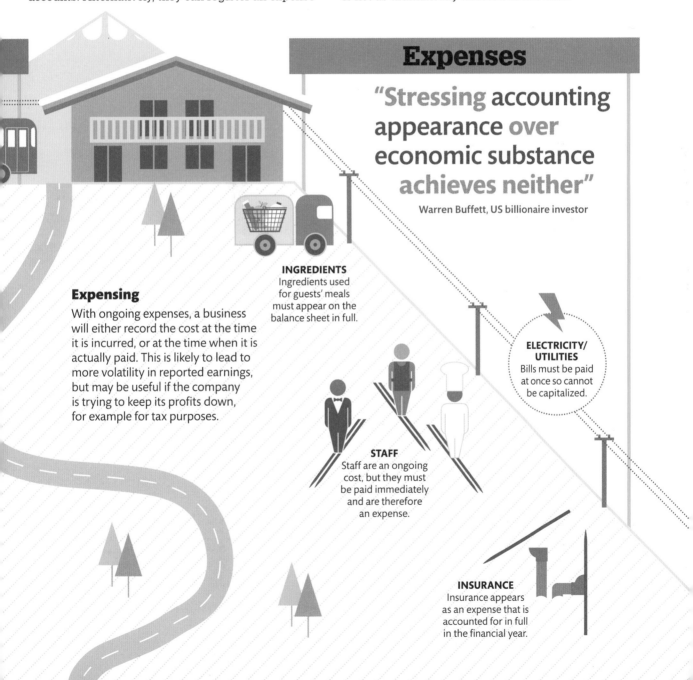

Expenses

"Stressing accounting appearance over economic substance achieves neither"

Warren Buffett, US billionaire investor

Expensing

With ongoing expenses, a business will either record the cost at the time it is incurred, or at the time when it is actually paid. This is likely to lead to more volatility in reported earnings, but may be useful if the company is trying to keep its profits down, for example for tax purposes.

INGREDIENTS
Ingredients used for guests' meals must appear on the balance sheet in full.

ELECTRICITY/ UTILITIES
Bills must be paid at once so cannot be capitalized.

STAFF
Staff are an ongoing cost, but they must be paid immediately and are therefore an expense.

INSURANCE
Insurance appears as an expense that is accounted for in full in the financial year.

Depreciation, amortization, depletion

The cost of a company's assets and its use of natural resources can be deducted from its income for accounting and tax purposes. Depreciation, amortization, and depletion allow the company to spread this cost.

Calculating depreciation

A delivery company buys a van for €25,000. Over time, the vehicle will need to be replaced. The company can record the reduction in the value of the vehicle in its accounts as depreciation.

$$\frac{\text{PURCHASE VALUE} - \text{SCRAP VALUE}}{\text{USEFUL ECONOMIC LIFE (YEARS)}} = \text{ANNUAL DEPRECIATION (€)}$$

$$\frac{€25,000 - €5,000}{5} = €4,000$$

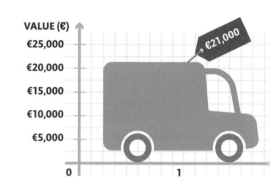

Calculating amortization

A company buys the patent for a computer design. The initial cost of this intangible asset can be gradually written off over several years and can be used to reduce the company's taxable profit.

$$\frac{\text{INITIAL COST}}{\text{USEFUL LIFE}} = \text{ANNUAL AMORTIZATION (€)}$$

$$\frac{€21,000}{7} = €3,000$$

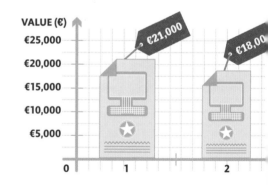

Calculating depletion

A forestry company knows that it has a finite number of trees. Depletion records the fall in value of the forest with its remaining reserves, as the product – wood pulp – is extracted over time.

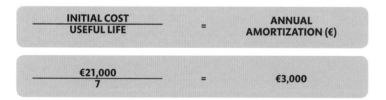

$$\frac{\text{COST} - \text{SALVAGE VALUE}}{\text{TOTAL UNITS}} \times \text{UNITS EXTRACTED} = \text{DEPLETION EXPENSE (€)}$$

$$\frac{€10,000,000 - €1,000,000}{60,000} \times 6,000 = €900,000$$

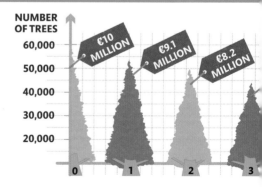

How it works

Depreciation is used to calculate the declining value of tangible assets (such as a machine or vehicle). It is a measure of how much the value of an asset falls over time, particularly due to use, or "wear and tear". Amortization is a term used in accounting to describe how the initial cost of an intangible asset (one without a physical presence, such as a patent) can be gradually written off over a number of years. Depletion is the reduction in value of an asset which is a natural resource. Unlike amortization, which deals with non-physical assets, depletion records the fall in value of actual reserves. It could be applied to coal or diamond mines, oil and gas, or forests, for example.

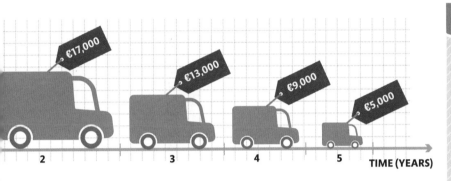

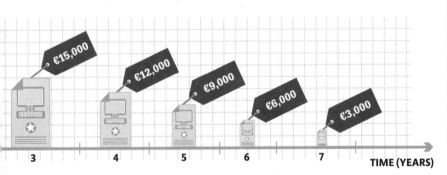

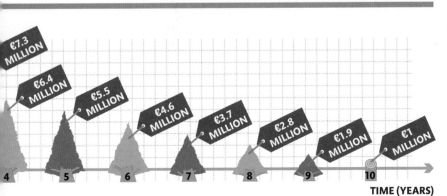

! WARNING

> **Country differences** There are different ways of allowing for depreciation, and accounting methods vary from one country to another. When working out how much a company is allowing for the cost of depreciation, it is important to know which method is being used in its accounts.

> **Purchasing vs leasing assets** Business owners have to make a choice between buying assets which they own but which will fall in value over time, or leasing equipment on which they will pay rent. As they do not own leased equipment, they cannot record its depreciation in value over time and there is no depreciation charge to be used to reduce the company's taxable profit.

60%
the value the average car loses after 3 years on the road

Smoothing earnings

A business practice aimed at reducing volatility in company income and reported profit, smoothing earnings involves the use of accounting techniques to limit fluctuations in a company's income.

How it works

Investors like to see companies demonstrate a steady increase in income and profits over time, rather than large fluctuations in income between good and bad years.

It is possible for companies to smooth their earnings to avoid these sorts of large fluctuations. For example, managers can manipulate figures by choosing when to make provision (set aside money) for large expenses. Rather than making large investments, paying back loans, or making provision for big costs in a year in which income has been low, they can instead decide to make provision for those costs in a subsequent year, when the company's income has increased.

Smoothing earnings is generally a legal and legitimate practice, and is a way of spreading profits over a number of years. By using this accounting practice, the financial statements of a company will show regular and steady growth, which encourages people to invest in it. However, it is sometimes used illegally, to disguise or hide losses, encouraging investors to buy into a company that is insolvent.

Volatile earnings

Company A does not keep money in reserve to pay for large expenses or to cover its running costs in case of a downturn in profits. It is therefore more vulnerable to fluctuations in its income.

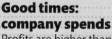

SPEND

Good times: company spends
Profits are higher than anticipated, so the company spends money on new equipment, staff bonuses, and advertising. It does not keep any money in reserve.

Slump: company has no reserves
The company suffers an unexpected downturn in profits, but has no money set aside. It may struggle to meet its running costs and will be less attractive to investors.

EMPTY

FAMOUS ACCOUNTING SCANDALS

Even large, well-known companies can be guilty of manipulating their profit-and-loss accounts. The biggest scandals of recent years included that of Enron, at the time one of the top seven US companies.

ENRON (2001)
Shareholders in this large US company lost a combined US$74 billion. When the company collapsed, accountants found that the balance sheet had huge hidden debts that had not been declared.

WORLDCOM (2006)
This communications company appeared to have far more assets than it actually owned, thanks to false entries detailing sales that never existed. It may have inflated its assets by as much as US$11 billion.

BERNIE MADOFF (2008)
Investors were paid returns out of their own money, and the business was only sustained via the recruitment of new investors. Investors in the scheme lost around US$65 billion.

LEHMAN BROTHERS (2008)
This investment bank, founded in 1850, had US$50 billion of losses in the form of worthless assets on its balance sheet. It went bankrupt, a major factor in the global financial crisis.

Smoother earnings

Company B smooths its earnings by setting money aside during profitable years to use at a later date, for example to repay a loan or cover any unexpected large expenses.

Figures are managed
Income is higher than usual, so company stockpiles the extra revenue and pushes it on to the following year. Profits therefore appear to be steadily increasing.

! WARNING

Reading a company's financial statement does not always give the full picture. Some of the biggest global corporate finance scandals have involved hidden losses, loans made to look like income, and misstated profits that have made the company in question appear solvent when it is not.

"We're not managing profits, we're managing businesses."

Jack Welch, former CEO of General Electric

Cash flow

The money coming into and going out of a business is called cash flow. Inflows arise from financing, operations, and investment, while outflows include expenses, payment for raw materials, and capital costs.

Capital
Investment and lump sums

❯ The main source of cash inflow for start-ups

❯ An additional cash injection after the initial start-up

❯ Revenue from flotation (going public) of private companies, and from shares issued by public companies

❯ Also known as cash flow from investing activities

Sales revenue
Cash for goods and services sold

❯ Revenue generated by core operations

❯ Profit that does not have to be repaid, unlike loans or capital

❯ Payment received for goods and services provided

❯ Also known as cash flow from operating activities

CASH IN

CASH IN

Cash in hand

CASH OUT

CASH OUT

CASH OUT

Salaries and wages
Payments to employees

❯ Money paid to employees who are directly involved in the creation of goods or the provision of services

❯ Salaries paid to staff as a fixed monthly or weekly amount (based on an annual rate)

❯ Wages paid to contractors for hours, days, or weeks worked

Overheads
Payment of bills

❯ The rental cost of commercial property; utility bills (water, electricity, gas, telephone, and internet); office supplies and stationery

❯ The salaries and wages of employees not directly involved in creating goods and services (known as indirect labour)

Loan repayments
Debt servicing and shareholder profit

❯ Interest on long-term loans for asset purchases and on short-term loans for working capital

❯ Repayments on loans

❯ Commission paid to factoring (payment-collecting) companies

❯ Share repurchases and dividend payments to shareholders

How it works

Cash flow is the movement of cash into and out of a business over a set period of time. Cash flows in from the sale of goods and services, from loans, capital investment, and other sources. It flows out to pay rent, utilities, employees, suppliers, and interest on loans. Timing income to correspond with outgoings is key.

Loans
Bank loans and overdrafts

❯ Working-capital loans to meet shortfalls, using anticipated income as collateral

❯ Advances on sales invoices from factoring (payment-collecting) companies

❯ Short-term overdrafts

❯ Also known as cash flow from financing activities

Other revenue
Grants, donations, and windfalls

❯ Grants from institutions or government, usually for research and development

❯ Donations and gifts (not-for-profit organizations)

❯ Sales of assets and investments

❯ Repayments received for loans made to other organizations

❯ Tax refunds

CASH IN

CASH IN

or stock

CASH OUT

CASH OUT

CASH OUT

Suppliers
Payments for materials and services

❯ The cost of raw materials needed to manufacture goods for sale

❯ The cost of stock – local or imported

❯ Fees for services (consulting or advertising) to generate revenue

❯ Payments to contractors involved in providing goods and services

Tax
Payments to tax authorities

❯ Corporation tax based on profits shown in annual financial statements

❯ Payroll tax paid by employers on behalf of employees

❯ Sales tax and/or VAT on goods or services

❯ The type and rate of taxes vary depending on national tax laws

Equipment
Purchase of fixed assets

❯ The cost of company buildings and equipment, such as phones and computers, office furniture, vehicles, plant, and machinery

❯ Such costs are offset by depreciation.
See pp.32–33.

Cash flow management

The survival of a business depends on how it handles its cash flow. A company's ability to convert its earnings into cash – its liquidity – is equally important. No matter how profitable a business is, it may become insolvent if it cannot pay its bills on time. A new business may even become a victim of its own success and fail through "insolvency by overtrading" if, for example, it spends too much on expansion before payments come in, and then runs out of cash to pay debts and liabilities.

In order to manage cash flow, it is essential for companies to forecast cash inflows and outflows. Sales predictions and cash conversion rates are important. A schedule of when payments are due from customers, and of when a business has to pay its own wages, bills, suppliers, debts, and other costs, can help to predict shortfalls. If cash flow is mismanaged, a business may have to hand out money before it receives payment, leading to cash shortages. Smart businesses, such as supermarkets, receive stock on credit, but are paid in cash – generating a cash surplus.

Positive and negative cash flow

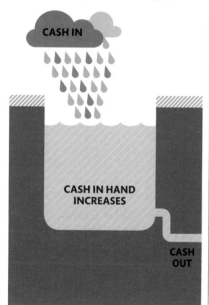

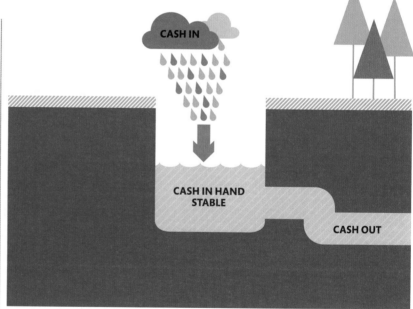

Positive cash flow

Cash flowing into the business is greater than cash flowing out. The stock, or reserve of cash, increases. A business in this position is thriving.

Stable cash flow

Cash flows into the business at the same rate at which it flows out. A business doing well may decide that it can afford to increase its investments or pay higher dividends. Despite these extra expenses, the fact that its cash stock remains stable is a sign that a business is healthy.

✓ NEED TO KNOW

> **Factor** A third party which, for a commission, collects payment from a business's customers.

> **Accounts payable** Payments a business has to make to others.

> **Accounts receivable** Payments a business is due to receive.

> **Ageing schedule** A table charting accounts payable and accounts receivable according to their dates.

> **Cash flow gap** The interval between when payments are made and when they are received.

> **Cash conversion** Successful businesses convert their product or service into cash inflows before their bills are due.

> **Operating cash flow** Inflows and outflows relating to a company's day-to-day activity.

> **Investing cash flow** Movement of money into and out of a company from investments in bonds, businesses, or stock markets.

> **Financing cash flow** Payments due to or from debitors and creditors.

80%
of small business start-ups fail due to poor cash flow management

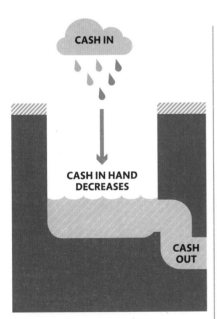

Negative cash flow

Less cash is flowing into the business than is flowing out. Over time, the available stock of cash will decrease and the business will face difficulties.

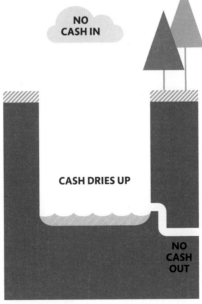

Bankruptcy

If cash flowing out continues to exceed cash flowing in, cash levels will drop so low that the business will become insolvent, having no cash to pay its bills.

HANDLING THE FLOW

A business with a cash surplus might:

> Invest or move excess cash into an account where it will earn interest.

> Upgrade equipment to improve production efficiency.

> Take on new staff, develop products, or buy other companies to expand the business.

> Pay creditors early or pay down debt before it is due to improve credit credentials.

A business with a cash shortage might:

> Lower prices to increase sales, or raise them to increase profit.

> Invoice promptly and chase outstanding payments.

> Ask suppliers to extend credit.

> Offer discounts in return for quicker payment.

> Use an overdraft or short-term loan to pay off pressing expenses.

> Continue to forecast cash flow and plan to avert future problems.

Gearing ratio and risk

COMPANY HAS MORE DEBT
A high proportion of debt to equity is also described as a high degree of financial leverage. Typical examples of debt are loans and bonds.

Capital gearing is the balance between the capital a company owns and the funding it gets from short- or long-term loans. Investors and lenders use it to assess risk.

EQUITY

Low gearing

EQUITY

How it works

Most businesses operate on some form of gearing (also called financial leverage), funding their operations in part by borrowing money via loans and bonds. If the level of gearing is high (that is, the business has taken on large debt in relation to its equity), investors will be concerned about the ability of the business to repay the debt. However, if the company's profit is sufficient to cover interest payments, high gearing can provide better shareholder returns. The optimum gearing level depends on how risky a company's business sector is, the gearing levels of its competitors, and the maturity of the company. Gearing ratios vary from country to country. Firms in Germany and France often have higher ratios than those in the US and UK.

Equity finance (shares)

Pros

❭ Low gearing is seen as a measure of financial strength

❭ Low risk attracts more investors and boosts credit rating

❭ Finance from shares does not have to be repaid

❭ Shareholders absorb losses

❭ Angel investors share expertise

❭ Good for start-ups, which may take a while to become profitable

Cons

❭ Shared ownership, so company founders and directors have limited control of decisions

❭ Profit is shared in return for investors risking their funds

❭ There is a legal obligation to act in the interests of shareholders

❭ Can be complex to set up

Gearing ratio calculation

Analysts and potential investors assess the financial risk of a company with this calculation, presented as a percentage.

$$\frac{\text{LONG-TERM DEBT}}{\left(\begin{array}{c}\text{SHARE CAPITAL +}\\\text{RESERVES +}\\\text{LONG-TERM DEBT}\end{array}\right)} \times 100$$

Low gearing

A software company is going public. Its ratio of 21.2 per cent tells investors that it has relatively low gearing and is well positioned to weather economic downturns.

$$\frac{\text{€1.2 MILLION}}{\left(\begin{array}{c}\text{€2 MILLION + €2.455 MILLION +}\\\text{€1.2 MILLION}\end{array}\right)} \times 100 = 21.2\%$$

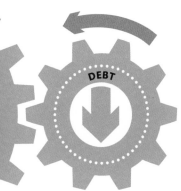

High gearing

COMPANY HAS LESS DEBT
A low proportion of debt to equity is also described as a low degree of financial leverage. Equity typically comes from reserves and share capitals.

Debt finance (loans)

Pros

› Debt payments do not change with profitability

› Interest payments are tax-deductible

› Debt does not dilute ownership

› The company retains control of decision-making

› Repayment is a known amount that can be planned for

› Quicker and simpler to set up

› Small-business loans at favourable rates may be available to start-ups

Cons

› High gearing is considered a measure of financial vulnerability, as debt payments must be made even if profits are low

› The risk may put off investors and adversely affect credit rating

› Loans and interest must be paid, even if the operating profit shrinks

› Debt may be secured on the fixed assets of the company. Unpaid lenders can seize assets and force bankruptcy

› Tax authorities and lenders are first to be paid in the event of insolvency

✓ NEED TO KNOW

› **Interest cover ratio** An alternative method of calculating gearing: operating profit divided by interest payable.

› **Overleveraged** A situation in which a business has too much debt to meet interest payments on its borrowing.

› **Deleverage** The immediate payment of any existing debt in order to reduce gearing.

› **Creditors** Those to whom a debt is due or a payment needs to be made (shareholders are always behind loan-holders in the order of repayment).

› **Dilution** Angel investors – people who provide finance and invest in the future of a start-up company – will usually receive shares in return. This is known as diluting ownership, as the angel investors will own part of the company and may hold sufficient shares to have a controlling stake.

High gearing

A water company is the only water provider in the area, with several million customers. Although high, the ratio of 64 per cent is acceptable for a utility company with a regional monopoly and a good reputation.

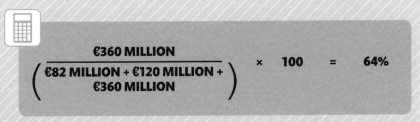

$$\left(\frac{€360 \text{ MILLION}}{€82 \text{ MILLION} + €120 \text{ MILLION} + €360 \text{ MILLION}} \right) \times 100 = 64\%$$

25% the ratio at or below which a company is traditionally said to have low gearing

How companies use debt

When a company wants to expand, it has two main funding options – to borrow money or to issue shares to investors. Borrowing money at a fixed price enables it to budget for costs and calculate potential profits.

How it works

By taking on debt – in other words, borrowing money – a firm receives a lump sum of cash, paying back the full amount with interest in regular payments over a fixed term to its creditors. It also retains control over its business strategy, unlike if it were to issue shares.

By issuing shares, a company is selling ownership (equity) stakes in the business. A firm that raises money via issuing shares may have to allow larger shareholders a say in how the business is run. If the company then makes a profit, it may have to pay dividends to shareholders. Unlike loans, shares do not get "paid off", dividends are paid as long as shares exist.

Firms may use both methods to fund investment, and each approach has different pros and cons, but without the facility to borrow, a company would be unable to take on large projects and make long-term commitments.

If a lender is concerned about how a company is being run, or its future ability to pay its debt, it may have the option to withdraw the loan or ask the company to reschedule its debt, thereby paying a higher rate of interest to compensate the lender for the increased potential risk.

Business expansion

Some companies, for example those in air travel, car manufacturing, or house building, tend to have higher levels of debt because they have to purchase stock, raw materials, or land well before they sell their products or services.

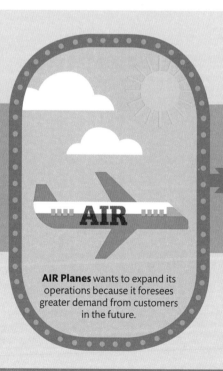

AIR Planes wants to expand its operations because it foresees greater demand from customers in the future.

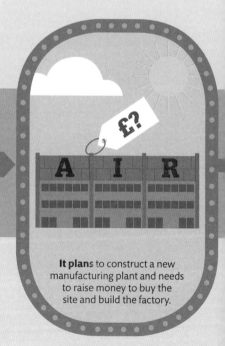

It plans to construct a new manufacturing plant and needs to raise money to buy the site and build the factory.

NEED TO KNOW

> **Creditors** Banks, loan companies, and individuals to whom a firm owes money.

> **Dividends** Profits paid to a company's shareholders.

> **Interest payment** The amount of interest charged on a loan. This is usually fixed and has to be paid on time in instalments – even if the company is struggling and losing money.

> **Lifecycle** The "debt phase" a company is in. Start-ups tend to be funded by bank loans and seed capital, and at a later stage in their lifecycle turn to venture capital, which may involve issuing shares.

GETTING THE BALANCE RIGHT

A company that borrows money as opposed to issuing shares has fixed liabilities and a timescale for repayment. It retains more independence as the creditors do not have a share of the profits or a say in how the company is run. There are also tax advantages – it is cheaper for a firm to bear the cost of debt than equity.

Too much debt and potential lenders will think the company is too risky. But using debt enables it to retain more profits.

Too little debt and the company may be forced to give away too much control and profits to new shareholders.

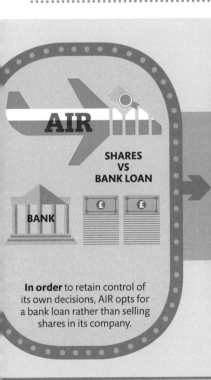

In order to retain control of its own decisions, AIR opts for a bank loan rather than selling shares in its company.

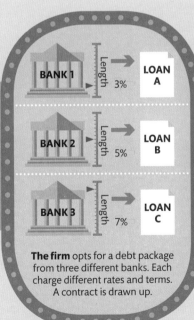

The firm opts for a debt package from three different banks. Each charge different rates and terms. A contract is drawn up.

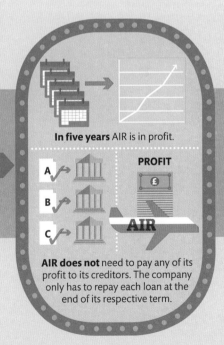

In five years AIR is in profit.

AIR does not need to pay any of its profit to its creditors. The company only has to repay each loan at the end of its respective term.

Financial reporting

Financial reporting is when a company publishes a set of statements showing its assets (what it owns), its liabilities (what it owes), and its financial status. This information is used by investors to keep track of the company's progress.

How it works

There are legal requirements surrounding financial reporting to ensure that a company gives a full and fair statement of its financial affairs. The company must show its performance over the year or half year, any significant changes to its financial position, and whether it has made money or incurred liabilities or losses during the year.

Two financial reports are usually issued per year – the half-year report and the annual report. For firms which are publicly owned – i.e. their shares are traded on the stock market – the annual report must be made public and freely available for investors to read.

Companies usually publish a number of documents: an annual report showing the firm's activities during the year; a balance sheet showing its current assets and liabilities, and the working capital (the difference between the two); and financial details on its website for investors. This information is used by investors to keep track of the company's progress.

Case study: **balance sheet**

This example, from a water company, shows how a balance sheet works.

ASSETS, LIABILITIES, AND CAPITAL

Fixed assets

Intangible assets

Tangible assets

Investments

Current assets

Stock and work in progress

Debtors

Cash at the bank and in hand

Total current assets

Creditors – amounts falling due within one year

Net current assets

Total assets less current liabilities

Creditors – amounts falling due after more than one year

Provisions for liabilities and charges

Retirement benefit obligations

Deferred income

Net assets

Capital and reserves

Issued share cap

Retained profit

Shareholders' funds

SYMBOLS FOR DEBITS AND CREDITS
Accountants use a number of different terms and symbols to indicate debits and credits. Some use "Dr" for debits and "Cr" for credits, others use "+" for debits and "–" for credits. On this balance sheet, brackets are used to show credits (negative numbers).

⚠ WARNING

A balance sheet is a snapshot of a company's financial position on one particular day. Although it is a good guide to the financial health of a company, doctored reports can, and in the past have been used to, hide large debts or liabilities, and not reveal them to the auditors who are checking the annual report or balance sheet. Auditors may be alerted to fraud by a number of "red flags" or warning signs – these could be anything from negative cash flows that miraculously become positive the following year, to sales registered before they have been made, to an unusual rise in gross margin.

	Year 2013 £m	Year 2012 £m
	0	0
	2,167.1	2,069.2
	–	–
	7.0	6.3
	162.6	153.9
	181.0	211.0
	350.6	371.2
	(198.8)	(171.7)
	151.8	199.5
	2,318.9	2,268.7
	(1,891.5)	(1,811.9)
	(114.9)	(115.3)
	(93.1)	(83.0)
	(17.2)	(17.9)
	202.2	240.6
	81.3	81.3
	120.9	159.3
	202.2	240.6

Fixed assets (or non-current assets) cannot easily be converted into cash and are usually bought for long-term use. They are either tangible, such as land, or intangible, such as brand logos.

Intangible assets are assets that are not physical – for example intellectual property (IP) or trademarks. They have a value but are distinct from tangible assets such as stock, property, and premises.

Current assets include all assets that could be converted into cash – cash reserves within the business and petty cash; stock; insurance claims; office equipment; accounts receivable.

Debtors are individuals or companies that owe the firm money. Debtors will usually have an agreement with their creditors about terms of payment.

Creditors are the individuals or organizations to which the company owes money. Here, the money must be repaid in the current financial year.

Net current assets are current assets after money due to creditors has been deducted.

Total assets less current liabilities are all the assets that the company owns which are not likely to be exchanged for cash, as well as cash, and other liquid assets, minus liabilities.

Liabilities due are loans, mortgages, or outstanding debt which the company owes, and on which it is likely to have to pay interest.

Net assets are the company's total assets minus the total liabilities it has. It is the amount of value left and is sometimes called shareholders' equity.

Issued share cap is the total number of shares held by the company's shareholders.

Retained profit is profit that has not been paid out as dividends to shareholders and may be reinvested or used to pay debt in the long term.

Shareholders' funds, or owner's equity, is the company's remaining net capital; this can be reinvested or paid out annually as a dividend.

Financial instruments

A financial instrument is something that has value and can be traded. This might be cash or currency, shares, assets, or debts and loans. It can include evidence of an ownership of interest in a company or other entity. Many records of financial instruments are now held electronically.

How they work

Financial instruments are legal agreements that require one party to pay (or promise to pay) money – or something else which has a value – to another person or organisation. There are usually conditions attached to an agreement. These conditions might cover the amount and timing of payments of interest, cash, capital gains, premiums, or provision of insurance cover as part of the agreement. As proof that you own a financial instrument, you might hold an actual document, such as a share certificate, an insurance policy, or a contract for a debt or a loan; however, shares can also be held in an online account.

WHY HOLD FINANCIAL INSTRUMENTS?

Growth and dividends

Investors buy and trade financial instruments in order to receive a straightforward capital gain, or to receive interest from a bond or from dividends of shares.

Risk control

Buying assets that perform independently of each other (such as shares from one country, and government bonds from another) can help to reduce a portfolio's risk.

Preparing for the unexpected

An investor wishing to hedge their portfolio might buy insurance against that portfolio falling in value. Holding an insurance certificate gives protection against losses that have been set out and agreed in the policy.

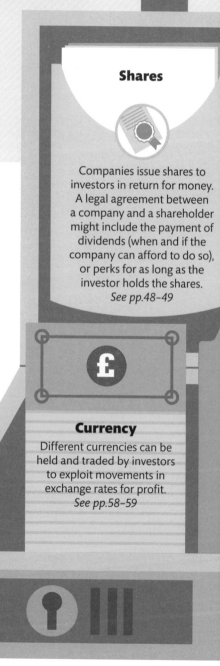

Shares

Companies issue shares to investors in return for money. A legal agreement between a company and a shareholder might include the payment of dividends (when and if the company can afford to do so), or perks for as long as the investor holds the shares.
See pp.48–49

Currency

Different currencies can be held and traded by investors to exploit movements in exchange rates for profit.
See pp.58–59

16%

rise in the value of Google shares in a single day on Friday 17th July, 2015

Derivatives – options and futures

The value of derivatives depends on the performance of an underlying asset. They are traded to provide capital growth, or to limit risk within a business or a portfolio. Professional investors may use them to hedge their portfolios. *See pp.52–53*

Bonds and loans

These are IOUs between a company and an investor. The investor effectively loans a company or government money and, in return, the borrower pays interest to the investor over a set period, at a set rate, with a specified date for the return of the capital. *See pp.50–51*

NEED TO KNOW

> **Capital gain** Profit from the sale of assets such as shares.
> **Risk** The chance that an investment's return may be lower or different than expected.
> **Portfolio** A range of investments held either by an individual or by an organization.

Insurance

An insurance policy involves a company or individual paying a premium to an insurance company, entering into a contract that promises monetary compensation in the event of them suffering a pre-agreed loss scenario. *See pp.78–79*

Funds

An investment fund (such as a Unit Trust) is a pool of capital belonging to a group of investors. This money is invested by the fund in the hope that the fund's value will increase, netting the investors a capital gain. It may also pay interest. *See pp.80–81*

Shares

Shares are small slices of a company that are available for investors to buy or sell. Companies create shares in order to raise capital, which they can invest to grow their business.

How it works

Shareholders are investors who buy the shares a company creates, and who therefore own a part of that company. When shareholders buy a share, it is usually an "ordinary share", which means that they can vote in the election of the company's executive team, approve or vote against new share issues and other money-raising activities, and in some cases receive profit-linked payouts known as dividends. Shareholders are entered on the company's share register, which is a list of all the investors who hold a stake in it.

Investors buy shares for capital growth (hoping the underlying value or price of the shares will rise), and for income if the shares pay dividends. Share prices rise and fall based on a company's financial performance, general economic news, and how investors feel about a company or the wider economy. If a share price fluctuates in a short space of time it is said to be volatile. If one company's share price is volatile it can indicate that investors are worried about that company; if volatility affects all share prices it can be a sign of instability in entire markets.

Issuing shares

Companies issue shares when they need money to invest or pay off costs. When an investor buys a share, they become a shareholder and own a small part of the company.

A company needs money to expand its operation. It decides to offer shares to the public via flotation on the stock market.

The company issues shares at 100p per share. The shares are made available via an Initial Public Offering (IPO) at an agreed price.

Individual investors receive their shares at the issue price, in this case 100p. The shares can then be bought and sold on the stock exchange.

UNDERSTANDING SHARES

Once shares have been issued they can then be traded on the stock market.

Shareholders buy part of a company. If share values fall there is no guarantee that they will get their money back.

The price of a share favoured by investors tends to rise; the price tends to fall if investors lose confidence.

If a company goes bust, shareholders will probably lose most or all of their initial capital investment.

If a company does well, shareholders share in the returns. This is what makes buying shares so exciting to investors.

If a company fails, shareholders lose their investment but they are not responsible for a company's debts.

¥2.25 trillion

average daily turnover of the Tokyo Stock Exchange

STOCK EXCHANGE

Shares for sale

100p per share

COMPANY SHARES

JUNE

110p (value rises 10p per share)

Share

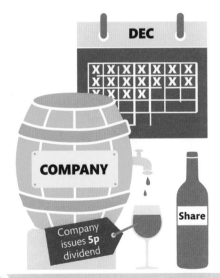

DEC

COMPANY

Company issues 5p dividend

Share

After the IPO allocations the company makes the shares available on the stock exchange where prices are affected by market performance.

Over six months the shares gain 10 per cent in value. Shareholders who sell shares bought at 100p have now made a profit of 10p per share.

After another six months the company pays a dividend of 5p per share. Investors still holding their shares receive this 5p profit per share.

Bonds

Companies and governments sell bonds to raise money without issuing shares. They are effectively fixed-term loans bought by investors who receive interest until the end of that term.

How it works

Bonds are securities for long-term debt, though they are not always held until the end of their term. The price of a bond rises and falls depending on current interest rates, and on how likely investors feel the bond issuer is to repay the initial sum invested. There are different kinds of bonds such as savings bonds, company bonds, and government bonds (also known as gilts), and some can be traded between investors. In savings bonds, investors deposit a lump sum with a retail savings institution (such as a bank or building society), receive regular interest, and are repaid the original sum in full. In other types of bonds, repayment of the original sum is not guaranteed, since the issuer could go bust. Because the risk of government default is so small, gilts are seen as the least risky bond type.

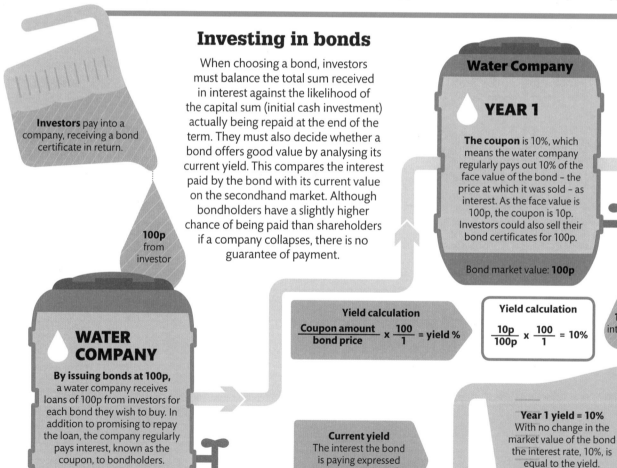

Investing in bonds

When choosing a bond, investors must balance the total sum received in interest against the likelihood of the capital sum (initial cash investment) actually being repaid at the end of the term. They must also decide whether a bond offers good value by analysing its current yield. This compares the interest paid by the bond with its current value on the secondhand market. Although bondholders have a slightly higher chance of being paid than shareholders if a company collapses, there is no guarantee of payment.

Investors pay into a company, receiving a bond certificate in return.

100p from investor

WATER COMPANY

By issuing bonds at 100p, a water company receives loans of 100p from investors for each bond they wish to buy. In addition to promising to repay the loan, the company regularly pays interest, known as the coupon, to bondholders.

Water Company

YEAR 1

The coupon is 10%, which means the water company regularly pays out 10% of the face value of the bond – the price at which it was sold – as interest. As the face value is 100p, the coupon is 10p. Investors could also sell their bond certificates for 100p.

Bond market value: **100p**

Yield calculation

$$\frac{\text{Coupon amount}}{\text{bond price}} \times \frac{100}{1} = \text{yield \%}$$

Yield calculation

$$\frac{10p}{100p} \times \frac{100}{1} = 10\%$$

10p interest

Current yield
The interest the bond is paying expressed as a percentage of its market value.

Year 1 yield = 10%
With no change in the market value of the bond the interest rate, 10%, is equal to the yield.

NEED TO KNOW

> **Face value** The initial price at which the bond was issued.

> **Market value** The price at which a bond is traded.

> **Coupon** The amount of interest paid to bond investors.

> **Yield** A general term that relates to the return on the capital invested in a bond.

> **Savings bonds** Cash deposits on which a regular interest rate is paid.

> **Securities** Financial instruments, such as bonds, that can be traded.

> **Junk bonds** Bonds of very risky companies.

> **Default** When a company fails to honour a repayment on a bond that it has sold to an investor.

10.8%
highest ever bond rate offered by German banks due to high interest rates in the 1980s

Water Company

YEAR 2

The company does well and is seen as a safe investment so the bond's market value – the price other investors will pay for it – increases. Some investors may choose to sell their bond certificates for a 20p profit, but others will keep them for the regular interest.

Bond market value: **120p**

Yield calculation

$$\frac{10p}{120p} \times \frac{100}{1} = 8\%$$

10p interest

Year 2 yield = 8%
Although the bond's market value has increased to 120p the interest rate remains the same, 10p, so the yield falls to 8%.

Water Company

YEAR 3

After a difficult year the company looks less reliable, so the market value of its bonds decreases. The bond still provides regular interest. Any new investors would receive the same interest payment – a higher rate of regular interest for a lower initial investment.

Bond market value: **80p**

Yield calculation

$$\frac{10p}{80p} \times \frac{100}{1} = 12.5\%$$

10p interest

Year 3 yield = 12.5%
The interest the bond pays remains at 10p, but the market value of the bond is now 80p. The yield therefore rises to 12.5%.

Water Company

YEAR 4

At the end of the bond's term, the company repays the original capital sum, plus any interest that has accrued, on a specified date known as the maturity date. The bondholder receives no further interest once the bonds have matured.

Bond market value: **Maturity**

Repayment **100p**

Return on bond = 130p
The bondholder receives the full redemption of 100p, plus the total interest of 30p that has been accrued over the three years.

Derivatives

A type of financial contract between two or more parties, the value of a derivative is derived from fluctuations in the price of an underlying asset. They are used to insure against risk and to speculate on price movements.

How it works

Used to fix a price in advance for a deal in the future, derivatives can be used to hedge against fluctuations in, for example, the foreign exchange market, interest rates, or the prices of shares or products. Derivatives can also be used for speculation, essentially betting on the future price of an asset. Investors may buy derivatives to reduce the amount of volatility in their portfolios because they can gain exposure to a market via a smaller outlay than if the actual underlying asset was bought. Often highly leveraged products, the most common are futures and options.

Futures

Used by companies to minimze risk, with a futures contract the parties agree a price in the present for a deal that will, in effect, happen in the future. For example, companies that rely heavily on a product, and wish to stabilize their costs, may buy a futures derivative to hedge against unexpected rises or falls in that product's price.

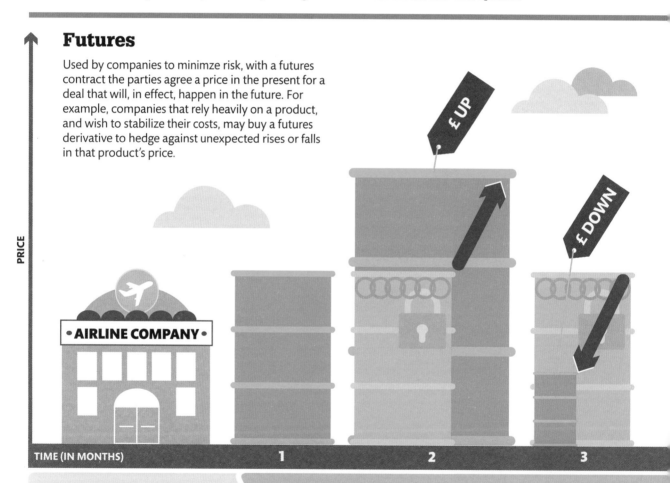

PRICE

£ UP

£ DOWN

• AIRLINE COMPANY •

TIME (IN MONTHS) 1 2 3

A UK-based airline company reviews its stock levels and decides that it will need to buy jet fuel for its fleet of planes in three months' time.

To protect itself from potential future price rises, it can arrange to buy fuel at today's prices for delivery and payment at a future date, known as a forward transaction. If the price of fuel then falls instead of rising, however, the company will still be locked in to paying a higher price.

WARNING

Referred to as financial weapons of mass destruction, derivatives can be volatile. Relying on debt leverage, they use complex mathematical models and not all traders clearly understand the risks they are taking. They can suffer large and catastrophic losses as a result.

£**827** million
was lost **in** derivatives trading by Barings Bank in 1995

Options

As with futures, options fix the price for a future deal but with options the buyer is not obliged to make the transaction. For a small cost, options offer speculators the chance of generating a profit by betting on future changes in the value of an asset, and the size and timing of these changes.

AIRLINE COMPANY

Options to buy

50p

Available for limited time period: 50p option on £5 share price.

£10

£5

£ PROFIT

AIRLINE COMPANY

Options to buy
Expired

£5

£1

SMALL LOSS
£

An investor notices a company's share price going up and buys an option on the shares – a right to buy shares at a future date.

If share prices do rise, the investor can profit by buying at the fixed option price and selling at the current higher price.

If share prices fall, the investor can sell the option or let it lapse, losing a fraction of the value of the asset itself.

Financial markets

The flow of money around the world is essential for businesses to operate and grow. Stock markets are places where individual investors and corporations can trade currencies, invest in companies, and arrange loans. Without the global financial markets, governments would not be able to borrow money, companies would not have access to the capital they need to expand, and investors and individuals would be unable to buy and sell foreign currencies.

Financial markets in action

Thanks to the global financial markets, money flows around the world between investors, businesses, customers, and stock markets. Investors are not restricted to placing their money with companies in the country where they live, and big businesses now have international offices, so money needs to move efficiently between countries and continents. It is also important for the growth of the global economy that people are able to invest money outside their domestic markets.

Inside the stock exchange

Buying and selling occurs in real time, and prices change by the second.

Brokers trade shares, bonds, commodities (raw materials), and specialist financial products on the markets.
See pp.60–61

Buyers specify which share or asset to buy, at what price, and in what volume.

Investors buy via brokers, who set prices and make commission on sales.

When shares are easy to buy and sell, the market is said to be liquid. When there are fewer buyers and sellers, the market is said to be illiquid.

A stock is known by its "ticker" – usually a shortened version of its trading name.

Buying shares or options
Investors study data to decide whether to buy or sell financial assets. Data is updated regularly to reflect changes in supply and demand. *See pp.62–63*

FINANCIAL MARKETS AROUND THE WORLD

New York, US

The New York Stock Exchange (NYSE) is the largest in the world (market capitalization – the market value of its outstanding shares: £14.14 trillion), followed by the NASDAQ, which is also based in New York, (£5.63 trillion).

Toronto, Canada

The Toronto Stock Exchange (TSE) in Canada is run by the TMX Group (£1.45 trillion).

Tokyo, Japan

The Japan Exchange Group (JPX), based in Tokyo, is the largest exchange in Asia (£3.73 trillion).

China

China has three stock exchanges: the Shanghai Stock Exchange (SSE), ($2.9 trillion); Shenzhen Stock Exchange (SZSE) (£2.36 trillion); and the Stock Exchange of Hong Kong (SEHK) (£2.32 trillion).

London, UK

The London Stock Exchange (LSE) is Europe's largest (£2.68 trillion).

European Union

Euronext has headquarters in Amsterdam, Brussels, Lisbon, London, and Paris (£2.56 trillion).

Frankfurt, Germany

Deutsche Börse is based in Frankfurt (FWB) (£1.24 trillion).

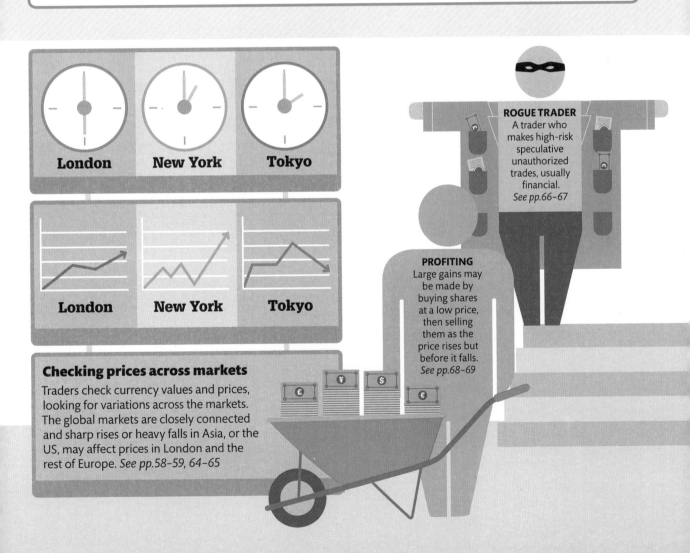

London **New York** **Tokyo**

London **New York** **Tokyo**

Checking prices across markets

Traders check currency values and prices, looking for variations across the markets. The global markets are closely connected and sharp rises or heavy falls in Asia, or the US, may affect prices in London and the rest of Europe. *See pp.58–59, 64–65*

ROGUE TRADER
A trader who makes high-risk speculative unauthorized trades, usually financial.
See pp.66–67

PROFITING
Large gains may be made by buying shares at a low price, then selling them as the price rises but before it falls.
See pp.68–69

The money market

Banks and companies use the money market to buy and sell financial assets that have short maturity dates, and which are easy and quick to exchange.

How it works

Unlike the stock market, which has a physical trading floor, money market deals are done electronically or by phone. Banks, financial institutions, and governments trade directly on the money market, without brokers, and use the market to access the loans that they need to carry out their day-to-day operations. For instance, banks may sometimes need to borrow in the short term to fulfil their obligations to their customers, and they use the money market to do so.

Most bank deposit accounts have a relatively short notice period and allow customers access to their money either immediately, or within a few days or weeks. Because of this short notice period, banks cannot make long-term commitments with all of the money they hold on deposit. They need to ensure that a proportion of it is liquid (easily accessible) and investing in the money market allows them to do this.

Banks may also find that they have greater demand for mortgages or loans than for savings accounts at certain times. This creates a mismatch between the money they have available and the money they have loaned out, so the bank will need to borrow in order to be able to fulfil the demand for loans.

Who uses the money market?

The primary function of the money market is for banks and other investors with liquid assets to gain a return on their cash or loans. These investors provide borrowers such as other banks, brokerages, and hedge funds with access to short-term funding. The money market is dominated by professional investors, though retail investors with more than £50,000 can also invest. Smaller deposits can be invested via money market funds. Banks and companies use the financial instruments traded on the money market for different reasons, and they carry different risks.

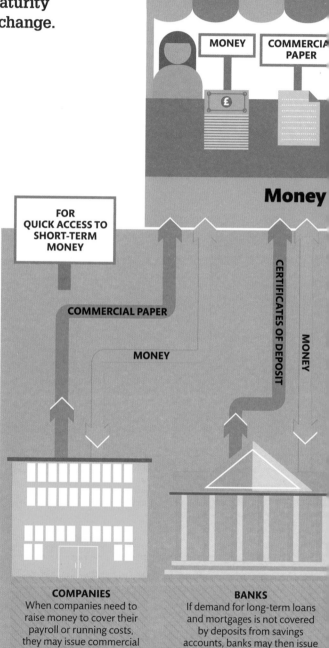

MONEY

COMMERCIAL PAPER

Money

FOR QUICK ACCESS TO SHORT-TERM MONEY

COMMERCIAL PAPER

MONEY

CERTIFICATES OF DEPOSIT

MONEY

COMPANIES
When companies need to raise money to cover their payroll or running costs, they may issue commercial paper – short-term, unsecured loans for £100,000 or more that mature within 1–9 months.

BANKS
If demand for long-term loans and mortgages is not covered by deposits from savings accounts, banks may then issue certificates of deposit, with a set interest rate and fixed-term maturity of up to five years.

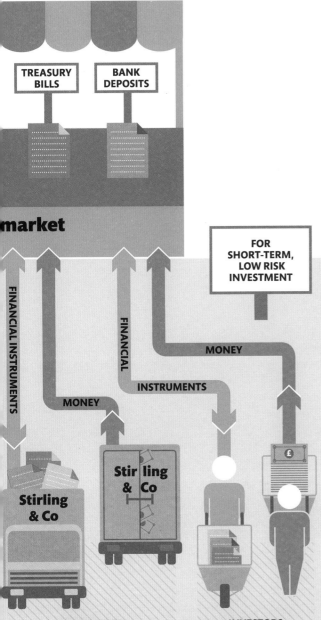

TREASURY BILLS

BANK DEPOSITS

market

FINANCIAL INSTRUMENTS

FINANCIAL

MONEY

INSTRUMENTS

MONEY

FOR SHORT-TERM, LOW RISK INVESTMENT

Stirling & Co

Stirling & Co

Stirling & Co

£

COMPANIES
A company that has a cash surplus may "park" money for a time in short-term debt-based financial instruments such as treasury bills and commercial paper, certificates of deposit, or bank deposits.

INVESTORS
Individuals seeking to invest large sums of money at relatively low risk may invest in financial instruments. Sums of less than £50,000 can be invested in money market funds.

WHAT IS TRADED ON THE MONEY MARKET?

LEAST RISK

> **Treasury bills** Short-term government securities that mature within three months to one year of issue, also known as T-bills. They are acquired at a discount on their face or "par" value, which is then paid in full on maturity. T-bills are considered effectively risk-free.

MEDIUM RISK

> **Certificates of deposit** Fixed-term savings certificates issued with a set interest rate by banks. Rates depend on length of maturity, with longer terms getting better rates. The main risks are being locked in to low interest rates if rates rise, and early withdrawal penalties.

> **Bank deposits** Money deposited in banks, often for a fixed term. Interest rates vary, based on the amount deposited and on deposit liquidity. Risk depends on bank creditworthiness, and whether it is covered by a government-run deposit protection scheme.

HIGH RISK

> **Commercial paper** Short-term, unsecured debt issued by a company. Only companies with good credit ratings issue commercial paper as investors are reluctant to buy the debt of financially compromised companies. They tend to be issued by highly rated banks and are traded in a similar way to securities. Asset values are tens or hundreds of thousands of pounds.

✓ NEED TO KNOW

> **Money market funds** Collectives that offer "baskets" of financial instruments to individual investors, allowing them to invest in the money market with a sum of less than £50,000.

> **Libor** London interbank offered rate – the benchmark rate for lending between international banks, which affects liquidity.

Foreign exchange and trading

Known as forex, foreign exchange and trading refers to the buying and selling of currencies. This trading of currencies can occur between banks, financial institutions, governments, and individuals.

Forex profit and loss

A trader wants to sell some UK pound sterling (GBP) and buy euros (EUR) because they think that the value of the pound is going to fall against the euro. If their prediction is right, they can sell the euros on for a profit, but if their prediction is wrong, they will make a loss when they sell. Investors who intend to speculate on the forex market may use a forex broker and give them a deposit, or borrow money (known as margin) from them to buy currency.

WARNING

Forex markets usually trade on small differences – for example the US dollar–euro rate changing by a few cents – so sudden shocks can catch investors unprepared. On 15 January 2015, the Swiss National Bank (SNB) unexpectedly announced that it would not be continuing to hold the Swiss franc at a fixed exchange rate with the euro. This caused panic in the forex markets; meaning that at one point on that day the Swiss franc rose 30 per cent against the euro and 25 per cent against the US dollar.

1

Investor A looks at the price of the two currencies on the forex market. The EUR/GBP is trading at £0.79 to buy and £0.77 to sell.

2

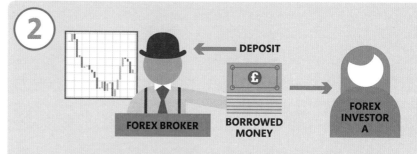

Investor A thinks that this is a good price and decides to trade, borrowing £79,000 to do so.

3

Currency trading at: Buying £0.79/€1, Selling £0.77/€1

Investor A buys €100,000 for £79,000 from Investor B. They do this via a currency brokerage, which charges them both a commission.

How it works

The forex market provides a service to banks and other financial institutions, individuals, businesses, and governments who need to buy or sell currencies other than that used in their country. This might be in order to make investments in another country, pay for import products, convert export earnings, or for foreign travel. It is also a marketplace in which currencies are bought and sold purely to make profit via speculation. When trading very large volumes of currency even small fluctuations in price can provide profits or losses.

The forex market is open 24 hours, five days a week, which makes it unusual, as equity markets have set daily trading hours and are closed overnight.

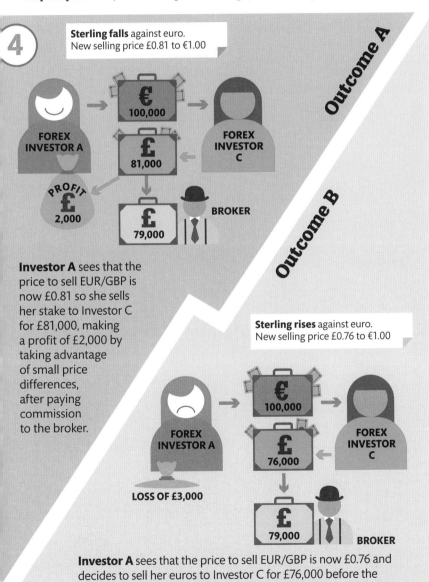

Sterling falls against euro.
New selling price £0.81 to €1.00

FOREX INVESTOR A

€ 100,000

FOREX INVESTOR C

£ 81,000

PROFIT £ 2,000

£ 79,000 BROKER

Outcome A

Investor A sees that the price to sell EUR/GBP is now £0.81 so she sells her stake to Investor C for £81,000, making a profit of £2,000 by taking advantage of small price differences, after paying commission to the broker.

Outcome B

Sterling rises against euro.
New selling price £0.76 to €1.00

FOREX INVESTOR A

€ 100,000

FOREX INVESTOR C

£ 76,000

LOSS OF £3,000

£ 79,000 BROKER

Investor A sees that the price to sell EUR/GBP is now £0.76 and decides to sell her euros to Investor C for £76,000 before the rate slides any lower, making a loss of £3,000. She still has to pay commission to the broker even though she lost money on the trade.

10%

drop in value of UK£ against US$ the morning after Brexit vote

✓ NEED TO KNOW

› **Currency pair** Two currencies that are being traded – for example US dollar and the euro.

› **Spread** The difference between the price at which one of a currency pair is sold, and the price at which it can be bought; spreads change depending on the liquidity of the markets and the demand for the currencies being traded.

› **Leverage** The option for individuals to trade higher values of currency than the cash in their forex account would cover.

› **Stop loss** An order placed with a broker to sell currency once it reaches a certain price, to limit the losses investors experience when the market moves against them.

› **Margin call** A request from a forex broker for an investor to increase their deposit, as the value of their investment has fallen below a certain point.

Primary and secondary markets

In order for shares to be bought and sold, there needs to be a market where they can be traded. There are different types of market, depending on the type of share involved and the size of the trade.

Primary market

A private company may decide to issue shares because it needs money to expand and grow, and it wants access to a wide pool of potential investors. The company sells (or "floats") these new shares in the primary market in an Initial Public Offering (IPO). A company that is preparing to float will use the services of several investment banks to gauge and gather support for the sale of its shares from institutional and private investors before setting a price. The shares are then sold to the public and institutional investors by the company using the services of a specialist broker.

Company
The public and investors can buy shares of a public company in the primary market.

SHARES

MANAGING THE SALE
Prospective buyers of the shares will be able to read about the company in its prospectus. Specialist brokers handle the sale.

Public

Broker

Investor

SETTING VALUE
The value of share issues in the primary market is fixed before flotation.

⚠ WARNING

There must be a secondary market for selling on shares bought in the primary market. If no one is interested in buying them, or there is no place to trade them, the market for them becomes illiquid. Investment scams often involve investors being sold securities that cannot be sold on in a secondary market because they are not listed on the exchanges or have no intrinsic value or potential. A share is only tradeable when other investors want to buy or sell it.

US$25 billion
the amount raised by the Alibaba Group's IPO, the largest in history

How it works

The primary market is where new shares are created and first issued, whereas the secondary market is where shares that have already been issued are traded between investors. When a company is preparing to float on the primary market, investment banks will set a price at which the new shares will be offered. They may also underwrite the Initial Public Offering (IPO) and guarantee to take on unsold shares. The issue price is fixed, but shares may be resold at a different price on the stock exchange (in the secondary market) from the first day of issue.

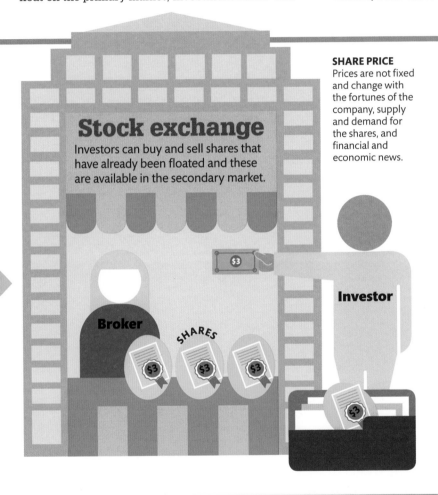

Stock exchange
Investors can buy and sell shares that have already been floated and these are available in the secondary market.

SHARE PRICE
Prices are not fixed and change with the fortunes of the company, supply and demand for the shares, and financial and economic news.

Broker

SHARES

Investor

Secondary market

When investors talk about shares being bought and sold, they are usually talking about transactions taking place in the secondary market. This is where shares are traded between investors. Trading is facilitated by brokers or dealers who take commission on trades. Dealers also earn profit on the spread, or difference, between the price at which they buy shares and the price at which they then sell those shares. These dealers are known as "market makers" and maintain liquidity by offering buy and sell prices at which they will accept trades. The secondary market includes the London Stock Exchange, the Nasdaq, the New York Stock Exchange, and other stock exchanges in countries around the world.

THIRD AND FOURTH MARKETS

Institutional investors, such as pension funds or hedge funds, tend to trade stocks and shares in large volumes. The third and fourth markets cater for these higher-volume trades. The third market operates between large investors and broker-dealers. The fourth market caters for large investors who buy and sell to each other. The cost of trades tends to be lower than in primary and secondary markets as there are no brokers' commissions. Although the stocks and shares may be listed on the main stock exchanges, the trades that take place in these markets are not put through them, and large trades can be made anonymously.

Predicting market changes

Being able to predict what might happen in the stock market is extremely useful for investors looking to profit from buying financial assets.

How it works

Investors use analysis in an attempt to understand where a company, share, or stock market might be heading. They want to determine whether it is likely to increase in value or whether there are factors that signal an impending fall in price or downward cycle. Investors also need to know how markets and economies are behaving, and how that behaviour is likely to affect the performance of other sectors or companies, before deciding to buy shares of companies that they think will do well in the hope of achieving capital growth.

However, prediction techniques are far from foolproof and there is no statistically significant evidence to show that correct predictions are based on anything other than luck.

Predicting the stock market

Traders try to use accurate market analysis to guide their decisions. In theory, analysis can indicate when to buy or sell shares, identify profitable regions for investment, and warn against potential losses.

Professional traders have developed ways to evaluate the future direction of a company, share, or index. Two approaches are often used: technical analysis and fundamental analysis.

Fundamental analysis

INTERIM REPORTS
Financial results give investors potentially valuable information about a company's profits, challenges, market position, and prospective growth.

Investment
Sales
Production

Company A

vs

Company B

COMPETITORS
Investors can gain clues to help predict price movements by tracking the fortunes of rival firms.

Investors use fundamental analysis to educate themselves about a company's challenges, profits, market position, and prospective growth. They study its annual and interim reports and balance sheet, and analyse its past and projected performance. They compare its revenues with its costs and debt, look at its profit margins, and take into account the quality and experience of its management in order to help them gauge its probable future profitability.

Debt

Costs

REVENUES
Investors can assess a company's financial health by examining the fundamentals: how much debt and income a company has.

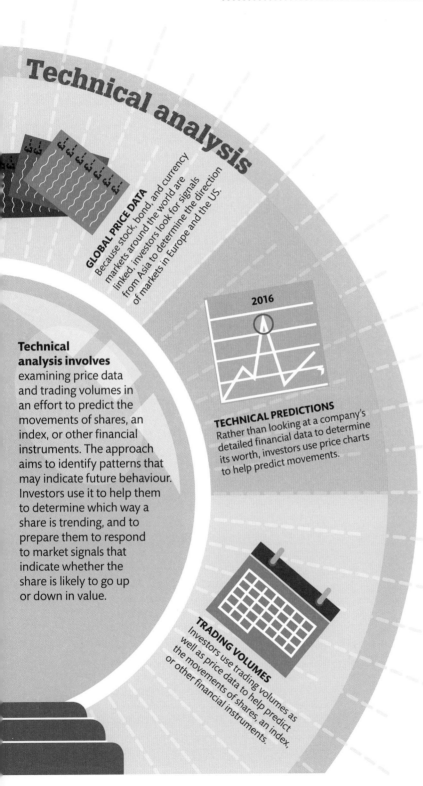

Technical analysis

GLOBAL PRICE DATA

Because stock, bond, and currency markets around the world are linked, investors look for signals from Asia to determine the direction of markets in Europe and the US.

TECHNICAL PREDICTIONS

Rather than looking at a company's detailed financial data to determine its worth, investors use price charts to help predict movements.

2016

Technical analysis involves examining price data and trading volumes in an effort to predict the movements of shares, an index, or other financial instruments. The approach aims to identify patterns that may indicate future behaviour. Investors use it to help them to determine which way a share is trending, and to prepare them to respond to market signals that indicate whether the share is likely to go up or down in value.

TRADING VOLUMES

Investors use trading volumes as well as price data to help predict the movements of shares, an index, or other financial instruments.

GLOBAL DATA ANALYSIS

Asian markets open up to 8 hours ahead of European and US markets due to the time difference. Because stock, bond, and currency markets around the world are closely linked, what happens on the Asian markets can affect markets in the Eurozone, UK, or US, and have a bearing on opening prices when these markets begin trading later in the day. For this reason, investors often look for signals from Asia to determine the likely direction of other markets.

✓ NEED TO KNOW

❯ **Hedging** A strategy that involves investors buying shares they think are likely to rise in price while also selling shares they think will fall, in order to maintain a market-neutral position.

❯ **Technical analysis** Research aimed at identifying patterns that indicate if a share is trending up or down.

❯ **Fundamental analysis** An assessment of revenues, costs, debt, profit margins, and management.

Arbitrage

When there are price differences between two similar assets being traded on different exchanges across the world, traders may seek to take advantage of the discrepancy in order to make a profit. This practice is known as arbitrage.

Transatlantic trades

When a company is listed on both the UK and US exchanges, arbitrage may be possible. For example, if a trader can buy shares in Company A on the US exchange for US$2.99 each and sell them on the UK exchange for £2.30 each – a sum equal to US$3.013 – the trader will make a profit of US$0.023 per share. In practice, arbitrage works by exploiting small price differences such as these at high volumes, using computer programs to trade almost instantaneously. These trades take place so quickly that the biggest profits are made by the organizations with the fastest computers.

HIGH-FREQUENCY TRADERS (HFT)

Computing power enables HFT to search the markets for tiny anomalies to exploit. A computer program evaluates and carries out a large number of trades at high speeds – faster than any person could do. It is possible to make a lot of money from very small price differences in this way.

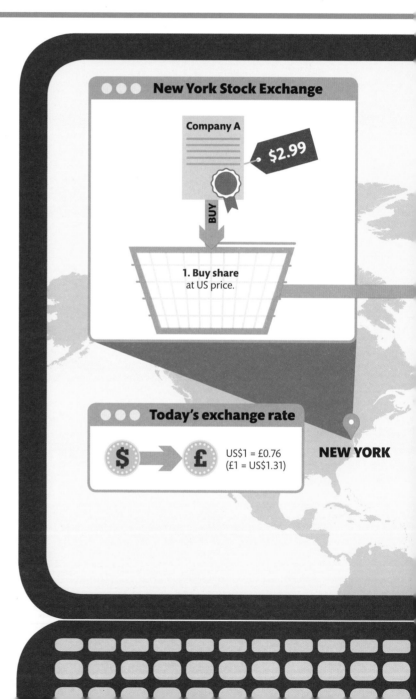

New York Stock Exchange

Company A

$2.99

BUY

1. Buy share
at US price.

Today's exchange rate

$ → £ US$1 = £0.76
(£1 = US$1.31)

NEW YORK

How it works

Arbitrage is the practice of buying a tradeable asset in one market and almost simultaneously selling it at a higher price in a different market. Conversely, it is also the practice of selling an asset in one market and buying it for a cheaper price in another. Arbitrage, as currently practised in stock and bond markets, is only possible due to the computing power now available, so large volumes of transactions can exploit small differences in prices within milliseconds.

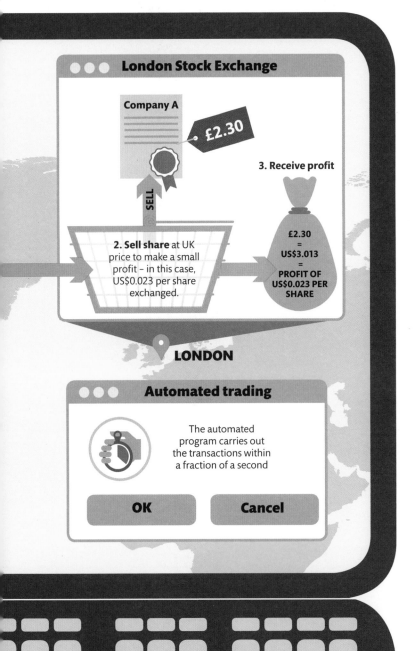

London Stock Exchange

Company A

£2.30

SELL

3. Receive profit

2. Sell share at UK price to make a small profit – in this case, US$0.023 per share exchanged.

£2.30
=
US$3.013
=
PROFIT OF
US$0.023 PER
SHARE

LONDON

Automated trading

The automated program carries out the transactions within a fraction of a second

OK   Cancel

WHEN ARBITRAGE GOES WRONG

In 1998, hedge fund Long-Term Capital Management (LTCM) lost US$4.6 billion as a result of arbitrage trades in bonds that went wrong.

The price difference between the bonds being traded was relatively small, so in order to make a profit LTCM had to carry out large volumes of trades. These trades were also highly leveraged – LTCM was borrowing billions of dollars from other financial companies.

This high leverage combined with the 1998 Russian financial crisis prompted investors to call in their loans and move their capital to less risky investments. LTCM sustained huge losses and was in danger of defaulting on its loans. The US government had to intervene in order to prevent a collapse of the debt markets and damage to the global economy.

60%
of US equity trading **was estimated to be High-Frequency Trading at its height in 2009**

Manipulating the stock market

Stock market manipulation can take many forms – such as artificially fixing prices higher or lower – with the aim of interfering with the market for personal gain.

How it works

A trader can manipulate the market by processing a lot of small sell orders in an atteept to drive down the price of a share. This can cause other shareholders to panic and sell their shares, sending the price down even further.

Conversely, a large number of small buy orders may push a share price up to convince other investors that good news will be announced. Market manipulation is highly unethical but not always illegal.

Pushing share prices down

- **Large sales** If a large investor sells off its stock, prices may fall because of an increase in supply. That same investor can then buy the stock back later at a lower price, having profited from the initial sale.
- **Short selling** Traders borrow shares that are sold at a high price, then manipulate the price down so that they can buy the shares back at a lower price to return to the original owner.
- **Bad news** If a company issues a profits warning, or a negative report, shares may fall in price.

WARNING

Investors often like to discuss shares they own or are thinking of buying with like-minded individuals on bulletin boards and investment forums. While these can be a good source of investment ideas, they can also be used by unscrupulous traders who post negative or positive information to inflate or deflate prices.

TRADER

PUSHING SHARE PRICES UP

BUY!

GO FOR GOLD

THE LIBOR SCANDAL

Manipulation can affect other areas of the market as well. A recent example is the Libor rigging scandal. Libor is a benchmark rate that banks charge each other for short-term loans and is regarded as an important measure of trust between major global banks. The scandal involved traders at 10 firms, which the UK's Serious Fraud Office alleged had conspired to manipulate the Libor benchmark between 2006 and 2010 in order to keep it artificially low.

Pushing share prices up

> **Stock liquidity** With less liquid stocks, a relatively small number of buy orders can move the price up. This makes it easier to exaggerate price movements through manipulative trades such as "pump and dump", where a rogue trader encourages investors to buy shares, pushing the price up so the trader can then sell their own shares at a high price.

> **Good news** Posting positive information about a company or stock on a bulletin board or in an investor chat room can encourage other investors to buy.

Day trading

Day trading is the buying and selling of shares, currency, or other financial instruments in a single day. The intention is to profit from small price fluctuations – sometimes traders hold shares for only a few minutes.

How it works

Investors typically buy or sell a share based on their analysis of economic or market trends, research into specific companies, or as part of a strategy to benefit from the regular dividends that companies issue. Unlike such investors, day traders look for small movements in prices that they can exploit to make a quick profit. They may hold shares only momentarily, buying at one price and selling when the price rises by a few pence (or cents), perhaps only minutes later.

Day traders make profits by trading large volumes of shares in one transaction, or by making multiple trades during the course of the day. They buy (or sell) shares and then sell (or buy) them again before payment is due, and usually "close out" all trades (selling the shares they have bought, or vice versa) at the end of the day in order to protect themselves from out-of-hours movements in the market. This is different from long-term investing, in which assets are held for longer periods in order to generate capital growth or income.

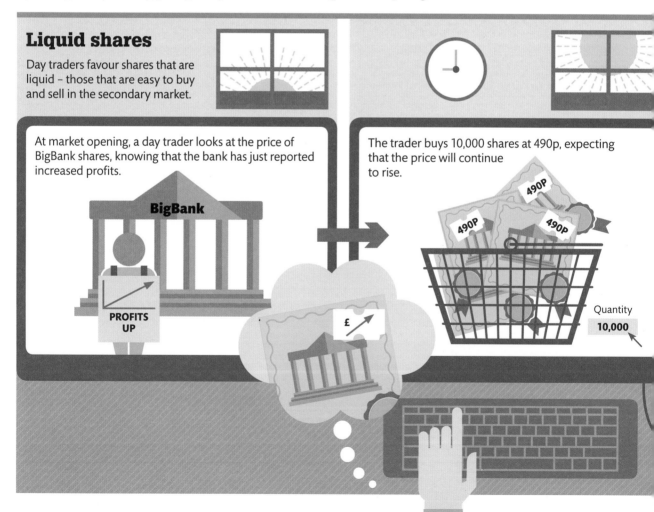

Liquid shares

Day traders favour shares that are liquid – those that are easy to buy and sell in the secondary market.

At market opening, a day trader looks at the price of BigBank shares, knowing that the bank has just reported increased profits.

BigBank

PROFITS UP

The trader buys 10,000 shares at 490p, expecting that the price will continue to rise.

490P
490P
490P

£

Quantity
10,000

⚠ WARNING

> **High risk** Day traders typically suffer severe losses in their first months of trading, and many never graduate to profit-making status.

> **Stress** Day traders must watch the market non-stop during the day, concentrating on dozens of fluctuating indicators in the hope of spotting market trends.

> **Expense** Day traders pay large sums in commissions, for training, and for computers.

✓ NEED TO KNOW

> **Scalping** A strategy in which traders hold their share or financial asset (known as their "position") for just a few minutes or even seconds.

> **Margin trading** A method of buying shares that involves the day trader borrowing a part of the sum needed from the broker who is executing the transaction.

> **Bid–offer spread** The difference between a price at which a share is sold, and that at which it is bought.

> **Market data** The current trading information for each day-trading market. Rather than using market data that is available free of charge but can be up to an hour old, day traders pay a premium for access to real-time data. Day traders must be able to trade on news or announcements quickly, so they need to watch the market and stay close to their trading screens at all times.

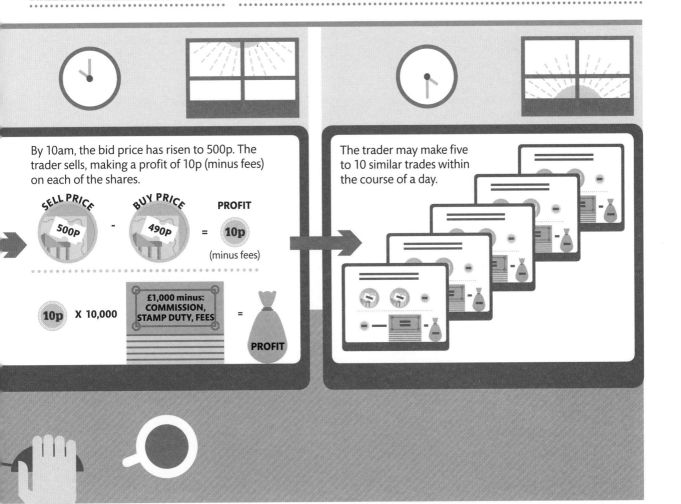

By 10am, the bid price has risen to 500p. The trader sells, making a profit of 10p (minus fees) on each of the shares.

SELL PRICE **500P** − BUY PRICE **490P** = PROFIT **10p** (minus fees)

10p X 10,000 £1,000 minus: COMMISSION, STAMP DUTY, FEES = PROFIT

The trader may make five to 10 similar trades within the course of a day.

Financial institutions

Around the globe, money moves between banks, businesses, governments, organizations, and individuals, crossing time zones, continents, and cultures. At the heart of the global financial systems are the banks, hedge funds, pension funds, and insurance companies that hold and invest the world's money. Without the liquidity that banks provide, organizations and individuals would find it hard to borrow or save money, invest in existing businesses, or start up new companies.

Services and fees

Financial institutions make money primarily by lending out cash at a higher interest rate than the one they are paying to their depositors. They also make money by investing the cash entrusted to them by customers, and by buying and selling assets for clients and charging a fee for this service. They lose money when debts are not repaid, or only partially repaid, or in the event that they make the wrong investment decision.

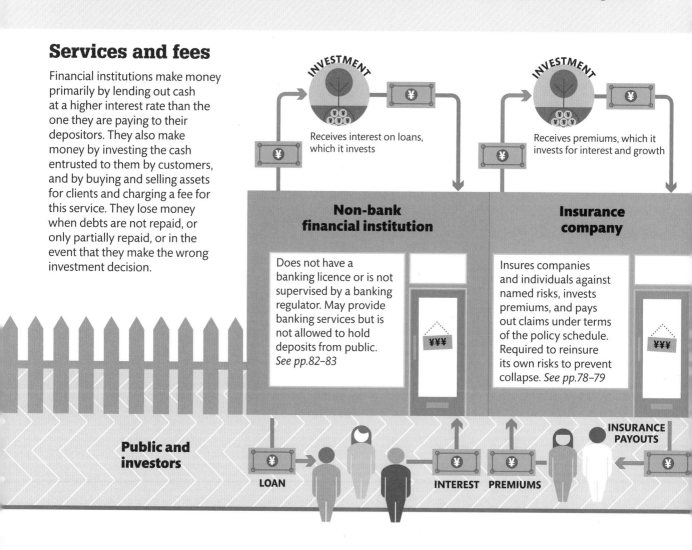

INVESTMENT

Receives interest on loans, which it invests

INVESTMENT

Receives premiums, which it invests for interest and growth

Non-bank financial institution

Does not have a banking licence or is not supervised by a banking regulator. May provide banking services but is not allowed to hold deposits from public. *See pp.82–83*

Insurance company

Insures companies and individuals against named risks, invests premiums, and pays out claims under terms of the policy schedule. Required to reinsure its own risks to prevent collapse. *See pp.78–79*

Public and investors

LOAN

INTEREST   PREMIUMS

INSURANCE PAYOUTS

INTERRELATED INSTITUTIONS

The worldwide markets are all interconnected and rely on each other. A shock in one market can have an adverse effect in another.

❯ **When Greece was renegotiating** its debt write-off the European stock markets were negatively affected, especially when it seemed as if Greece might leave the euro.

❯ **Fears that the Chinese economy** was slowing down fed into fears about global market growth.

❯ **Uncertainty after the Brexit** vote in 2016 led to a sharp drop in the value of the pound.

US$639 billion
value of Lehman Brothers investment bank when it filed for bankruptcy in 2008

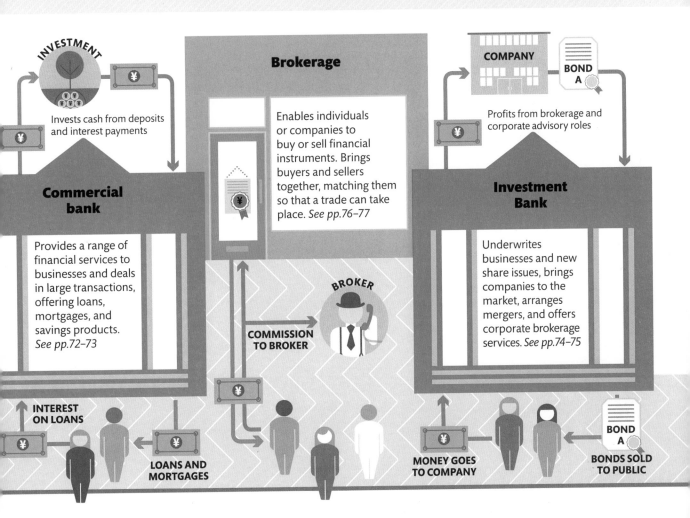

INVESTMENT

Invests cash from deposits and interest payments

Brokerage

Enables individuals or companies to buy or sell financial instruments. Brings buyers and sellers together, matching them so that a trade can take place. *See pp.76–77*

COMPANY

BOND A

Profits from brokerage and corporate advisory roles

Commercial bank

Provides a range of financial services to businesses and deals in large transactions, offering loans, mortgages, and savings products. *See pp.72–73*

Investment Bank

Underwrites businesses and new share issues, brings companies to the market, arranges mergers, and offers corporate brokerage services. *See pp.74–75*

BROKER

COMMISSION TO BROKER

INTEREST ON LOANS

LOANS AND MORTGAGES

MONEY GOES TO COMPANY

BOND A

BONDS SOLD TO PUBLIC

Commercial and mortgage banks

Banks make money by providing loans and charging interest on them. They also pay out interest – at a lower rate – on deposits that they hold for savers. To remain solvent, banks must maintain a balance between the two.

How it works

Banks need to continually make money in order to pay costs and expenses, maintain or increase their market share, make profits, and make regular dividend payments to shareholders.

Commercial banks provide loans to individuals and sell products to customers such as loans, savings accounts, credit cards, overdrafts, and mortgages for prospective home-buyers.

Commercial banks advise and lend to businesses, to retail or small-business customers, to business start-ups that need capital to grow, and to large businesses that need multi-million-pound funding for major projects.

Banks can vary the rates they offer to customers in order to boost demand for their products. They do this either because central bank interest rates have been raised or lowered, or because they want to undercut competitors and increase their market share. For example, in order to attract custom one bank might offer a mortgage loan at a rate that is lower than that offered by its competitors.

A fine balance

The banking business is constantly in flux, but banks have to protect themselves against the possibility of a sudden significant outflow of savers' money. If this happened it could lead to a run on the bank, which might in turn cause the bank to collapse. In order to guard against this eventuality, banks keep large capital reserves and offer competitive savings rates in notice accounts. Notice, usually of between 30 and 180 days, has to be given before money can be withdrawn from such accounts.

PROFITABLE INTEREST RATES

Banks constantly adjust the interest rates they charge on debt and the interest they pay on savings and current account balances, depending on market factors and their business objectives. To make a profit, a bank needs to charge a higher rate on the money it lends than it pays on the savings and deposit accounts it offers. In the example on the right, the bank pays savers and deposit holders 2% on the money they hold with it. At the same time it charges mortgage borrowers 5%, enabling it to achieve an overall profit margin of 3%.

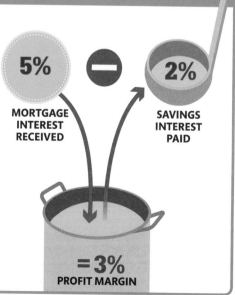

5%
MORTGAGE INTEREST RECEIVED

2%
SAVINGS INTEREST PAID

=3%
PROFIT MARGIN

10%
capital reserve requirement of largest US banks

INTEREST PAID ON MORTGAGES

Making money

Banks make money from loans by charging interest, on current accounts by charging fees and overdraft penalties, and from business accounts through transaction charges.

INTEREST PAID ON LOANS

Attracting new customers

It is cheaper and easier for banks to sell products to existing customers – a practice known as cross-selling – as they know more about those customers' individual financial circumstances.

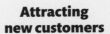

INTEREST RATES ON SAVINGS ACCOUNTS

DIVIDENDS TO SHAREHOLDERS

Paying money

Banks pay interest on savings accounts, and usually on credit balances in current accounts. They also pay dividends to shareholders out of their profits.

OVERDRAFT CHARGES

MONTHLY OR ANNUAL FEES ON SAVINGS ACCOUNTS

CHARGES FOR TRANSACTIONS ON BUSINESS ACCOUNTS

Capital reserve

Banks hold large sums of money that they are not permitted to lend or invest. Banks keep capital reserves to protect themselves in the event of mass withdrawals by customers or heavy losses from bad loans. The reserves are typically only a fraction of deposits.

ANNUAL FEES AND MONTHLY CHARGES ON CREDIT CARDS

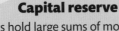

Bank

Investment banks

An investment bank offers distinct financial services, and deals with much larger and more complicated financial deals than retail banks.

How it works

Investment banks work with large companies, other financial institutions such as investment houses, insurance companies, pension funds, hedge funds, governments, and individuals who are very wealthy and have private funds to invest.

Investment banks have two distinct roles. The first is corporate advisory, meaning that they help companies take part in mergers and acquisitions, create financial products to sell, and bring new companies to market. The second is the brokerage division where trading and market-making – in which the investment bank provides mediation between those who want to buy shares and those who want to sell – take place. The two are supposed to be separate and distinct, so within an investment bank there is a so-called "wall" between these divisions to prevent conflict of interest. The different areas of responsibility are called "front office" and "back office".

Areas of business

While the brokerage and corporate advisory divisions of an investment bank are theoretically distinct, there is inevitably overlap between the two areas of, for example, market-making and underwriting new share issues, or mergers and acquisitions advisory and research.

⚠ WARNING

> **Although investment banks** help to keep money moving around the world, if they run into difficulties it can affect cash flow across geographical boundaries.

> **Investment banks** are exposed both to the inherent risks in the assets that they hold, and also the risk that other financial companies with which they are connected might fail. This is called counterparty risk.

Brokerage

Proprietary trading

Investment banks have their own funds, and they can both invest and trade their own money, subject to certain conditions.

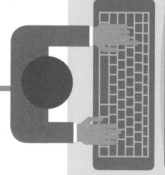

Acting as a broker

Banks can match investors who want to buy shares with companies wanting to sell them, in order to create a market for those shares (known as market-making).

Research

Analysts look at economic and market trends, make buy or sell recommendations, issue research notes, and provide advice on investment to high net-worth and corporate clients.

Corporate advisory

Bringing companies to market

Investment banks can raise funds for new issues, underwriting Inital Public Offerings (IPOs) in exchange for a cut of the funds they raised.

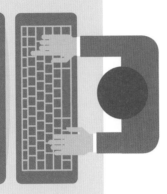

Bringing companies together

Banks facilitate mergers and acquisitions (M&A) by advising on the value of companies, the best way to proceed, and how to raise capital.

Structuring products

Clients who want to sell a financial product to the public may bring in an investment bank to design it and target the retail or commercial banking market.

NEED TO KNOW

❯ **Hedge fund** An investment partnership consisting of a fund manager and wealthy investors, aiming to make money whether the market rises or declines by using investment techniques to "hedge" against losses.

❯ **Underwriting** The covering of a potential risk – in return for a fee or percentage.

❯ **Guarantees** The commitment that, in a new share issue, shares will be sold for a minimum price. If the new issue is not popular, the bank may be left holding the shares on its books and may have to sell them at a loss in the future; if the new shares are in demand and the open market price rises above the issue price, the bank will make a profit.

HOW BANKS MAKE AND LOSE MONEY

Making money

❯ Banks receive fees in return for providing advice, underwriting services, loans and guarantees, brokerage services, and research and analysis.

❯ They also receive dividends from investments they hold, interest from loans, and charges on the financial transactions that they facilitate.

Losing money

❯ The advisory division may end up holding unwanted shares if the take-up of an IPO is lower than expected.

❯ The trading division of a bank may make the wrong decisions and end up losing the bank money.

❯ In a year of little corporate activity, banks may have to rely on trading profits to bolster their returns.

❯ Banks may create financial products which they fail to sell on to other investors, leaving them holding loss-making securities or loans – as in the run-up to the 2007–2008 financial crisis.

Brokerages

A broker is the middleman who brings buyers and sellers of stocks and other securities together, and acts as an intermediary for trades.

How it works

A brokerage firm enables companies or individuals to buy or sell different financial instruments. Traditionally, brokerages research markets, make recommendations to buy or sell securities, and facilitate those transactions for their clients. A stockbroker then makes the trade in the market on behalf of the client, for a commission. Larger institutional trades are still often done in this way, with a broker being instructed to buy or sell a large amount of stock on behalf of a client.

With the advent of the internet, discount and online brokers have automated this process for the wider retail market (private investors), dispensing with the need for stockbrokers to place trades by phone or in person. Online brokers enable retail clients to trade financial securities instantly via an online trading platform, but these brokerage companies may not give advice or provide research. This allows them to offer a much cheaper execution-only service.

Brokerages may also make money by charging fees for managing clients' portfolios and executing trades for them. This is known as a discretionary service, and may involve transaction fees and a management fee taken as a percentage of the value of the client's portfolio.

The broker's role

When an investor wishes to sell some of their shares, they first contact their broker and ask them to quote a price. The broker checks the market and tells them the bid price at which the share is trading – that is, the price at which the broker would be willing to buy from a client. It is generally lower than the offer price at which the broker is willing to sell to a client. The difference in price is known as the bid–offer spread, and it is how brokers make money on their deals. The seller then specifies whether they want to go ahead at that price, wait, or sell "at best", which is whatever price the broker can secure for them in the market at the current time (prices for certain assets can change within seconds on busy trading days). The broker then proceeds to carry out the trade on the investor's behalf.

Sells for £400

WHY THE BID–OFFER SPREAD MATTERS

Investors need to be aware of the bid–offer spread when trading securities or other financial products. This is the difference between the buying and selling price of a security. For example, one investor wants to buy shares and is given a price – the offer price – of 210p. Another investor wants to sell and is quoted a sell, or bid price, of 208p. The 2p difference is the bid–offer spread. Securities that are frequently traded, for example those listed on the FTSE 100 index of leading shares, tend to have smaller spreads and are called "liquid" because it is easy to find a buyer or seller for them. Those traded less frequently – for example the shares of smaller companies – may have a bigger spread and are therefore less liquid. Liquidity is generally defined by "normal market size", which is the number of shares for which a retail investor should be able to receive an immediate quote.

1994 year the first online broker launched

Real-time trading

If a retail investor is using an online trading platform, the price at which they can buy or sell the security is displayed online. They have a finite amount of time to decide whether or not to accept that price and trade at that level.

OFFER PRICE
£420

BID PRICE
£400

Bid–offer spread: £20

Transaction fee: £20
Commission: 1% = £4.00
Total: £24.00

Broker

Acts as an intermediary, charging a flat fee and/or commission on the trades they execute, as well as profiting from the bid–offer spread.

Seller

Contacts the broker, who may provide recommendations or simply process trades for a fixed fee.

Buyer

Must be in credit before the brokerage puts through a buy order. Corporate clients may be able to negotiate loans or credit.

Buys for £420

Insurance risk and regulation

Insurance is in essence a form of risk management, by which individuals and other entities pay a fee to transfer a potential financial loss to an insurer in exchange for compensation if the loss occurs.

How it works

Insurance mitigates risks that can be quantified and anticipated as potentially or possibly likely to happen. All types of insurance – life, home, corporate, business, and motor – work in the same way, by pooling risk.

Without insurance, individuals would be exposed to unexpected events leading to financial hardship, such as premature death, accidents, fire, and theft. Businesses would be vulnerable to closure, governments to bankruptcy, and companies unable to grow and develop.

Insurance companies take on the risks of individuals, companies, and governments in exchange for a fee, or premium, which represents a small proportion of the value of the risk they have agreed to cover.

Premium sizes are based on the insurer's past experience, known as a claims history, which is related to both that particular risk, and also the client's risk-level as an individual or business.

Relatively small premiums paid by a large group of people are used to fund the payouts required when a small number of those customers make a claim.

Insuring a business

If a business wants to insure itself against the risk of adverse events, such as a fire that destroys its premises, it pays a premium to an insurance company, which promises to pay out a certain amount of money should such an adverse event happen. The circumstances on which the insurance company will pay out are listed in the contract between the business and the insurance company, which is known as the policy schedule. The premium gives cover for all the risks specified in the policy schedule. Risks which are not covered are classed as "exclusions".

INSUREES
Individuals or businesses will each pay a premium – a fraction of the financial value of the risk insured – to cover them against events such as fire, death, accidental damage to their property, and theft.

POLICY SCHEDULE
Shows cover extent, limits, exclusions, and excesses.

REGULATION

It is important for the insurance industry to be well regulated in order for it to work properly.

Regulators monitor the industry to make sure that insurers can pay claims made by insurees. They require insurance companies to buy their own insurance – called reinsurance – to ensure they can meet their financial liabilities in full.

Reinsurance covers the insurance companies' own risks so that if, for example, they have a lot of claims at once, or if one client has a huge and unexpected loss, they can afford to pay without experiencing financial difficulties.

✓ NEED TO KNOW

❭ **Premium** The amount of money an insurance company charges to provide the cover described in the policy or bond.

❭ **Excess** The financial contribution the customer must bear on an insurance premium.

❭ **Surplus** Insurance companies are required to hold a surplus in reserve.

❭ **Profit** The return received by insurers from the growth and interest from their investments, or by selling insurance to customers at the right price, or by having few claims.

❭ **Loss** A result of not charging enough in premiums, a fall in the price of investments, or by having large claims to pay out to customers.

❭ **Investment portfolio** A collection of assets bought with the money insurance companies receive from premiums. Portfolios make money from interest, dividends, and capital gains on trade stocks.

❭ **Investment income** The income an insurance company receives from the investment of premiums and reserves.

❭ **Policy** The contract between an insurance company and its customer.

CLAIMANTS

If an adverse event happens to a claimant, they will receive monetary compensation from the insurance company. As part of the contract between the insurer and the insuree, all risks must be disclosed at the start of the policy or a claim may be invalid.

Pooled premiums

The insurance company pools the receipts from premiums, investing the premiums in the expectation of making money from investment returns. It pays out only in the event of a claim.

PAYOUTS
As not all customers will experience an adverse event, the insurance company can afford to pay those that make a valid claim.

Investment companies

Investment companies buy and sell equities, bonds, and other financial assets on behalf of their clients, and with their clients' cash. Investors buy a stake in a fund and their money is pooled to buy a range of assets.

Investment companies and diversification

Diversified investment companies invest in a wide range of assets and in various different securities (cash, bonds, and stocks) within each kind of asset, whereas non-diversified companies invest in a single industry or asset. A diversified portfolio will spread risk, and limit the impact of any market volatility.

INVESTORS' INPUT

Property

Commodities

FUND MANAGER'S FEE

Investment fund

A fund manager's objective is to create capital growth, or income, or both, for their shareholders and investors. They assess and adjust investments as required.

If the property market is expected to do well, the fund manager might create a portfolio with more exposure to it. Property is often considered to be a good investment for safe, long-term growth.

A fund manager will buy commodities – income-producing assets like gold, natural gas, or beef not usually traded alongside bonds and equities. Investing in them can be a good way of diversifying a portfolio.

How it works

Investment companies pool investors' funds to invest in different businesses and assets, potentially giving clients access to markets they could not afford to enter alone. Fund managers analyse the market, deciding when to buy, sell, or hold. They respond to economic and world news, and try to anticipate movements in global stock markets to make money for clients.

5%

the maximum amount of total assets a diversified investment company can hold in a single security according to US law

WARNING

> **Charges** Investing in a fund can include administrative charges, management fees, and entry and exit fees, in addition to the cost of the units in the fund.

> **Performance** Despite the fact that they are actively managed by professionals, many funds do not provide a better return than basic market trackers.

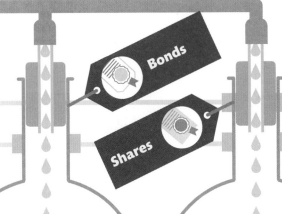

Bonds

Shares

The fund manager aims to spread risk while creating returns. Fixed income from interest payments is provided by bonds that form part of the investors' portfolio.

Shares are selected by company, country, or sector. The fund may be an income fund that pays out dividends on shares, or a capital growth fund, which aims to grow the original sum invested.

AMOUNT RETURNED TO INVESTORS

Return

The income and growth from a fund is known as the return. This is the net amount after deducting dealing costs, fund management fees, and other costs. Fees are charged to the fund regardless of whether or not the underlying asset value has fallen.

REINVESTED IN FUND

Non-bank financial institutions

A non-bank financial institution (NBFI) is an organization that does not have a banking licence, and is not supervised by a banking regulator. It may provide banking services, but it cannot hold deposits from the public.

As a consequence of the financial crisis of 2008–09, regulatory authorities have been reconsidering their approach to financial supervision. In the UK, banks are now required to be more stringent about their lending criteria and to hold higher levels of reserve cash. They are also required to conduct credit checks on their borrowers. In meeting these requirements, traditional banks have tended to reduce the number of customers on their books who are at a medium or high risk of not being able to pay back their loan or mortgage. Increasingly, non-bank lenders have moved into the space that has been vacated by the banks.

Types of NBFI and their business areas

In the last few years, the number of NBFI companies has greatly increased. NBFIs are not subject to the tougher criteria that traditional banks must meet when they lend to individuals or businesses, and may also offer lower interest rates and larger amounts of credit than banks are allowed to provide. There are numerous types of NBFI.

Commercial loan providers

These companies provide funding to businesses but may not accept deposits, and they are not allowed to provide overdrafts. Their lending criteria may be less stringent than that of a bank. Their services are not aimed at individuals.

Peer-to-peer lenders

These lenders act as middle-men, uniting lenders with borrowers. The idea is that each will receive a better rate – lenders receive more interest than they would on a bank savings account, while borrowers will often pay less interest than they would on a bank loan.

OTHER TYPES OF NBFI

The kinds of NBFI available will vary from country to country.

CREDIT UNIONS
These member-owned, non-profit financial cooperatives, pool their members' deposits to finance their loans.

BUILDING SOCIETIES
These mutual companies offer savings accounts to their members. The money is then pooled to offer mortgages.

SPECIALIST LENDERS
Able to charge high interest rates, these may target those with poor credit ratings or with court judgements against them.

PAWNBROKERS
These offer secured loans to people who put up an asset, such as a car or jewellery, as collateral on the debt.

WARNING

NBFIs are not accompanied by the same guarantees that are built into products and companies regulated by the government watchdog, the Financial Conduct Authority (FCA) in the UK. For the borrower, loan terms may be less favourable, while lenders may find it more difficult to establish the creditworthiness of the individuals to whom they are intending to lend.

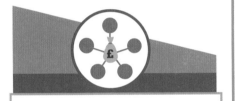

Crowdfunding

This is an emerging means of raising capital in which small projects or businesses can seek investment from individuals, bypassing traditional finance sources. Crowdfunding platforms allow investors to spread risk between projects, though there is a chance the investment will fail.

42% of consumers will use NBFIs over the course of a year

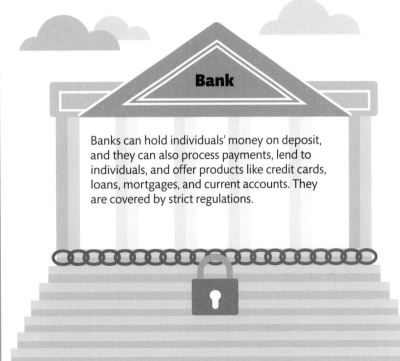

Bank

Banks can hold individuals' money on deposit, and they can also process payments, lend to individuals, and offer products like credit cards, loans, mortgages, and current accounts. They are covered by strict regulations.

GOVERNMENT FINANCE AND PUBLIC MONEY

> The money supply > Managing state finance
> Attempting control > Why governments fail financially

The money supply

The money supply is the total amount of money in the economy at a given time. The government monitors this supply, because of its impact on economic activity and on price levels. It may decide to change financial policy to influence the money supply – for example, by raising or lowering the amount that banks must hold in reserve as actual cash. If the money supply is too low, such as during a recession, or a depression, the government may take steps to try and increase it.

How the money supply is measured

Types of money in an economy are classified in "M" groups. The most liquid, or easily available, form of money is called "narrow" money, and includes classes M0 and M1. The definition of "broad" money includes other less liquid forms. These are classed as M2, M3, and also M4. How these classes are defined, and what they include or exclude, varies between countries.

> "He who controls the money supply of a nation controls the nation"
>
> James Garfield, US president 1841

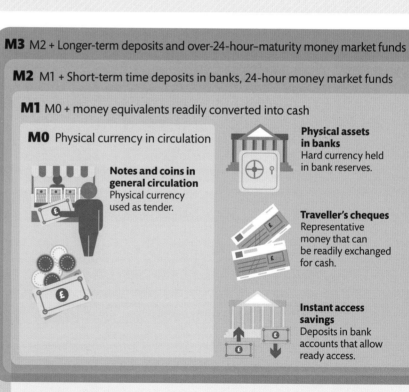

M3 M2 + Longer-term deposits and over-24-hour–maturity money market funds

M2 M1 + Short-term time deposits in banks, 24-hour money market funds

M1 M0 + money equivalents readily converted into cash

M0 Physical currency in circulation

Notes and coins in general circulation
Physical currency used as tender.

Physical assets in banks
Hard currency held in bank reserves.

Traveller's cheques
Representative money that can be readily exchanged for cash.

Instant access savings
Deposits in bank accounts that allow ready access.

Narrow money
M0 and M1 make up the narrow money group. This is money in a form that can be readily used as a medium of exchange, and includes notes, coins, traveller's cheques, and some types of bank accounts.

MORE LIQUID

FIAT CURRENCY VS REPRESENTATIVE CURRENCY

The word *fiat* is Latin for "let it be done", and refers to the fact that fiat money is legal tender only because it is backed by a government decree. Unlike a currency backed by a commodity, such as gold, fiat money does not represent anything, nor can it be redeemed for a set amount of another commodity. It has no intrinsic value.

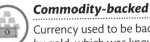

Commodity-backed
Currency used to be backed by gold, which was known as the gold standard.

❯ **Based on a commodity** The value of money is tied to that of a commodity, such as gold.

❯ **Redeemable** Currency is redeemable for an equivalent amount of gold.

❯ **Limited** Money supply is limited by the supply of gold.

Government-backed (fiat)
The state backs paper and digital money – another type of fiat currency (*see pp.88–89*).

❯ **Not based on a commodity** Value is based on faith in the government and economy.

❯ **Not redeemable** Fiat money is not redeemable for anything.

❯ **Unlimited** The government is free to print more if it wishes.

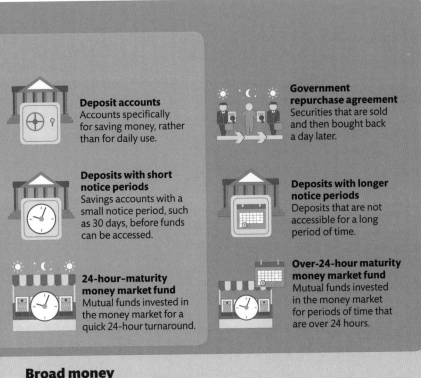

Deposit accounts Accounts specifically for saving money, rather than for daily use.

Deposits with short notice periods Savings accounts with a small notice period, such as 30 days, before funds can be accessed.

24-hour-maturity money market fund Mutual funds invested in the money market for a quick 24-hour turnaround.

Government repurchase agreement Securities that are sold and then bought back a day later.

Deposits with longer notice periods Deposits that are not accessible for a long period of time.

Over-24-hour maturity money market fund Mutual funds invested in the money market for periods of time that are over 24 hours.

Broad money
M2, M3, and M4 constitute broad money. This includes forms of money that are not immediately available in a spendable format, and which take time to access.

LESS LIQUID

TAKING THE MEASURE OF THE ECONOMY

The government or the central bank decides which definition of money to use when assessing the money supply. For instance, the US government measures supply by M2, and, since 2006, no longer includes data on M3. Once the data is gathered, the state may decide to make adjustments to the reserve amount that banks must hold (*see pp.90–91*) or increase the money supply (*see pp.92–93*).

M0
M1
M2
M3 £

Increasing money circulation

Most of the money in the economy occurs in the form of bank deposits – the appearance of funds in bank accounts. Banks increase money circulation whenever they make loans.

How it works

When a bank issues a customer with a loan, it will credit their account with the agreed amount. From the moment the loan shows up electronically in that customer's account, they will expect to be able to withdraw it as cash, so the bank must have that cash available in order to be able to hand it over to the customer on demand. Similarly, if the customer wants to use the loan to pay money into a different bank account in a different bank – having for example paid for goods with a debit card – the issuing bank must be able to persuade the second bank to accept the transfer of credit money. Because the issuing bank is liable to meet demands such as these, the deposit money that it has credited to the customer's account is seen as a liability as the bank will have to pay this money out. By contrast, the loan is regarded as an asset for the bank. This is because the bank can expect to recoup the money it has issued as a loan, along with the accrued interest, and it has a legal right to enforce the repayment should the customer refuse to pay. The bank records this transaction using a system of accounting called double-entry bookkeeping, which reflects the equal and opposite effects that the issuing of the loan will have on the bank's accounting books (*see right*).

BANK ASSETS AND LIABILITIES

Assets

An asset is something that is owned that can be used to pay debts. Assets usually produce a return over time. A bank's most important asset is its customer loan book, since customers pay interest on loans.

Liabilities

A liability is an obligation that is legally due to be paid. A bank's major liabilities are its customers' bank accounts, since all of its customers expect to be able to withdraw their money at some moment in time.

Balancing the books

Banks increase money circulation when they issue a loan in the form of money deposited in a customer's account. Although the loan and its repayment is an asset, the extra account money is a liability, because if the bank fails to make the money available on demand, it could collapse. To prevent this from occurring, banks maintain tight control of their balance sheets, making sure that their liabilities always match their assets. They carefully assess customers who apply for loans to ensure they will be able to make repayments. Central banks (*see pp.100–103*) exist to oversee the whole system and support banks when they face difficulties.

ASSETS

97%
of money in circulation is in the form of credit

BANK BALANCE SHEET: **LOANS**

Creating credit A balance sheet shows how liabilities are balanced by assets. When a bank makes a loan to a customer, the asset to the bank (the amount of the loan) is balanced exactly by the liability to the bank (the credit deposited in the customer's account).

The balance sheet records assets in one column and liabilities in the other.

Assets	Liabilities
Loan to customer **£1,000**	New money in the customer's account **£1,000**

The value of the loan in the customer's bank account.

The loan to the customer is an asset on which interest will be paid.

The credit in the customer's account is a liability that could be demanded in cash at any time.

The value of credit in the customer's bank account.

Assets	Liabilities
Additional loan to customer **£100**	Additional new money in the customer's account **£100**
Total loan to customer **£1,100**	Total new money **£1,100**

Further sums borrowed by the customer add to the bank's assets.

Further sums lent to the customer add to the bank's liabilities.

The bank is now owed an additional £100 on which interest will be paid.

The bank is now liable to pay an additional £100.

DOUBLE-ENTRY BOOKKEEPING

In accounting, this bookkeeping system requires that every business transaction is entered twice in at least two accounts to demonstrate that each entry has an equal and opposite effect. In practice this means that every debit in an account must be matched and offset by a credit. The sum of all debits must therefore equal the sum of all credits.

LIABILITIES

Banking reserves

Banks are not allowed to loan out all the money they receive as deposits, but instead are required by law to hold a set percentage of their deposits in reserve as hard currency, that is available to depositors.

How it works

The central bank sets the reserve requirement for commercial banks. This is the minimum percentage of total deposits that banks must hold as actual currency, in case some depositors wish to withdraw deposits as cash. Reserve amounts of hard currency may be stored in bank vaults on site, or held by the central bank in the form of deposits. The reserve amount held by a bank is usually around 10 per cent of its total deposits. The remaining 90 per cent of deposits, the excess reserve, can be loaned out to other customers. Freeing up capital for loans helps to create wealth in the economy. However, it also means that commercial banks would be unable to honour all withdrawals should all of its depositors try to withdraw their money as cash at the same time. This is a scenario that commercial banks count on as very unlikely; however, in such an event, they can appeal to the central bank for additional reserves. The central bank manipulates the reserve rate to influence how much money commercial banks are able to loan. In theory, a low reserve rate makes it cheaper for banks to lend, and vice versa (*see pp.100–103*). Banks are paid interest on their reserves held by the central bank.

How fractional reserves work

A reserve rate of five per cent means that a bank must retain five per cent of a £100,000 deposit; that is, hold £5,000 in reserve. The depositor's account will thus be credited with the full deposit amount of £100,000, and the bank then loans out £95,000 to another customer, crediting their account with £95,000. Now the bank holds £5,000 in cash against claims of £195,000.

CENTRAL BANK SETS RESERVE RATIO AT **5%**

COMMERCIAL BANK

Total bank reserves **£100,000**

£95,000
Excess reserves are loaned out to other customers, or can be used by the bank to make investments.

£5,000
Required reserves are held in a bank's vault as hard currency (and used for cash withdrawals), or held with the central bank.

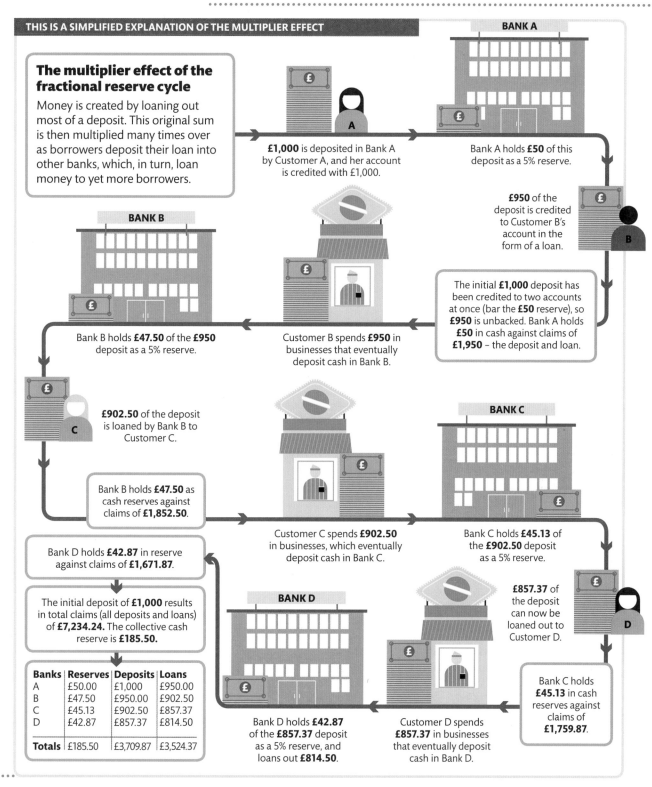

THIS IS A SIMPLIFIED EXPLANATION OF THE MULTIPLIER EFFECT

The multiplier effect of the fractional reserve cycle

Money is created by loaning out most of a deposit. This original sum is then multiplied many times over as borrowers deposit their loan into other banks, which, in turn, loan money to yet more borrowers.

BANK A

£1,000 is deposited in Bank A by Customer A, and her account is credited with £1,000.

Bank A holds £50 of this deposit as a 5% reserve.

£950 of the deposit is credited to Customer B's account in the form of a loan.

The initial £1,000 deposit has been credited to two accounts at once (bar the £50 reserve), so £950 is unbacked. Bank A holds £50 in cash against claims of £1,950 – the deposit and loan.

BANK B

Bank B holds £47.50 of the £950 deposit as a 5% reserve.

Customer B spends £950 in businesses that eventually deposit cash in Bank B.

£902.50 of the deposit is loaned by Bank B to Customer C.

Bank B holds £47.50 as cash reserves against claims of £1,852.50.

BANK C

Bank C holds £45.13 of the £902.50 deposit as a 5% reserve.

Customer C spends £902.50 in businesses, which eventually deposit cash in Bank C.

£857.37 of the deposit can now be loaned out to Customer D.

Bank D holds £42.87 in reserve against claims of £1,671.87.

The initial deposit of £1,000 results in total claims (all deposits and loans) of £7,234.24. The collective cash reserve is £185.50.

BANK D

Bank C holds £45.13 in cash reserves against claims of £1,759.87.

Banks	Reserves	Deposits	Loans
A	£50.00	£1,000	£950.00
B	£47.50	£950.00	£902.50
C	£45.13	£902.50	£857.37
D	£42.87	£857.37	£814.50
Totals	£185.50	£3,709.87	£3,524.37

Bank D holds £42.87 of the £857.37 deposit as a 5% reserve, and loans out £814.50.

Customer D spends £857.37 in businesses that eventually deposit cash in Bank D.

Recession and the money supply

The way money is used in an economy will change depending on how well or how badly that economy is performing. In a recession, the money supply is restricted, which affects the economy as a whole.

Recessionary cycle

Everything in the economy is linked to everything else through buying and selling, so it is possible for an economic downturn to lead to an ongoing pattern of decline – known as a recessionary cycle. Once a few households or firms (or the government) begin to cut their spending, other firms will start to sell less. In turn, they will want to reduce the amount they are spending on labour, or raw materials, to limit the impact of falling sales. They may also put off making longer-term investment decisions as profits are uncertain, meaning that they contribute even less money to the economy. This can add up to a powerful negative cycle.

If the money supply slows, the wheels of the economy turn more slowly, further restricting the movement of money around the economy, which creates a recessionary cycle.

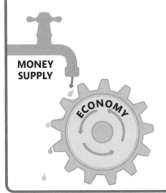

MONEY SUPPLY

ECONOMY

Consumers have less money to spend. They feel less confident about the future, and so may try to save more and spend less.

In response to decreased demand, producers cut wages and hours, lay off workers, and buy fewer raw materials.

Investors fear that company profits, and the value of stocks, will decrease, and are less willing to invest in new companies.

THE CREDIT CRUNCH

In the early 2000s, banks and other financial institutions began lending money on a vast scale. Regulations were loosened and low interest rates encouraged borrowing. The US and UK were particularly badly affected, with easily available credit encouraging spending by consumers and causing rapid economic growth. However, the very large amount of lending by banks meant that some loans were going to riskier borrowers. In the US, this took the form of "sub-prime mortgages", where people who were denied a conventional mortgage by banks were loaned money by certain lenders. When a number of these borrowers were unable to repay their loans, the heath of the whole system was at risk. Financial institutions stopped lending to each other, and, at the same time, consumer lending dried up in the "credit crunch" of 2008. As money was harder to get hold of, spending slowed, and the world economy fell into a recession.

How it works

A recession is a period during which the economy, as measured by its GDP, is shrinking, meaning that less is being bought and sold in that economy. This will usually also lead to falling wages and higher unemployment. As more people are out of work, or earning less than they previously were, they have less money to spend. They begin to save their money, fearing for their economic future, which has a further negative effect on the economy as a whole, as it reduces the overall money supply. Demand for goods can fall further, companies may be forced to cut costs and production, and the recession can worsen, setting up a vicious circle of decline.

As economic activity decreases people's expectations about the future worsen. They borrow less money and banks, in turn, may cut lending for fear that anyone borrowing money is less likely to repay it.

Unemployed workers have less money to spend, and by spending less they cause demand for consumer goods to fall still further. Workers on reduced hours and lower wages will also spend less and try to save more.

Companies produce fewer consumer goods, which further reduces their demand for labour and raw materials, slows their growth rate, and causes their profits to fall. Firms begin to fear for their futures and invest even less.

Fewer capital goods, such as machinery and equipment, are sold as companies reduce investment and spending. This hits the profits of the companies producing capital goods and reduces their demand for labour.

✓ NEED TO KNOW

❯ **Expansionary policy** Attempts by a government to make an economy grow faster – for example by cutting taxes, raising government spending, cutting interest rates, or making money easier to borrow.

❯ **Contractionary policy** Attempts by a government to slow an economy down, usually to try to avoid inflation – for example by raising taxes, cutting government spending, or both. It usually involves raising interest rates and making money harder to borrow.

5%
the amount by which the UK economy shrank in 2009

Recession to depression

A sustained period of deep recession is known as a depression. During a depression a country's GDP (the value of all the goods and services it produces) can fall by up to 10 per cent and unemployment levels soar.

Case study: The Great Depression, 1929–41

The worst economic crisis of the 20th century, economists still debate what caused the Great Depression, how it spread around the world, and why recovery took so long.

1. Prosperity in the US during the "Roaring Twenties" leads to overconfidence and reckless investment. Thousands of ordinary Americans buy stocks and shares, and the increasing demand inflates their value.

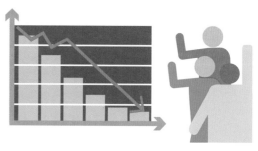

2. By late 1929 there are signs the US economy is in trouble: unemployment is rising, consumer spending is declining, and farms are failing. But still confident of getting rich quick, some people continue to invest.

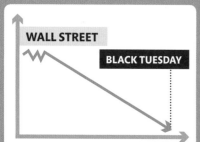

WALL STREET

BLACK TUESDAY

3. Over six days in October 1929, shares on Wall Street's New York Stock Exchange crash. In total US$25 billion is lost, and with it people's confidence in the stock market. Many investors go bankrupt, banks lose money, and trade collapses.

4. There are a series of runs on the banks, as shaken customers want to hold on to all their cash (*see right*). Many banks lose their reserves and by 1933 more than half have shut. Banks contract their loans, and the deposits they create, further reducing the US money supply.

CLOSED

5. Loss of confidence, less money, and increased borrowing costs result in reduced spending and demand for goods. Manufacturing slows, workers are laid off, and wages are lowered, further reducing spending power.

CLOSED

How it works

A depression occurs following a protracted period of deep recession, and when an economy is stuck in a perpetual cycle of decline there can be catastrophic results. Banks crash, stock markets plummet, the money supply shrinks, prices fall, investments are rendered almost worthless, there is an increase in defaults and bankruptcies, and unemployment levels rise as individuals and businesses stop spending. Government attempts to stimulate the economy by pumping more money into it no longer work, and low interest rates no longer encourage consumer spending. Instead, government investment to stimulate employment and growth is needed.

6. The depression spreads around the world as the US, having lent a lot of money to European countries, recalls loans, pulls out of foreign investments, and increases taxes on foreign imports. European banks collapse and unemployment rises.

NEW DEAL

7. In 1932, US President Franklin D Roosevelt introduces the New Deal, to fight the depression through economic and social reforms. In Europe, right wing parties emerge, such as Hitler's National Socialist Party, which promises to restore the economy.

40%
the amount the average US income fell between 1929 and 1932

LIQUIDITY TRAP

People tend to hold on to money in economically unstable times because it is a reliable store of wealth that can be exchanged quickly for other assets – a good insurance against an uncertain future. Holding on to money also becomes more profitable when prices are dropping, as a given amount of money will buy ever more goods.

When the desire to save is so great that it overwhelms normal spending activity, the economy can become stuck in a liquidity trap. Any increase in the money supply fails to stimulate economic activity, as people continue to hoard money while they wait for the economy to improve. However, this hoarding slows the economy further and, if it persists, can potentially help to cause a depression.

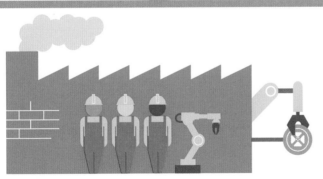

8. Countries that leave the gold standard early, and so can depreciate their currencies to combat deflation, tend to begin recovery sooner. For the US, WWII brings an increase in employment (in industrial production and military service) and government spending, which speeds recovery.

Managing state finance

In spending money to provide the services that people expect, governments must aim for maximum cost efficiency. They therefore plan to finance their budget from a combination of taxation, borrowing, and (very occasionally) printing new money. Taxation in all its forms is the primary source of funding, with borrowing used as a means to make up the shortfall. Printing money is rare as it risks undermining confidence in the value of the currency itself.

Balancing the books

Government spending today is largely to meet demand, and typically accounts for around one-third of a country's economy. In some countries (such as those in Scandinavia), government spending accounts for a much greater proportion than this. Financing this degree of spending can be a difficult task. While governments aspire to balance their budgets, most borrow a proportion. What matters is that the level of borrowing is controlled so that people have confidence that government debts will always be repaid.

CENTRAL BANK
A country's central bank manages the currency and money supply, holds central bank reserves, and implements economic targets set by the government.
See pp.100–103

PRINTING MONEY
Modern governments very rarely print currency to finance themselves, since doing so carries significant risks.
See pp.124–125

TAXES
Taxation is the safest means of raising money, but is unpopular as it represents a loss of money to the people being taxed.
See pp.106–107

BORROWING
This is a costly option as interest will be charged, and money borrowed must be paid back.
See pp.108–109

Government revenue

PRINTING MONEY

Governments can issue their own money, either by printing it or by creating it electronically. However, creating money in this way carries a risk. Since money depends on trust, when a government issues increasing amounts of currency, people may have less confidence in the value of that currency. If their trust collapses completely, then hyperinflation may occur (*See pp.132–135*). This is what took place in Germany in the 1920s, for example.

US$6.7 trillion
the amount the US government spent in 2016

A BUDGET IN BALANCE
The government budget balance is the overall difference between its revenues and its spending.

CONSUMPTION AND INVESTMENT
Government spending is a mixture of paying for the immediate costs of running services, and investment in things such as roads, hospitals, and universities. Services such as pensions, healthcare, education, welfare, and defence are all major elements of annual spending.
See pp.130–131

DEBT REPAYMENT
Governments must repay their debts. Paying interest on debt can be a significant budget cost.
See pp.110–111

Government spending

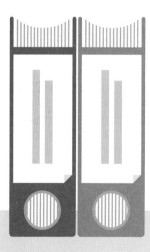

Governments and money

A country's government and central bank play a key role in the circulation of money in the economy. They monitor money supply, send funding to key sectors of society, and ensure that cash flows back to them for state spending.

How it works

A healthy economy requires a good money supply. Although it is difficult to control the supply of money directly, government monetary policy can help to influence it. The most important institution in determining monetary policy is the central bank (*see pp.100–103*), which is critical in influencing interest rates and can be used to inject more money into the economy via open market operations (*see pp.102–103*) or through quantitative easing (*see pp.124–125*). Governments may also control the flow of money via taxes, and by restricting borrowing and lending. However, these mechanisms are imperfect in the modern monetary system, since commercial banks are largely free to decide the terms of their lending. Attempts to directly control money supply tend to fail.

Money supply and a healthy economy

Just as a healthy body depends on a good blood supply to receive nutrients, so a healthy economy relies on a good money supply to keep the cycle of spending going: as one person spends, another earns, then spends, and so on. If this cycle slows, the economy may begin to decline. The government, via the central bank – which is like the beating heart of the economy – helps to keep money flowing. Meanwhile, the government also ensures that funding reaches key areas of society, and collects revenues for state spending. Economic policies around interest rates, reserve ratios, open market operations, and quantitative easing are all focused on maintaining money supply. A body may have optimal blood supply, but it is down to the cells to effectively utilize the nutrients. In the same way, while a government can improve money supply, economic growth then depends on how effectively individuals and businesses are able to convert this money into useful goods and services to raise living standards.

Money flows out

The central bank uses financial institutions as a conduit to increase the money supply. At the same time, government spending makes up a huge part of the economy.

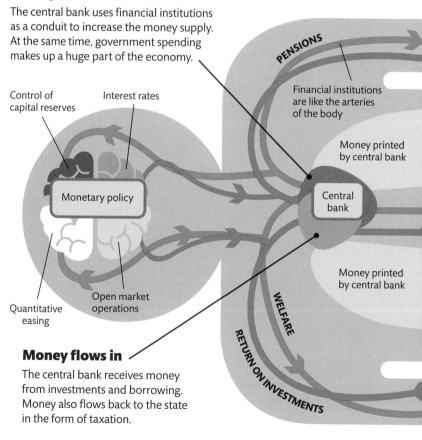

Control of capital reserves

Interest rates

Monetary policy

Quantitative easing

Open market operations

PENSIONS

Financial institutions are like the arteries of the body

Money printed by central bank

Central bank

Money printed by central bank

WELFARE

RETURN ON INVESTMENTS

Money flows in

The central bank receives money from investments and borrowing. Money also flows back to the state in the form of taxation.

✓ NEED TO KNOW

> **Money supply** The total amount of money circulating in a country, from currency to less liquid forms.

> **Central bank** An institution that provides financial services to the government and commercial banks, implements monetary policies, sets interest rates, and controls money supply.

> **Currency in circulation** Money that is physically used to conduct transactions between customers and businesses.

THE CASE FOR INDEPENDENT CENTRAL BANKS

Many central banks were made independent from the government in the early 2000s, although they are still required to be both transparent and accountable. The 2008 crash led some to question whether independent banks are desirable.

Pros

> **Monetary policy can be** more impartial as banks have no interest in maintaining electoral popularity.

> **As they are unaffected** by the electoral cycle they can plan and implement long-term policies.

> **Independent banks** have tended to maintain lower rates of inflation.

Cons

> **Unelected banks** cannot be voted out, arguably making them less accountable.

> **Central bank** controls may not be enough to avert financial crises without government aid.

> **Governments** may blame banks for recessions, so eroding trust.

"Monetary policy is not a panacea"

Ben Bernanke, US economist

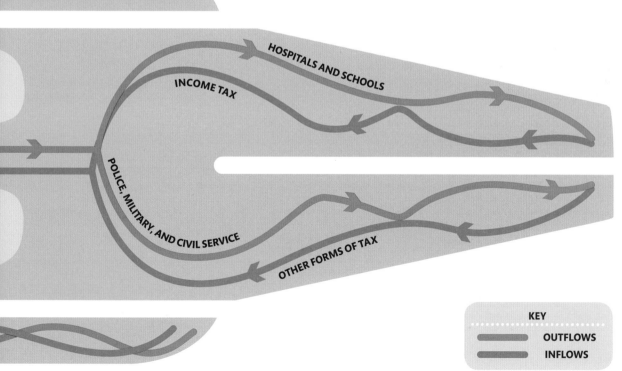

BORROWING

HOSPITALS AND SCHOOLS

INCOME TAX

POLICE, MILITARY, AND CIVIL SERVICE

OTHER FORMS OF TAX

KEY

OUTFLOWS

INFLOWS

The central bank

A central bank is the "bankers' bank", acting as guarantor for the rest of the banking system. Central banks play a critical role in setting a country's monetary policy and supporting government economic objectives.

How it works

A central bank manages a country's currency, interest rates, and money supply, and holds central bank reserves. Commercial banks rely on these central bank reserves to support their day-to-day operations. By altering both the amount of the reserves, and the cost of borrowing from them (via the rate of interest charged, known as the reserve rate or base rate), central banks can assert control over the country's money supply.

The base rate (see pp.120–121) is usually the cheapest rate of interest available for its currency, and because central bank reserves

are fundamental to commercial banks' ability to lend, the central bank helps to set interest rates for the entire economy. When the base rate rises or falls, interest rates on commercial bank loans do the same. As with the supply and demand of other commodities, when demand for reserve money is high, its price (here the reserve rate or base rate) rises. Conversely, when the demand for reserve money is low, its price falls.

Central banks often focus on regulating other specific economic targets – most typically the rate of inflation. They do this by meeting preset, publicly displayed targets.

LENDER OF LAST RESORT

Because banking contains an element of risk, the stability of the system depends on an institution that can provide protection to banks threatened with failure. Central banks, with their potentially unlimited quantities of central

reserves, play the role of "lender of last resort". When a failing bank presents too risky a prospect for lenders, it can still rely on loans from the central bank. This provides a safeguard against financial collapse that could damage the economy.

Monetary targets

The objective of a central bank's monetary policy is usually to deliver price stability (low inflation) and to support the government. Price stability has a role in achieving economic stability more generally, and provides the right conditions for sustainable growth. Central banks have a range of strategies to achieve this. One is to target the total amount of money in the economy: the money supply. A second strategy is to target a particular exchange rate by altering the amount of currency in circulation to affect the foreign exchange markets. A third is to target a particular interest rate, as illustrated opposite.

19 countries

in the **European Union** share a single central bank: the **European Central Bank**

Central bank

The central bank creates and supplies reserve money to commercial banks, giving it huge power over the day-to-day workings of the banking system. Usually, the central bank will try to maintain its target interest rate by pumping reserve money into or out of the banks. This affects demand for reserve money and, therefore, the price the central bank can charge commercial banks to borrow – the reserve rate.

Reserve rate too high

When the demand for central bank money is high, the reserve interest rate rises.

Reserve rate too low

When the demand for central bank money is low, the reserve interest rate falls.

Commercial bank reserves

PUSHING RATE DOWN
The central bank buys securities from the commercial banks, so increasing the amount of central bank reserves in the system. As more money is available, the cost of borrowing – the interest rate – decreases.

The central bank pumps more of its money into commercial bank reserves, lowering the interest rate, bringing it back in line with the target interest rate.

The central bank sucks reserve money out of the system, bringing the base rate up, back in line with its target.

PUSHING RATE UP
To increase the interest rate, it sells securities to commercial banks, so reducing the quantity of central bank reserves in the system. As a result, the demand for money and the cost of borrowing it goes up.

TARGET RESERVE INTEREST RATE

Managing the monetary system

By raising or lowering its reserve rate of interest, a central bank can influence the size of commercial banks' reserves, and thus their borrowing and lending rates, and the amount of money in circulation. This affects spending, and inflation, as when interest rates are lower, saving is less appealing and borrowing more, and when interest rates are higher, the opposite is true.

✓ NEED TO KNOW

❭ **Secondary market** The forum in which investors buy and sell bonds issued by the government.

❭ **Inflation** A general increase in prices and fall in the purchasing value of money.

❭ **The spread** The difference between the cheapest and the most expensive interest rate.

❭ **Credit guidance** A form of cheaper lending by the central bank that is designed to meet wider government objectives such as boosting key industries.

❭ **Reserve ratio** The percentage of depositors' balances that a bank must keep as cash. The reserve ratio is set by the central bank.

Increasing money in circulation

Lowering the reserve (base) rate of interest

The central bank can cut the reserve rate of interest to make it cheaper for commercial banks to borrow from its reserves. The idea is that the commercial banks will then in turn reduce their interest rates to the public.

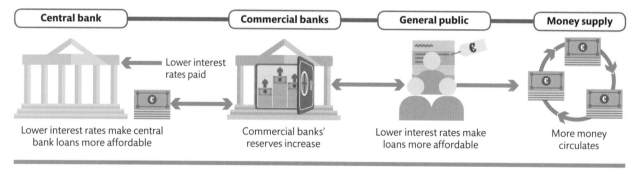

Central bank	Commercial banks	General public	Money supply

Lower interest rates paid

Lower interest rates make central bank loans more affordable

Commercial banks' reserves increase

Lower interest rates make loans more affordable

More money circulates

Open market operations: buying bonds

The central bank buys bonds on the open market. Investors deposit the money from the sales, which increases the amount of reserve money in the open market. Commercial banks then respond by lowering interest rates.

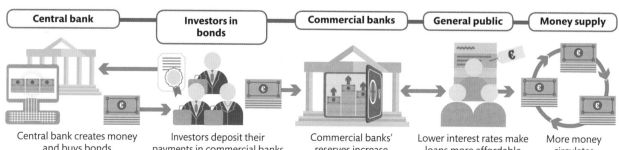

Central bank	Investors in bonds	Commercial banks	General public	Money supply

Central bank creates money and buys bonds

Investors deposit their payments in commercial banks

Commercial banks' reserves increase

Lower interest rates make loans more affordable

More money circulates

CENTRAL BANK CONTROLS

Credit guidance

The central bank's control of commercial banks' licences means that it is able to influence how commercial banks lend. It can, for example, give commercial banks incentives to encourage them to offer very low interest rates to important sectors of the economy.

Open market operations

The central bank buys and sells bonds in the open market to affect the short-term rates of interest.

Credit access

The central bank can restrict access to credit for commercial banks, for example by raising the amount of deposits they must hold as reserves.

1668

the year that the oldest central bank in the world, the Swedish Riksbank, was established

Decreasing money in circulation

Raising the reserve (base) rate of interest

The central bank can curtail commercial banks' lending to the public by raising its reserve rate of interest. This makes it more expensive for commercial banks to borrow from central bank reserves. Commercial banks then raise interest rates for borrowers.

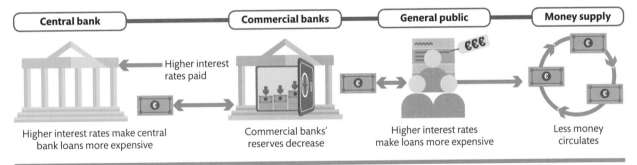

| Central bank | Commercial banks | General public | Money supply |

Higher interest rates paid

Higher interest rates make central bank loans more expensive

Commercial banks' reserves decrease

Higher interest rates make loans more expensive

Less money circulates

Open market operations: selling bonds

The central bank sells bonds back to the market in exchange for money, causing investors to make withdrawals to buy the bonds, lowering the amount of money in the banking system. Commercial banks respond by raising interest rates.

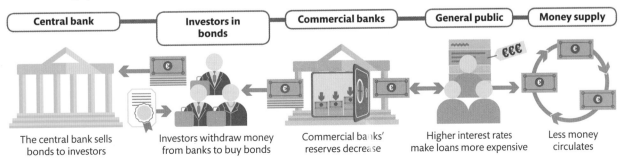

| Central bank | Investors in bonds | Commercial banks | General public | Money supply |

The central bank sells bonds to investors

Investors withdraw money from banks to buy bonds

Commercial banks' reserves decrease

Higher interest rates make loans more expensive

Less money circulates

Budget constraint

Governments have financial constraints just as individuals and companies do. When spending exceeds income, the government may need to borrow – or even print – money to cover the shortfall.

How it works

Governments need to pay for the public services they provide and for any other financial commitments they may have. To do this they tax the population, and borrow money if additional funds are needed. In extreme cases it is even possible for governments to print their own cash. Each strategy has its own costs – but printing money is so risky that it is very rarely used by governments.

The difference between a government's tax revenues and its spending is known as its budget (or fiscal) deficit. The budget deficit shows how much extra money the government needs to borrow (or print) to finance its spending. It is typical for some governments to run a small budget deficit on an ongoing basis.

Spending and the deficit

Ideally a government's spending commitments (inside the circle) should be covered by tax revenue and its other forms of income. However, when a proportion of spending is not covered (budget deficit), the extra funding has to be raised either from borrowing or by printing additional money. Small deficits can usually be dealt with by borrowing alone, but if a deficit grows too large, then the government may find itself in financial difficulties as it may need to borrow increasing amounts simply to keep up with existing payments (see pp.146–7).

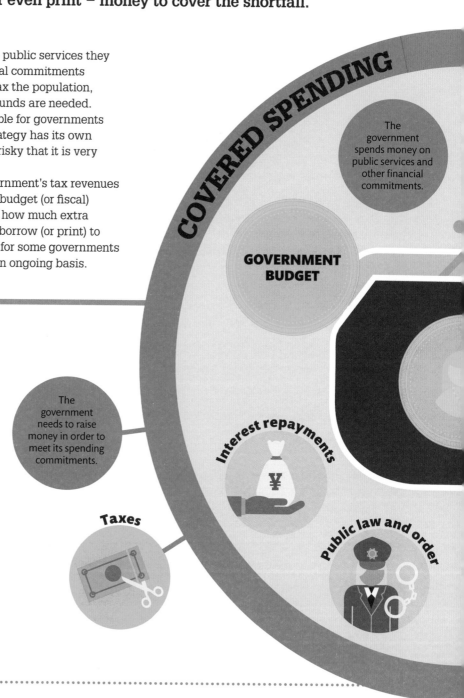

COVERED SPENDING

The government spends money on public services and other financial commitments.

GOVERNMENT BUDGET

The government needs to raise money in order to meet its spending commitments.

Interest repayments

Taxes

Public law and order

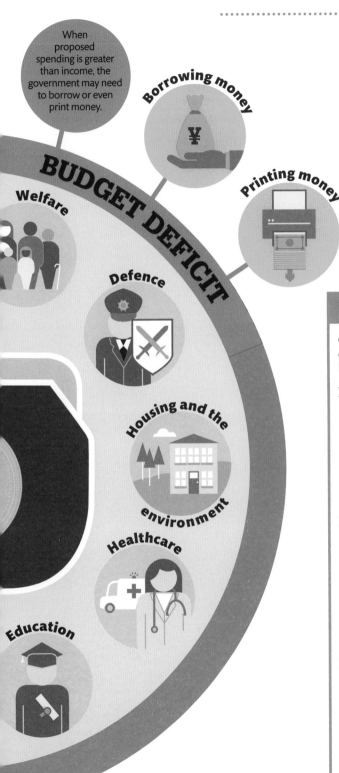

When proposed spending is greater than income, the government may need to borrow or even print money.

Borrowing money

Printing money

BUDGET DEFICIT

Welfare

Defence

Housing and the environment

Healthcare

Education

75%
of GDP: Libya's budget deficit – the worst in the world

HOW GOVERNMENTS RAISE MONEY

Governments can raise funds to meet their spending commitments in three different ways. Each strategy has its own advantages and disadvantages.

❯ **Taxes** Governments can levy taxes on what the population earns and owns, and on foreign trade. Taxes are safe, but unpopular.

SAFE   **UNPOPULAR**

❯ **Borrowing** Governments can borrow from their own citizens – through pension funds for example – or from abroad. But loans incur interest charges.

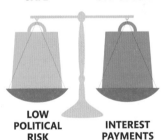

LOW POLITICAL RISK   **INTEREST PAYMENTS**

❯ **Printing money** A government can print its own money. This seemingly simple solution is rare because of the risks it entails (*see pp.144–5*).

LOOKS EASY   **HIGH FINANCIAL RISK**

How tax works

Taxation is the main way in which governments raise the revenue needed to pay for public spending. Governments may tax the public directly (such as with income tax) or indirectly (via VAT, for example).

How it works

Governments have the unique privilege of being able to demand that anyone in their country pay taxes. These can be divided into "direct" taxes, which are paid from earnings, either by people or by institutions, and "indirect" taxes, which are paid for out of consumer spending. Taxes can be levied as a share of spending or income, or as a flat rate. A progressive tax system is one in which richer individuals pay proportionately more tax.

Questions surrounding the level of taxation are hotly debated. As a result, taxation rates, and laws about who or what pays for which taxes, vary significantly from country to country.

TAXES AND BEHAVIOUR

Some taxes are designed to reduce the amount of revenue that goods earn. Because a newly-levied or increased tax on a product raises its price, that item becomes less attractive to buy. Where a product, such as cigarettes, is harmful, higher taxes can be a way to reduce public consumption. In cases in which the behaviour of consumers does not alter much in response to higher pricing, however, the extra tax is likely to raise much more money. This can make such taxes appealing for governments seeking revenues.

Direct and indirect taxes

People have to pay taxes on either their income, or on what they spend. Some typical taxes on an individual in the UK are shown below.

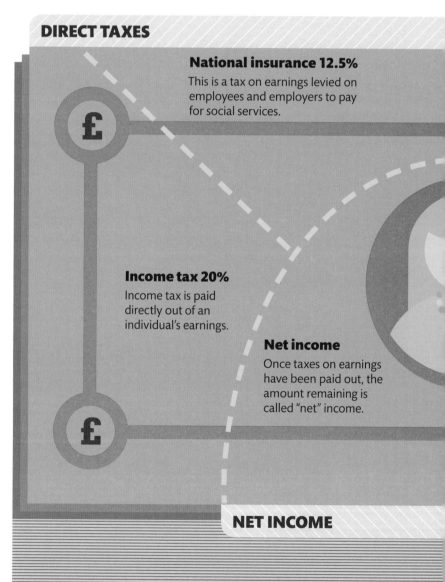

DIRECT TAXES

National insurance 12.5%
This is a tax on earnings levied on employees and employers to pay for social services.

Income tax 20%
Income tax is paid directly out of an individual's earnings.

Net income
Once taxes on earnings have been paid out, the amount remaining is called "net" income.

NET INCOME

US$**21** trillion
thought to be hidden in **tax havens abroad**

INDIRECT TAXES

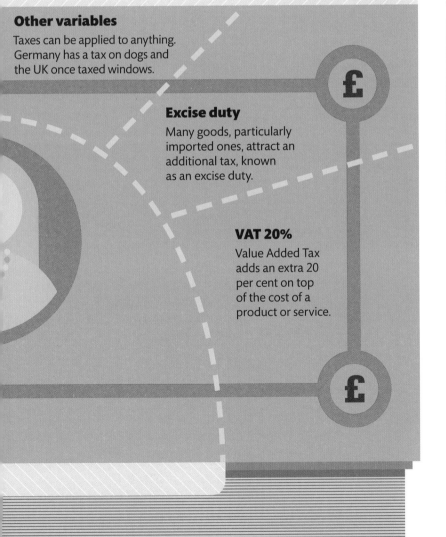

Other variables
Taxes can be applied to anything. Germany has a tax on dogs and the UK once taxed windows.

Excise duty
Many goods, particularly imported ones, attract an additional tax, known as an excise duty.

VAT 20%
Value Added Tax adds an extra 20 per cent on top of the cost of a product or service.

TAX EVASION AND AVOIDANCE

Because tax systems vary widely from country to country, it is possible for companies and some rich individuals to exploit the differences in international tax rates to reduce the total amount of tax they pay. This is termed tax "evasion" when done illegally, and tax "avoidance" when performed legally, although in practice the boundaries are blurred. Some jurisdictions deliberately set very low tax rates to attract investment; some also provide secrecy around the identity of those investing there. This has led to accusations that such areas are acting as "tax havens". This means that, instead of providing a legitimate location for economic activity, they are allowing major corporations and the very wealthy to avoid paying taxes they should be paying.

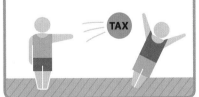

Government borrowing

The main way that governments pay for any spending, not already covered by taxation, is through borrowing. However, excessive borrowing will result in high levels of government debt.

Managing the debt

Governments keep a careful eye on their overall level of debt, since high levels of debt mean greater interest repayments. Very elevated levels of debt may even become impossible to repay if tax revenue proves insufficient to keep pace with elevated interest rates. Furthermore, a heavily indebted country that investors see as a risky prospect may find it difficult to borrow enough to cover day-to-day spending.

Borrowing

Governments typically borrow money by issuing bonds to individuals and financial institutions in exchange for a loan. The government will then pay a fixed rate of interest over a period of time to the investor, paying the bond back in full when it reaches maturity.

Government funds

A typical government receives most of its financing in the form of taxes, but borrowing is also often necessary in order to meet planned expenditures. Any borrowed money will need to be repaid eventually and so a significant portion of a government's budget is reserved for debt payments.

TAX

How it works

Governments will often want to spend more than they earn in taxes. This may happen during a recession, when there is higher unemployment and therefore lower tax revenues. The gap between government tax revenue and what it spends is called the deficit. Governments borrow in order to cover the deficit, maintain spending, and continue to provide services with the aim that debts will eventually be repaid with tax revenue. Most governments run a deficit from time to time, and may run one most of the time. If debts can be repaid, and interest payments are not large, this is not a problem, but there is a risk of default when repayment cannot keep pace with borrowing.

"A national debt, if it is not excessive, will be to us a national blessing"

Alexander Hamilton, first US Secretary of the Treasury

Repaying the deficit

The higher the deficit, the more of a government's budget is required in order to pay it off. Governments with a surplus can give more to their debt payments.

Repayment

Any debt that a government takes on must eventually be repaid, along with interest on that debt. A certain level of debt repayment must always be maintained by the government to avoid default or excess interest incurred on that debt.

Government default

If a government fails or refuses to pay back a debt in full it is said to have defaulted. This means that it is unable to keep up repayments on some of the debt it owes.

DANGER OF DEFAULT

Public debt

Public debt is the total sum of money owed by a country's government, including its historic debt. Nations with big economies and large tax-paying populations can carry more debt than those without.

How it works

The total amount borrowed by a country's government (and by all its previous governments) is known as the public or national debt. This is generally calculated as the total debt minus the government's liquid assets. Interest is due on this debt, and it can be substantial. If a government spends more than it collects in taxes in one year, it will be in deficit. Any money it borrows to cover this is then added to the public debt. When the government spends less than it collects in taxes in a year, it has a "surplus", which can be used to pay off the debt. Inflation can also help reduce a debt burden. A state that becomes unable to pay its debt is said to "default", and will find it hard to borrow again.

Carrying debt

Governments usually repay debt using taxes. The more money that they raise, the faster they can repay it. The larger a country's economy, the more debt it can safely hold, since a bigger economy is able to gather more taxes.

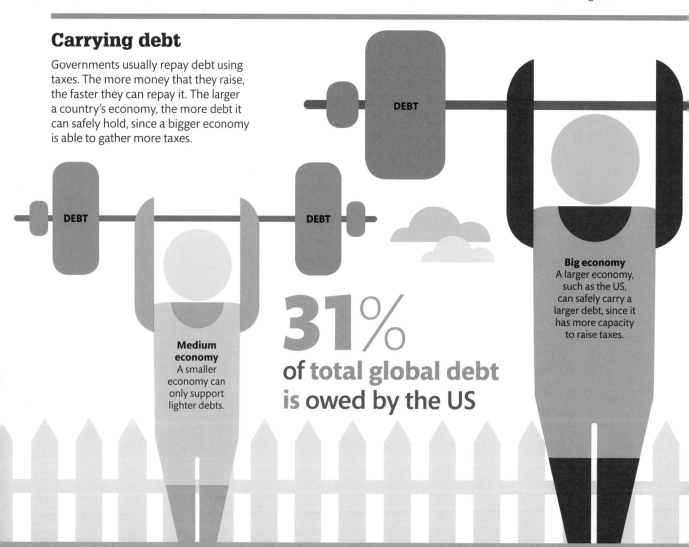

DEBT

DEBT

DEBT

Medium economy
A smaller economy can only support lighter debts.

31%
of **total global debt**
is owed by the US

Big economy
A larger economy, such as the US, can safely carry a larger debt, since it has more capacity to raise taxes.

GOVERNMENT DEBTS RISE IN WARTIME

War imposes exceptional demands on government spending. Governments typically finance this by borrowing money. The first ever government debts, in the 17th century, were a result of borrowing to fund military campaigns.

GOVERNMENT · DEBT

✔ NEED TO KNOW

> **Public/national/sovereign debt** Total debt owed by a government.

> **Internal debts** Money that is borrowed from within a government's own country.

> **External debts** Money that is borrowed from abroad.

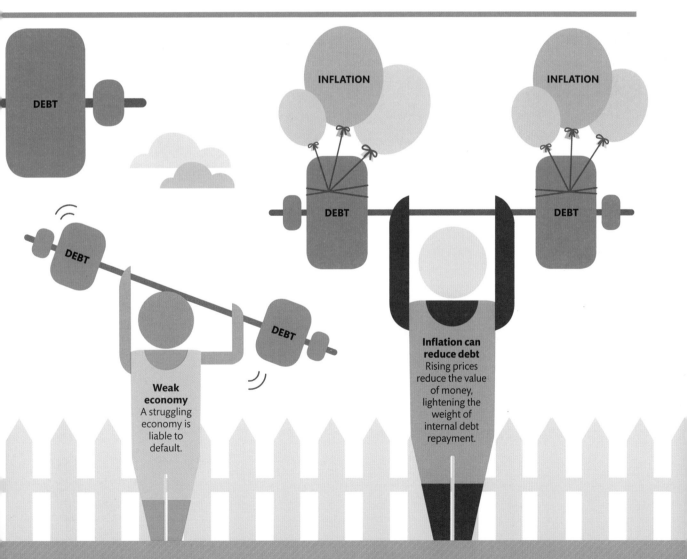

DEBT

INFLATION · DEBT

INFLATION · DEBT

Weak economy
A struggling economy is liable to default.

Inflation can reduce debt
Rising prices reduce the value of money, lightening the weight of internal debt repayment.

Accountability

Responsibility for economic policy is usually shared between a country's government and its central bank. By reporting their decisions to the public and to democratic institutions, they can be made more accountable to the people.

How it works

Democratic countries typically insist that governments report annually to their legislative bodies about their taxation and spending plans – their fiscal policy. The annual budget has become the central instrument of governments' economic policy, and its contents tend to dominate the debate during national elections. Before the 2008 crash, monetary policy – changing interest rates and influencing the money supply – had been increasingly left to central banks. However, since the crash, the policy, and the banking system's role in it, have been subject to more rigorous examination.

Media reports on budget

The media reports on changes to the government budget and how they will affect the public.

Public adjusts its spending habits

Knowledge about the budget may inform decisions by households and firms on spending and saving money.

Legislative body approves budget

A country's legislative body, typically an elected parliament, will debate the budget and potentially make changes.

Auditors inspect public finances
Many countries have an independent body that inspects the government's financial decisions.

Government draws up a budget

Typically an annual budget allocates spending across different resources.

FISCAL IMPACT
Government policymakers take a long-term perspective. To achieve the best economic outcomes, central bank policymakers need to be guided by this perspective.

MONETARY IMPACT
Central bank decisions on monetary policy affect government spending due to the impact of interest rates on employment and inflation in particular.

TRANSPARENCY AND ACCOUNTABILITY IN CENTRAL BANKS

The current trend in many countries is for an independent central bank. It is essential that an autonomous central bank is able to coordinate effectively with the government and keep it, and the public, appraised of economic projections. To this end, a central bank should demonstrate both transparency and accountability.

Transparency

❱ **Increased openness** is expected to lead to better-informed decisions.

❱ **Political, economic, and procedural policies** should all be clearly outlined.

❱ **Regular and comprehensive reports** must be made available to the public and the government.

Accountability

❱ **Rigorous standards of conduct** for the central bank's staff should lead to higher-quality decisions.

❱ **Audited financial statements** should be made publicly available.

❱ **Operating expenses and revenue** should be disclosed.

EXTERNAL FACTORS
Central bank decision-making must also take into account factors such as social attitudes, business considerations, and the volatility of the financial markets.

Central bank also oversees commercial banks Oversight of commercial banks gives the central bank large power in shaping the economy.

Report justifies and explains decisions

The central bank governor appears before the committee to give further explanation when required.

Central bank sets interest rates

Having consulted a range of financial indicators, the central bank decides on a set rate of interest.

Minutes of policy meeting published

Reports of the central bank's decision-making process are made publicly available.

Impact of policy is monitored and quantified

Financial institutions and the specialist press pay especially close attention to the central bank's decisions.

IMPACT ON THE PUBLIC
Interest rates affect saving, borrowing, and spending decisions. These feed through into output and employment, then producers' costs and prices, and eventually consumer prices.

IMPACT ON MONEY MARKETS
Interest rates affect the price of financial assets and the exchange rate, which affect consumer and business demand, and the return on a country's assets relative to their foreign-currency equivalents.

Attempting control

Governments can attempt to manage the economy by adjusting policies such as taxes and influencing interest rates. Each adjustment can affect a small part of the complete economic machine. However, the economy is usually beyond the direct control of a country's government, and its different elements interact with each other in different ways. Forecasting its behaviour, and attempting to balance competing demands for resources, is therefore a continual challenge.

Economic machine

This design is based on a real machine, the MONIAC, a hydraulic simulation of the UK economy built in 1949 by economist Bill Phillips. Based on the theory of national income, it showed the connections between the different parts of the economy using a system of tanks, pumps, and tubes, and could be used to make simple forecasts resulting from policy changes.

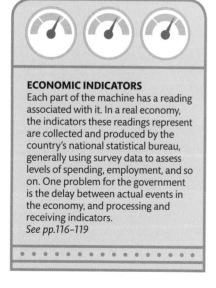

ECONOMIC INDICATORS
Each part of the machine has a reading associated with it. In a real economy, the indicators these readings represent are collected and produced by the country's national statistical bureau, generally using survey data to assess levels of spending, employment, and so on. One problem for the government is the delay between actual events in the economy, and processing and receiving indicators. *See pp.116–119*

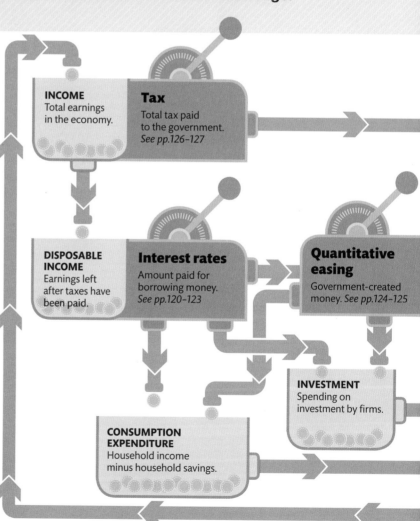

INCOME
Total earnings in the economy.

Tax
Total tax paid to the government. *See pp.126–127*

DISPOSABLE INCOME
Earnings left after taxes have been paid.

Interest rates
Amount paid for borrowing money. *See pp.120–123*

Quantitative easing
Government-created money. *See pp.124–125*

INVESTMENT
Spending on investment by firms.

CONSUMPTION EXPENDITURE
Household income minus household savings.

NATIONAL INCOME ACCOUNTING

National income

National income is the total amount earned by every sector of the economy and from the foreign balance (also known as the balance of payments). National income accounting is a method that a national government uses to measure the level of a country's economic activity in a given time period.

Income equals expenditure

The idea of national income means that every penny spent in one part of the economy must equate to a penny earned elsewhere, and the economy's total earnings must match its total spending. This basic idea allows economists to build and study models such as the MONIAC machine.

US$4.29 trillion

Japan's Gross National Income (GNI) in 2015

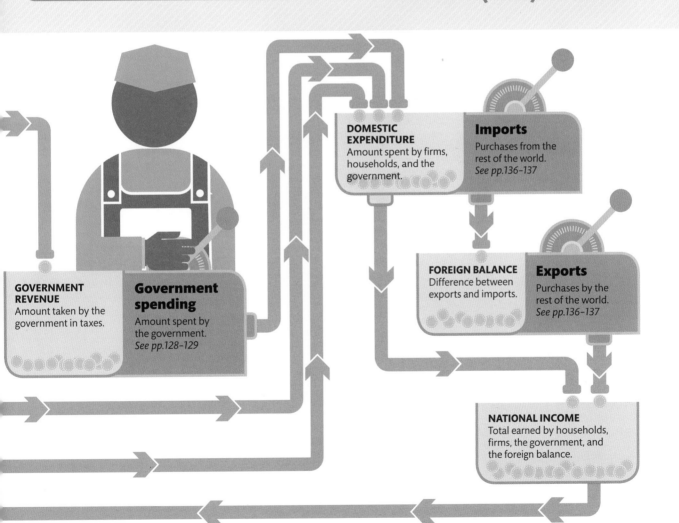

GOVERNMENT REVENUE
Amount taken by the government in taxes.

Government spending
Amount spent by the government.
See pp.128–129

DOMESTIC EXPENDITURE
Amount spent by firms, households, and the government.

Imports
Purchases from the rest of the world.
See pp.136–137

FOREIGN BALANCE
Difference between exports and imports.

Exports
Purchases by the rest of the world.
See pp.136–137

NATIONAL INCOME
Total earned by households, firms, the government, and the foreign balance.

Reading economic indicators

Using a few key indicators of performance, governments can monitor how parts of the economy are working and whether there are potential problems ahead. However, such indicators must be read with care.

Measuring performance

Indicators are usually shown as the rate of change over time, because the economy is very dynamic. But this means indicators are only estimates, based on surveys taken at a particular point in time.

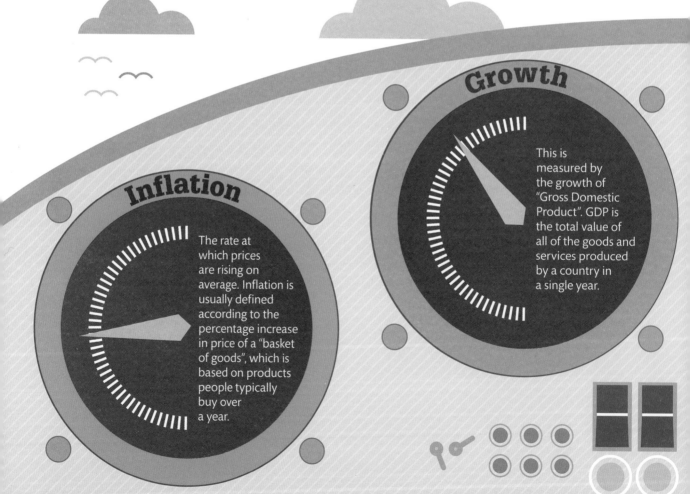

Growth

This is measured by the growth of "Gross Domestic Product". GDP is the total value of all of the goods and services produced by a country in a single year.

Inflation

The rate at which prices are rising on average. Inflation is usually defined according to the percentage increase in price of a "basket of goods", which is based on products people typically buy over a year.

How it works

The main indicators governments use to monitor the economy are based on surveys of individuals, businesses, and government departments. A national statistics agency is usually charged with running the survey, and then calculating the figures. The agency will look at the economy, business, industry and trade, the employment and labour markets, and society in general. The "headline indicators" generally relate to parts of the economy that have the most impact on people's daily lives, and might include assessments of the likelihood that individuals will find employment, whether their pay will go up or down, and whether businesses will be able to expand.

1884 the year the US Bureau of Labor Statistics was formed to analyse data

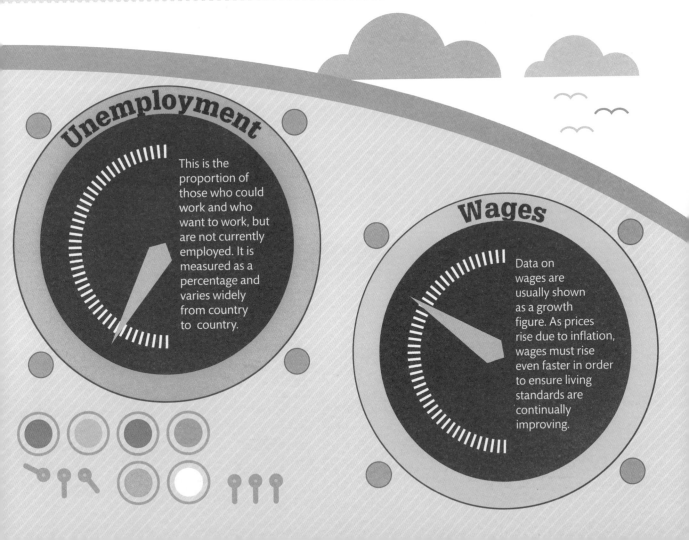

Unemployment

This is the proportion of those who could work and who want to work, but are not currently employed. It is measured as a percentage and varies widely from country to country.

Wages

Data on wages are usually shown as a growth figure. As prices rise due to inflation, wages must rise even faster in order to ensure living standards are continually improving.

Deciding on economic policy

Governments closely monitor data on the economy to establish which policies might improve its performance. There are numerous ways of intervening in the economy, each with their own pros and cons.

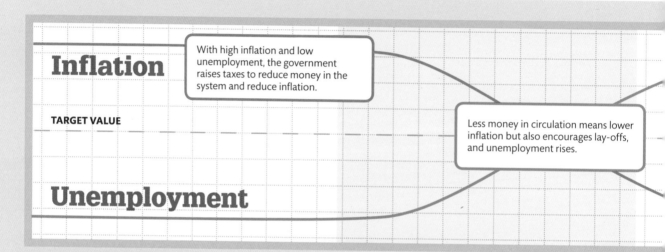

Inflation

With high inflation and low unemployment, the government raises taxes to reduce money in the system and reduce inflation.

TARGET VALUE

Less money in circulation means lower inflation but also encourages lay-offs, and unemployment rises.

Unemployment

Calibrating the economic machine

Governments have a number of different controls they can adjust to help the smooth running of the economy. The biggest are taxes, spending decisions, and interest rates. Each of these controls affects the economy in many different ways, and governments have to consider a range of potential outcomes when taking action.

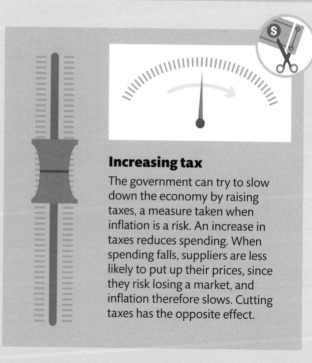

Increasing tax

The government can try to slow down the economy by raising taxes, a measure taken when inflation is a risk. An increase in taxes reduces spending. When spending falls, suppliers are less likely to put up their prices, since they risk losing a market, and inflation therefore slows. Cutting taxes has the opposite effect.

"**Inflation is the one form of taxation that can be imposed without legislation**"

Milton Friedman, US economist

How it works

Economic policy-making has been compared to trying to operate a finely balanced machine. By adjusting various policy "dials", the government aims for the best combination of key economic variables – usually, a combination of low inflation and unemployment levels. However, economists point to a trade-off between inflation and unemployment, with low unemployment coming at the cost of high inflation, and vice versa. More recently, economists have concluded that economies run best by themselves, with institutions such as central banks controlling monetary policy, while the state concentrates on "supply-side policies" such as making markets more efficient.

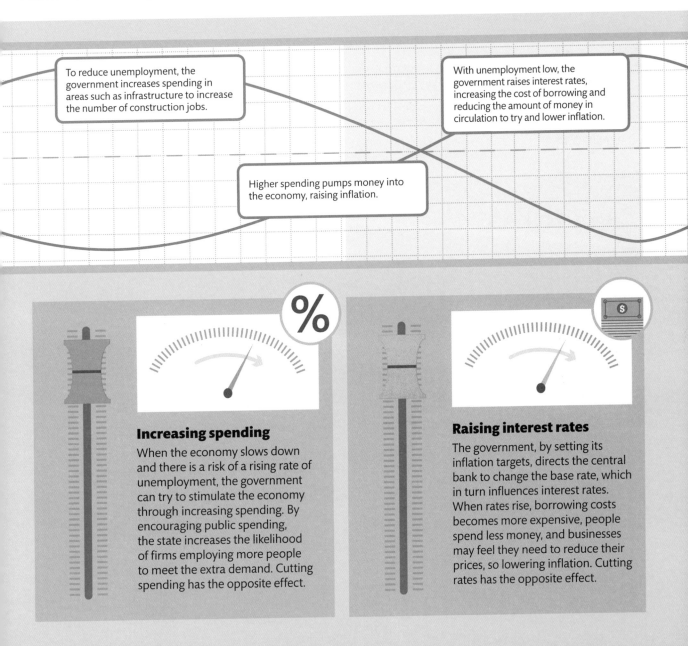

To reduce unemployment, the government increases spending in areas such as infrastructure to increase the number of construction jobs.

With unemployment low, the government raises interest rates, increasing the cost of borrowing and reducing the amount of money in circulation to try and lower inflation.

Higher spending pumps money into the economy, raising inflation.

Increasing spending

When the economy slows down and there is a risk of a rising rate of unemployment, the government can try to stimulate the economy through increasing spending. By encouraging public spending, the state increases the likelihood of firms employing more people to meet the extra demand. Cutting spending has the opposite effect.

Raising interest rates

The government, by setting its inflation targets, directs the central bank to change the base rate, which in turn influences interest rates. When rates rise, borrowing costs becomes more expensive, people spend less money, and businesses may feel they need to reduce their prices, so lowering inflation. Cutting rates has the opposite effect.

Interest rates

Interest is effectively the price charged by a lender to a borrower for the use of funds. The national reserve interest rate, set by the central bank, affects how easy it is to borrow or lend money in a country.

How it works

Lenders charge interest on the money or other assets that they loan. This is a charge levied to cover risks to the lender, should the borrower fail to repay the loan. Borrowers perceived to present a greater risk of failing to repay a loan may be charged more. Interest charges also compensate lenders for profits that they may have made if the money had been invested elsewhere. Interest charges with banks and other financial or business institutions are normally calculated as a percentage of the borrowed amount and expressed as a yearly figure – the annual percentage rate or APR (*see p.210*). The central bank plays a key role in setting national interest rates (*see pp.100–103*).

How interest rates are set

The base rate of interest is set by a country's central bank in response to inflation targets set by its government. Commercial banks respond to changes in the base rate by adjusting the interest rates of the different products that they offer.

The government

Each year, the government sets out its goals for economic growth and the rate of employment. One such aim is to achieve price stability, as this makes for stable economic growth. Prices are kept steady when inflation occurs at a limited rate, and so the government sets an inflation target, beyond which prices should not rise or fall. This is announced annually, expressed as a percentage of the Consumer Price Index (CPI). The CPI is measured as the cost of a selection of representative goods and services bought by a household, including food, transportation, clothing, and entertainment.

The central bank

The government's inflation target is passed on to the central bank, who then set the base rate – the interest rate that the central bank charges commercial banks to borrow from it. The central bank does this in order to encourage commercial banks to adjust their rates in line with the base rate. Commercial bank rates determine the ease with which customers and businesses can borrow, so it affects investment, spending, employment rates, and wage levels in the wider economy. These in turn influence prices charged for products, which affects inflation (*see pp.122–123*).

Base rate

Raising the base rate means that commercial banks pay higher interest on money they borrow from the central bank, making it more expensive for them to borrow. Lowering the base rate means that commercial banks pay less interest on the reserves they borrow from the central bank, which makes their borrowing cheaper.

HOW INFLATION AFFECTS INTEREST RATES

Interest rates and inflation are closely linked, and a change in one influences the other. Inflation is the decline of a currency's purchasing power due to an oversupply of money (*see pp.132–135*). A limited supply of goods and services, along with an oversupply of money, means that money devalues, and so more of it is required to obtain products.

A loan is a product and an interest rate the price paid for it, so if the value of money decreases, then commercial banks may charge a higher interest rate on their loans. Higher charges will make borrowing more expensive, resulting in fewer loans being taken out. This may ultimately impact on spending, causing the money supply to fall, as well as the rate of inflation.

Commercial banks

Banks need to make a profit, so if the cost for them of borrowing from the central bank increases (as the base rate goes up), or the inter-bank lending rate increases, they need to reflect this in the interest rates that they charge their customers for borrowing. Commercial banks set interest rates according to their own needs so some banks may choose not to pass lower interest rates on to customers taking out loans, while other banks may offer a higher interest rate on savings in order to attract new customers' money.

INTER-BANK LENDING RATE

Banks lend to each other at a slightly higher rate than the base rate.

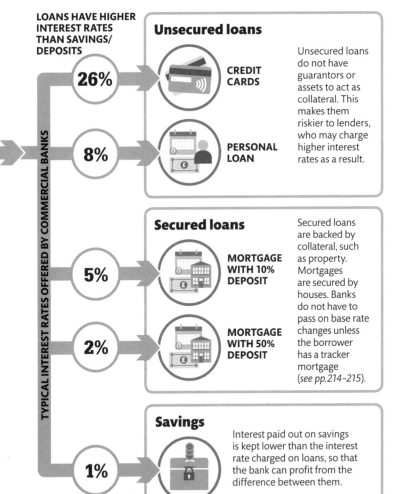

LOANS HAVE HIGHER INTEREST RATES THAN SAVINGS/ DEPOSITS

TYPICAL INTEREST RATES OFFERED BY COMMERCIAL BANKS

Unsecured loans

26% CREDIT CARDS

8% PERSONAL LOAN

Unsecured loans do not have guarantors or assets to act as collateral. This makes them riskier to lenders, who may charge higher interest rates as a result.

Secured loans

5% MORTGAGE WITH 10% DEPOSIT

2% MORTGAGE WITH 50% DEPOSIT

Secured loans are backed by collateral, such as property. Mortgages are secured by houses. Banks do not have to pass on base rate changes unless the borrower has a tracker mortgage (*see pp.214–215*).

Savings

1%

Interest paid out on savings is kept lower than the interest rate charged on loans, so that the bank can profit from the difference between them.

The impact of changing interest rates

If interest rates fluctuated all the time, the economy would become volatile. This is why the government and central bank work together to keep inflation and interest stable. Every time the interest rate is changed, it sends a signal to consumers to either spend or save – and may also increase or decrease confidence in the state of the economy. An increase in interest rates encourages saving, since higher interest will be paid on money in savings accounts, and investments can grow. Meanwhile, borrowing becomes less attractive as interest repayments increase, and banks are more selective about whom they lend to. This impacts on the affordability of obtaining or repaying an existing loan, such as a mortgage. By contrast, a drop in interest rates is intended to stimulate spending, since consumers can take out loans more cheaply, while savers will tend to spend or invest deposits that are attracting little interest. Interest repayments will also drop for those with mortgages tracking the base rate, leaving more cash for spending. While encouraging spending through very low interest rates might boost the economy, it can ultimately impact negatively on long-term savings plans, such as pensions.

When interest rates are raised

Higher interest rates make loans less affordable, while high interest on savings accounts encourages saving rather than spending. As spending slows, so does the economy, with demand for goods and services decreasing. This eventually affects businesses and employment levels.

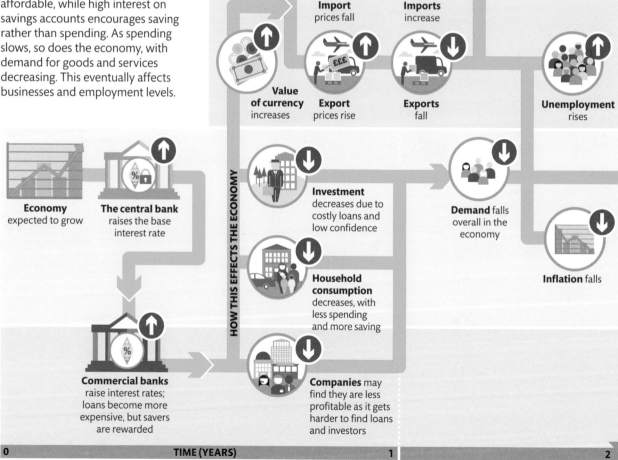

Import prices fall

Imports increase

Value of currency increases

Export prices rise

Exports fall

Unemployment rises

HOW THIS EFFECTS THE ECONOMY

Economy expected to grow

The central bank raises the base interest rate

Investment decreases due to costly loans and low confidence

Demand falls overall in the economy

Inflation falls

Household consumption decreases, with less spending and more saving

Commercial banks raise interest rates; loans become more expensive, but savers are rewarded

Companies may find they are less profitable as it gets harder to find loans and investors

0   **TIME (YEARS)**   1   2

NEGATIVE INTEREST RATE POLICY (NIRP)

In some countries, the central bank has experimented with cutting base interest rates to a negative figure, for instance, – 0.01 per cent. If this rate were passed on by commercial banks, it would mean that depositors must pay a percentage of their deposit to the bank. But while a central bank might impose a negative interest rate to encourage spending and investment, and discourage savers from hoarding cash, commercial banks usually tend to be reluctant to pass negative interest charges on to customers, and particularly small businesses, as depositors may be driven to withdraw their savings in cash to avoid fees. Large depositors, however, may pay negative rates for security and a stable currency account.

40.5%
Argentina's rate of inflation in April 2016, the world's highest

When interest rates are lowered

Lower interest rates make it cheaper to take out loans, and hence to spend more money, while saving becomes less attractive as interest rates are low. With more money in circulation, demand for products and services rise, stimulating businesses and increasing employment.

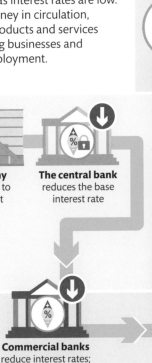

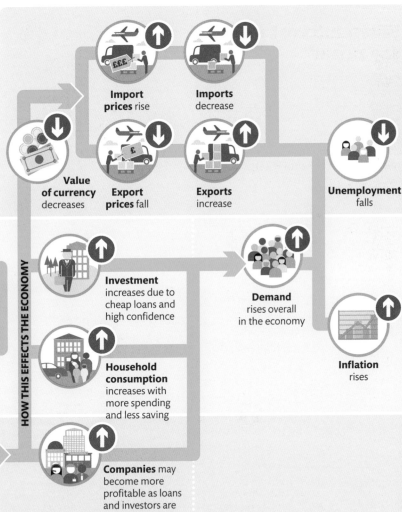

Economy expected to contract

The central bank reduces the base interest rate

Commercial banks reduce interest rates; loans are cheaper, but saving becomes less rewarding

HOW THIS EFFECTS THE ECONOMY

Import prices rise

Imports decrease

Value of currency decreases

Export prices fall

Exports increase

Unemployment falls

Investment increases due to cheap loans and high confidence

Demand rises overall in the economy

Household consumption increases with more spending and less saving

Inflation rises

Companies may become more profitable as loans and investors are easier to secure

EXCHANGE RATES

INTEREST RATES

CREDIT

0   TIME (YEARS)   1   2

Quantitative easing

Quantitative easing is a 21st-century strategy aimed at boosting the economy. It uses the central bank's powers to create new money in an effort to reduce interest rates and increase investment and spending.

How it works

Governments use a number of tools to try to manage the growth of the economy in a stable, balanced way. One of their key tools is their influence, via central banks, over interest rates. Lowering interest rates can encourage financial institutions to lend more to businesses and individuals, which encourages them to spend rather than to save.

In recent times quantitative easing (QE) has been used when economic activity is sluggish and there is a fear of deflation or recession. QE involves the creation of new money – usually taking the form of electronic currency – which the central bank then uses to buy government bonds, or bonds from investors such as banks or pension funds. The aim is to increase the liquidity of money in the economy, which will in turn lower interest rates and make lending easier and more attractive. This, in turn, should encourage businesses to invest and consumers to spend more, thus boosting the economy.

QE is still very much a monetary policy experiment in progress. There are concerns that it could lead to an inflation problem, and its detractors point out that its benefits are not being felt across the whole economy.

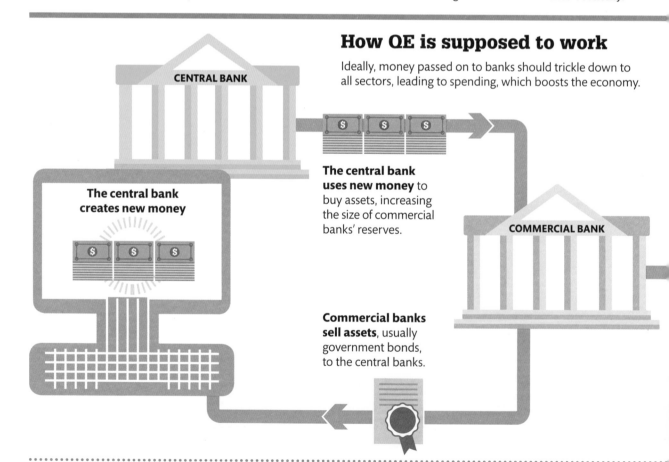

How QE is supposed to work

Ideally, money passed on to banks should trickle down to all sectors, leading to spending, which boosts the economy.

CENTRAL BANK

The central bank creates new money

The central bank uses new money to buy assets, increasing the size of commercial banks' reserves.

COMMERCIAL BANK

Commercial banks sell assets, usually government bonds, to the central banks.

POTENTIAL DANGERS OF QE

QE is a relatively new strategy so its effects are hard to measure. It is therefore still not known whether it can stimulate the economy without excessive risk.

 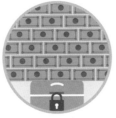 

The economy may not fail to respond as expected even to very large amounts of new money being created.

Inflation may occur due to high money supply – although it is unlikely to lead to hyperinflation.

Banks don't always pass on the money to businesses in need, but hoard it or invest it elsewhere.

🔍 CASE STUDY

UK

The UK began a QE programme in early 2009, after interest rates were cut to almost zero. Most of the new money has been used to purchase government debt. The effects of QE depend on sellers passing on the money that they receive from selling assets, and banks investing the additional liquidity they obtain. The Bank of England believes QE has boosted growth, but at the cost of higher inflation and increasing inequality of wealth, as prices rise.

US$**3.5** trillion
spent on **QE purchases** by the **US government**

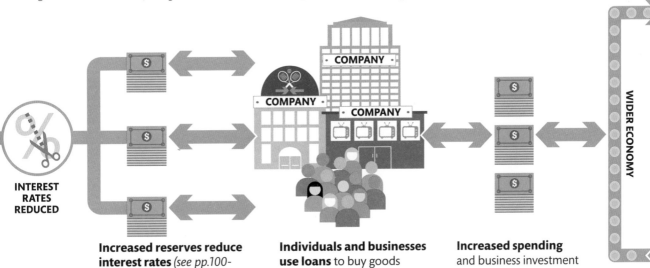

INTEREST RATES REDUCED

Increased reserves reduce interest rates *(see pp.100-101)*, leading individuals and businesses to borrow more.

Individuals and businesses use loans to buy goods and services and to invest in businesses.

Increased spending and business investment boosts economic activity.

WIDER ECONOMY

The level of taxation

It is difficult for governments to establish how much tax to levy. Too low and the government cannot provide the services people want. Too high and people will be unwilling to pay the tax.

How it works

Governments can impose taxes on a person's earnings, their buildings and homes, savings and investments, pensions, inherited property, or on what they spend. Most governments rely heavily on income taxes, usually with different proportionate levels for different levels of earnings. This makes the tax system fairer; however, introducing more complexity also increases the chances of tax avoidance. Some taxes are also levied in order to change behaviour. By taxing something viewed as negative or unhealthy, such as tobacco or alcohol, the government can help to persuade people to consume less of those things.

Pigouvian taxes in action

Standard economic theory says that if consuming goods or services causes harm, a tax should be applied to them until the value of the tax matches the cost of the harm done – for example, a tax on sugar should match the cost to public health services of obesity. This is a "Pigouvian tax", named after Arthur Pigou, the economist who proposed the idea.

✓ NEED TO KNOW

> **Effective tax rate** Many tax systems allow different "reliefs" – such as investment relief to encourage investment. More than one tax may also be levied at once, for example income and corporation tax. As a result, the effective (average) tax rate may differ from the headline (basic) rate.

> **Marginal tax rate** Describes the additional tax paid for undertaking a small amount of extra activity – for example the extra tax paid in earning £1 more. Decisions made "at the margin" influence the behaviour of individuals and businesses, such as whether it is worth working longer hours.

> **Grey economy** People who work for cash wages or fees and do not declare their income, in order to avoid paying tax.

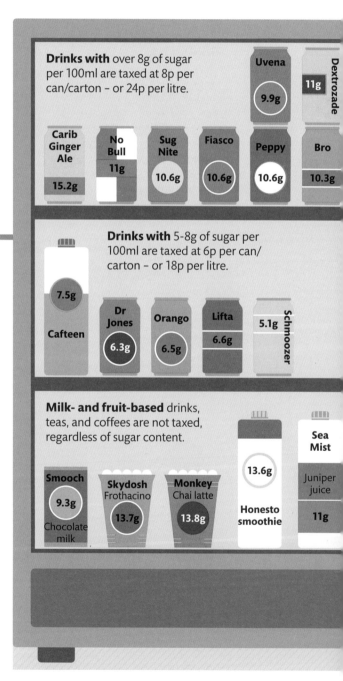

Drinks with over 8g of sugar per 100ml are taxed at 8p per can/carton – or 24p per litre.

Uvena 9.9g
Dextrozade 11g
Carib Ginger Ale 15.2g
No Bull 11g
Sug Nite 10.6g
Fiasco 10.6g
Peppy 10.6g
Bro 10.3g

Drinks with 5-8g of sugar per 100ml are taxed at 6p per can/carton – or 18p per litre.

Cafteen 7.5g
Dr Jones 6.3g
Orango 6.5g
Lifta 6.6g
Schmoozer 5.1g

Milk- and fruit-based drinks, teas, and coffees are not taxed, regardless of sugar content.

Sea Mist
Honesto smoothie 13.6g
Juniper juice 11g
Smooch Chocolate milk 9.3g
Skydosh Frothacino 13.7g
Monkey Chai latte 13.8g

THE LAFFER CURVE

The Laffer curve, named after US economist Arthur Laffer, illustrates the concept that there is an optimum level of taxation to maximize revenues. This is because at very high rates of taxation, more people will be looking to avoid or reduce the tax than will pay it. So, although tax revenues initially increase with rising tax rates, they will eventually decline. Controversy surrounds the idea because it is very hard to know where this optimum point might lie and also because it would seem to legitimize non-payment of taxes by high net-worth individuals, and tax avoidance by ordinary people who start to participate in the "grey economy".

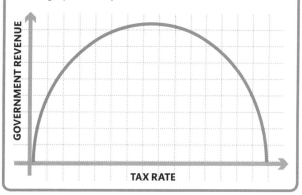

Unintended effects of tax

❯ Drinks taxed at the higher rate are actually taxed less per gram of sugar than those at the lower rate – so consumers may switch to more sugary drinks.

❯ Consumers may turn to untaxed sugary drinks such as milkshakes and smoothies.

❯ The tax increase may hit poorer consumers harder, making it a regressive tax.

❯ The profits of drinks companies may fall, affecting government tax revenue.

❯ If businesses are affected, this may lead to the loss of jobs.

❯ In Mexico, a 10 per cent tax on soft drinks has raised more than US$2 billion since 2014. While sales initially dropped they have started to rise again.

24%
estimated percentage of economic activity in Greece that went undeclared and untaxed in 2013

Government spending

Governments today spend a large part of what an economy produces, using money from taxes to prioritize their political commitments and potentially boost their country's economy.

How it works

Modern governments usually pay for a range of services that might typically include education, healthcare, pensions, and welfare payments. The electorate may also expect them to invest in roads, airports, water, electricity and gas supply, and other infrastructure.

However, governments cannot simply spend whatever they want. Healthy tax revenues depend on a thriving national economy. Most governments attempt to prioritize their spending depending on their political commitments, setting an annual budget to allocate spending from taxes they expect to receive.

Typical government spending

How a government spends money depends on its political priorities, the size of the government relative to the economy, and its level of debt. For instance, Scandinavian countries famously prioritize high welfare spending. Government spending can also boost the economy. By raising spending on infrastructure, governments can help to sustain economic activity. Funding scientific research aids product invention, feeding into economic growth, while spending on education can provide the training to make a workforce more productive.

SPENDING VS CUTS

Government spending can directly support the economy, such as expenditure on transport and communications. Scientific research is often funded by government, and spending on education helps to train workers. Some governments also subsidise and support key national industries. However, many governments since the 2008 financial crash have tried to cut their spending to reduce their deficits (*see pp.146–147*). These decisions are controversial, as the long-term effects on the economy are still unknown.

"Never spend your money before you have it"

Thomas Jefferson, former US president

Health 22%

Interest payments 5%

Transport 3%

Defence 6%

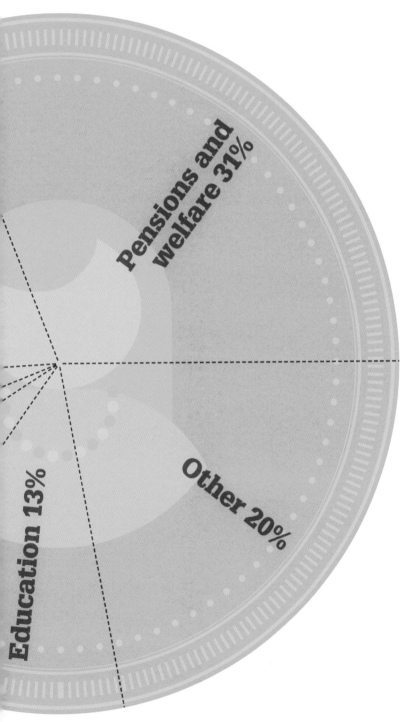

Pensions and welfare 31%

Education 13%

Other 20%

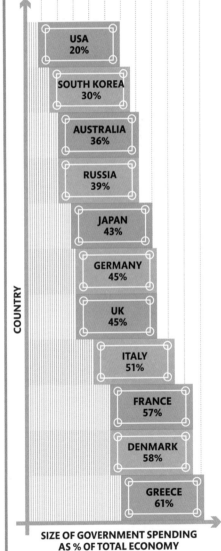

GOVERNMENT SPEND RELATIVE TO ITS ECONOMY

The size of a government's budget in relation to its economy, can vary. Typically, governments spend around 40 per cent of GDP. The graph below shows some of the variation. In South Korea the government spends 30 per cent of GDP, while in Denmark it spends 58 per cent.

USA 20%
SOUTH KOREA 30%
AUSTRALIA 36%
RUSSIA 39%
JAPAN 43%
GERMANY 45%
UK 45%
ITALY 51%
FRANCE 57%
DENMARK 58%
GREECE 61%

COUNTRY

SIZE OF GOVERNMENT SPENDING
AS % OF TOTAL ECONOMY

How governments provide for the future

Government spending can help to shape how an economy develops. By investing in productive activities, as well as day-to-day items, governments can help their economies to grow.

How it works

Governments usually take responsibility for providing the buildings public services use, and for building and maintaing essential national infrastructure such as railways, electricity and gas supplies, and roads.

Sometimes, governments will also invest in building new housing or sponsor research.

Spending on this is government investment, and appears as its "capital" spend in the national budget. It is equivalent to spending by private companies and

Government investment and returns

Governments can invest in many different areas of economic activity. The returns, such as those below, can benefit the government, or wider society.

TRANSPORT

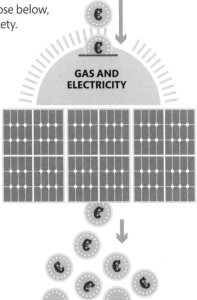

GAS AND ELECTRICITY

WATER, WASTE, AND

FLOODING

Returns to government

> **Direct** Passenger fares

> **Short-term** Tax on increased spending near stations

> **Long-term** A growth in businesses activity

> **Indirect** Economic growth

Returns to government

> **Direct** Cash from energy bills

> **Short-term** Lower energy costs for government

> **Long-term** More investment in infrastructure by business

> **Indirect** Economic growth

Returns to government

> **Direct** Cash from utility bills

> **Short-term** Cheaper utility costs for government

> **Longer-term** Health and environmental benefits

> **Indirect** Growth of cities

individuals on things such as machinery and buildings, and in the same way the investment will produce a return over its lifetime. In some cases this return is paid directly (for instance in passenger fares) and sometimes it appears indirectly (for instance in the many economic benefits of a new road, helping businesses to trade and resulting in more tax revenues). Governments justify such spending by showing it will produce returns.

CAPITAL SPENDING AND BORROWING

To fund their capital spending, governments (just like businesses) will often borrow money. This means adding to their overall debt, and so governments concerned with cutting debts will often look first at ways of reducing capital spending. However, this means missing out on the returns of an investment so, in order to lower the costs, many governments have began to use private funding. This allows the private investors to share in the returns. In some cases this means full privatization, in which a government allows a private firm to build and run the investment outright. When this is not possible or desirable, private investment may take the form of a deal between government and private investors to split the costs, risks, and profits of building and running the investment.

SOCIAL HOUSING

Returns to government
❯ **Direct** Rent from tenants
❯ **Short-term** Cheaper rents leading to a more stable society with less homelessness
❯ **Longer-term** Growing towns
❯ **Indirect** Economic growth

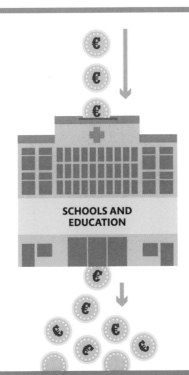

SCHOOLS AND EDUCATION

Returns to government
❯ **Direct** None
❯ **Short-term** Public opinion
❯ **Longer-term** A more productive workforce; better social cohesion
❯ **Indirect** Economic growth

SCIENCE AND INNOVATION

Returns to government
❯ **Direct** Revenue from research
❯ **Short-term** Tax revenues
❯ **Longer-term** New markets; investment in business
❯ **Indirect** Faster economic growth

Inflation

The general increase of average prices in an economy, accompanied by a decrease in the purchasing power of money, is called inflation. This leads to a rise in the cost of living.

How it works

Inflation is the year-on-year rise in general prices. This increase is usually measured by the cost of a basket of representative household goods. As more money is needed to buy the same goods and services, the value of money decreases, and day-to-day living becomes more expensive. There are various factors that influence inflation, but changes in the supply and demand of goods

and services, and of money, have a major impact. There are two main types of inflation: "cost-push" and "demand-pull". Cost-push inflation is driven by businesses experiencing rising costs, which are then passed on to their customers. A business's expenses might go up for a number of reasons, such as an increase in production costs or the need to raise the wages of employees. Demand-pull inflation

comes about when a high demand for goods exceeds firms' ability or willingness to provide them. Rather than increasing supply to match rising demand, businesses raise their prices instead. This alone would not cause demand-pull inflation, but if there is also an oversupply of money in the economy, then consumers will continue to pay elevated prices, raising them further.

Cost-push inflation

There are several factors that can cause costs to rise. An increase in the price of raw materials, for instance, can have a knock-on effect, leading to a rise in prices throughout the economy. Increased energy and transport costs can also push prices up. Higher salaries and taxes are other examples of expenses that are ultimately passed on to customers in the form of rising prices.

Cost of necessary materials increases
The availability of an essential commodity, oil, becomes limited, raising its price and the cost of transport, heating, and manufacture. This has an immediate and widespread impact on basic costs for businesses, particularly those that require the commodity for production, such as this car factory.

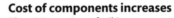

Cost of components increases
The rising price of oil increases the costs involved in making the components that are used to manufacture cars, raising the business's production costs.

"Inflation is always and everywhere a monetary phenomenon"

Milton Friedman, US economist

Price of product rises
Manufacturers respond to higher production costs by passing some of this on to customers.

Rate of inflation accelerates
If the price of goods and services increases across the economy, a higher rate of inflation results.

Higher wages
The employees demand better pay, as it appears that prices are rising. The company agrees and their overall costs increase.

✓ NEED TO KNOW

❯ **Nominal values** Prices, wages, and other economic variables that are not adjusted in order to take account of inflation.

❯ **Real values** Figures adjusted for inflation and used when looking at economic variables over a period of time to determine whether increases are influenced by inflation or economic growth.

CAUSES OF COST-PUSH INFLATION

Cost-push inflation is driven by a rise in running costs for businesses. This can have a number of causes.

❯ **Costs of raw materials** Rises might be due to a scarcity resulting from a natural disaster, or an artificial limit imposed by a monopoly – for instance, the oil embargo in the 1970s, which tripled prices.

❯ **Labour costs** Strikes, low unemployment – meaning that firms need to pay more in order to attract skilled labour – strong unions, and staff expectation that general prices will rise can all result in firms raising wages and shifting the extra cost to customers.

❯ **Exchange rates** When a country's currency drops against a trading partner, more money is required to purchase goods from abroad, which can cause inflation.

❯ **Indirect taxes** A rise in VAT or other tax on a product might be passed on to the customer.

Inflation and the velocity of money circulation

It is not just the supply of money that affects growth in an economy, but also the rate at which money changes hands. This is called the "velocity" of money. It is a measure of how many times a unit of money has been used in transactions for goods and services over a period of time. For instance, if the same unit of money, such as $1, is spent three times in one year in three separate transactions, the velocity of money would be three. If the money supply increases rapidly, as well as the velocity of money, the supply of goods and services may not be able to keep pace with demand – there will be more money chasing fewer goods. This can happen if the economy expands too rapidly, perhaps due to a sudden increase in money supply as a result of monetary policy. Companies respond by raising their prices, kickstarting demand-pull inflation.

However, a higher money supply may not necessarily result in an increase in velocity. If confidence in the economy is low, banks may limit loans, while individuals and businesses may hoard rather than spend their money. If less money is pumping around an economy, then inflation reduces.

NEED TO KNOW

❯ **Market power** A company's capacity to raise a product's price by manipulating levels of supply, demand, or both. Increased market power due to a strong brand may result in lower output.

❯ **Effective demand** This is an indication of what consumers are actually buying, dictated by their willingness to spend, available income, and need.

❯ **Latent demand** This represents customers who have a desire to buy a product, rather than those making actual purchases.

Demand-pull inflation

In an expanding economy, a phone company experiences a sudden increase in demand for their product. However, since the firm's resources are already at full capacity, they cannot increase their supply. Instead, they raise their product's price.

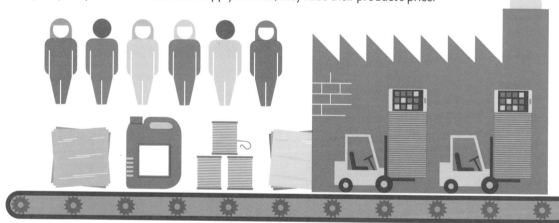

Demand rises
With more money available in the economy, there is a willingness to spend more money on products in general. This brand of mobile phone, a market leader, is particularly in demand.

Manufacture at maximum capacity
The factory is already producing at full capacity, with full employment. Without investment to increase production, which takes time, the supplier is unable to produce more.

Demand outstrips supply
Suppliers cannot increase output in the short term so consumer demand exceeds the number of products that can be supplied.

CAUSES OF DEMAND-PULL INFLATION

When an economy expands too rapidly, or unsustainably, an excess money supply can cause customer demand to overtake the supply of goods and services. A rise in spending is caused by several factors.

〉 **Monetary policy** A cut in interest rates, leading to a relaxation of loan restrictions, can increase the money supply, and result in more borrowing and spending.

〉 **Government spending** Increased investment and spending by the state can expand the money supply, resulting in more consumer activity.

〉 **Lower tax** A decrease in direct or indirect taxes can increase income.

〉 **Consumer confidence** If consumers and firms feel confident about the future, they may spend money they would otherwise have saved.

〉 **Property prices** High house prices can cause home owners to feel more wealthy, increasing their willingness to spend and thus their demand for consumer goods.

〉 **Rapid growth abroad** High export sales can increase the amount of money flowing into the country, with a knock-on effect on inflation.

2%
the US federal government's target level of inflation

Rising rate of inflation
If consumer spending increases generally across the economy, and businesses respond by raising prices, rather than output, then inflation will rise.

Prices rise
With an increased money supply and high consumer confidence, customers seem willing to pay more for a limited supply of the product, so the company raises its price. How high a price may rise depends on consumer demand for the product; if of demand is inelastic – the item is something that customers need and cannot do without – the price point may be pushed higher.

Effective demand
The rise in customer demand has an impact on the product's price, as it is an "effective demand": customers have the income to meet a higher price point and are willing to pay more for a product they perceive as valuable.

Balance of payments

A country's balance of payments (BOP) is a record of its international transactions over a set period of time. This record tracks goods, services, and investment into, and out of, the country.

COUNTRY

How it works

A country's balance-of-payments account provides a record of all of its international credits and debits. Transactions that result in money flowing into a country will appear as a credit, while transactions moving money out of the country will appear as a debit. The BOP account has three parts: the current account, which measures goods and services; the capital account, which tracks the movement of capital and non-financial assets; and the financial account, which looks at investment.

In theory, a country's BOP should total zero, as each credit to the current account will correspond with a debit to the capital account, and vice versa. In reality, as a result of variations in accounting practices and regular exchange rate fluctuations, this rarely happens.

International flow

A country's balance of payments includes transactions by individuals, businesses, and the government. Tracking these transactions helps the government determine how much money is coming into and leaving the country, and in which economic areas there is a deficit or surplus.

THE THREE PARTS OF A BOP ACCOUNT

A balance of payments account is separated into three main accounts, each of which track different types of international transactions into and out of the country. The three main accounts are, in turn, divided into sub-accounts, to chart specific areas of expenditure.

Current account

> Raw materials and merchandise
> Services, such as business, tourism, or transportation
> Income, including from property and shares

> Unilateral or one-way transfers, such as foreign aid or gifts

Capital account

> Capital transfers, such as money transfers or assets of migrants
> Non-produced, non-financial assets, such as natural resources and land

Financial account

> Assets held abroad, such as bonds, investment, and foreign currency
> Foreign-owned assets at home, including bonds, investment, and local currency

COUNTRY'S BOP		
CURRENT ACCOUNT	**CAPITAL ACCOUNT**	**FINANCIAL ACCOUNT**
Credit +€2bn	**Debit** −€1bn	**Debit** −€1bn
TOTAL: 0		

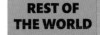

REST OF THE WORLD

Goods and services
€3bn

IMPORT

Current account

The current account is mainly concerned with the international exchange of goods and services.

€3bn - €1bn = €2bn

EXPORT

Goods and services
€1bn

Money transfers and land
€1bn

Capital account

This account is chiefly for recording the movement of money and non-financial, non-productive assets.

€1bn - €2bn = €-1bn

Money transfers and land
€2bn

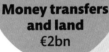

Currency and stocks
€1bn

Financial account

This account monitors international positions in local and foreign currency, bonds, and investment.

€1bn - €2bn = €-1bn

Currency and stocks
€2bn

Zero

Balance of payment

The sum of the "balance of payment" should equal zero, but this rarely turns out to be the case.

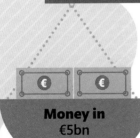

Money in
€5bn

Money out
–€5bn

International currency fluctuations

Exchange rates fluctuate according to supply and demand. If one country has a stronger, more stable economy than its trading partners, then its currency will be valued more highly.

How it works

A country's economic conditions change from day to day, which is why exchange rates also fluctuate continuously. These currency fluctuations are determined in foreign exchange markets around the globe when currencies are traded (a buyer selling one currency to buy another).

Buyers base their trading decisions primarily on the performance of a country's economy. They examine real-time data such as interest rates, and political and commercial events that will affect economic performance – such as elections, the crash of a financial institution,

or news of increased investment in manufacturing facilities. Four key economic factors – GDP (gross domestic production), inflation, employment, and interest rates – indicate how well a country's economy is performing, and determine its exchange rates.

Political stability is also crucial. If investors fear that a government is not capable of managing its country's economy, they will lose confidence, sell their investments in that country, and exchange the local currency for other currencies. This in effect pushes down the value of the local currency by increasing the supply of it and reducing the demand for it.

Currency fluctuations

The state of the economy in any country will dictate whether its currency will rise or fall against other currencies. Interest rates, inflation, productivity, and employment will all have a bearing on currency. Investor confidence also affects exchange rates – investors favour countries with a sound political regime, efficient infrastructure, educated workforce, and social stability.

Weak currency

Several economic factors – either by themselves or combined – can trigger a fall in the value of a country's currency.

LOW INTEREST RATES
Low rates encourage domestic growth, but do not attract investors to buy currency.

HIGH INFLATION
Inflation increases the cost of export goods, lowering demand for them and for the exporter's currency.

FALLING GDP
Shrinking production indicates that demand for a country's exports, and so for its currency, has fallen.

HIGH UNEMPLOYMENT
Rising unemployment may signal falling rates of production and a lack of competitiveness.

LOW CONFIDENCE
Nervous investors sell local currency and so depress the exchange rate.

US$5.3 trillion

the typical value of foreign exchange trades made each day

Bank actions

When a country's central bank expects the currency's value to drop, it tries to shrink the money supply.

INCREASING THE INTEREST RATE

Raising the interest rate attracts investors to buy the country's currency as they will benefit from the higher rate of interest.

SELLING FOREIGN RESERVES

Selling foreign reserves and retaining domestic currency increases demand for the domestic currency.

Strong currency

Several economic factors can signal a booming economy, and boost demand for the country's currency and increase its value.

HIGH INTEREST RATES

Higher rates attract foreign investors and increase the value of the currency.

STABLE INFLATION

Stable or falling inflation can help to boost the value of the local currency.

RISING GDP

High production rates demonstrate demand for a country's products, and thus its currency.

LOW UNEMPLOYMENT

Employment is linked to GDP, indicating that a country's products are in demand.

HIGH CONFIDENCE

Confidence in a nation's economy can be enough to keep its currency buoyant.

THE IMPORTANCE OF RESERVE CURRENCY

Reserve currency is a recognised safe foreign currency held by a country's central bank and financial institutions and used to make trade payments. Using the reserve currency avoids the need to change payments into local currency, minimizing the exchange-rate risk for both countries. Many central banks set a reserve ratio – the percentage of deposits that the bank must hold. The US dollar is the currency most commonly held in reserves worldwide.

Managing state pensions

Most governments use taxpayer money from current workers to fund pensions for those who have retired. Some governments also invest taxpayer money to increase the overall pension fund.

How it works

In most countries, it is the current working generation that is funding the pensions of those who have reached retirement age, as well as the pensions of those who are due to retire. This is the case in the UK, where National Insurance contributions from current workers go towards pensions for those who have retired. Governments need to ensure there is enough money to go around, a task that is all the more challenging because in most developed countries the population is ageing, which means that fewer workers are funding the pensions of an increasing number of older people. Measuring how well pension funds are likely to meet current and future liabilities is key to the successful management of state pensions.

Managing investments

In countries with state-owned investment funds, the government invests taxpayers' contributions to increase the available money in the fund. Investment is usually in core assets, which are less risky but can still fluctuate. If stock markets rise, so do pension funds, and vice versa.

Managing contributions

In some countries, such as Chile and Japan, and at state level in the US, pension managers invest the funds collected from taxpayers with the aim of keeping the amount of available money sufficiently high to meet predicted demand. In other countries, any surplus in the pension fund (such as the National Insurance Fund in the UK) may be lent to the government, but in general it is simply used to pay for the pensions of people who have already retired.

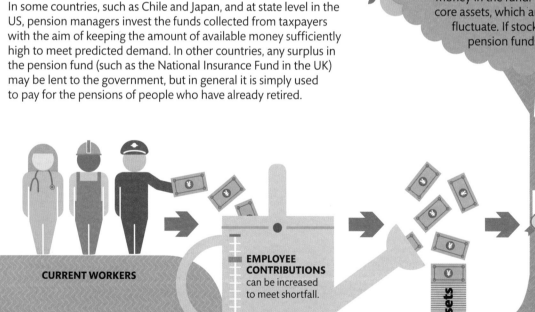

CURRENT WORKERS

EMPLOYEE CONTRIBUTIONS can be increased to meet shortfall.

Assets

CORE INVESTMENTS

MONEY MARKET

GOVERNMENT BONDS

STOCKS AND SHARES

INFRASTRUCTURE ASSET INVESTMENTS

"A pension is nothing more than deferred compensation"

Elizabeth Warren, US politician

LIABILITIES
Payments to pensioners will appear as a liability on the government balance sheet. Demographics influence the amount of money needed to meet this liability. For example, if the population is projected to live longer in old age, the amount needed for future payments will rise.

Increased assets from investments

PENSIONERS

Measuring health

Sufficient money must come in to the pension fund to maintain or improve it. The fund's performance can be assessed in two ways:

❯ Funding level The amount of money in a pension fund compared to the amount of pension that needs to be paid out. This can be expressed as a percentage or as a ratio (the assets divided by the liabilities). A funding level of 100%, or a ratio above 1, means that there will be enough money in the pension fund to meet the payment obligations. A funding level below 100%, or a ratio below 1, means there is not enough.

❯ Deficit The difference between the liabilities and assets in a pension fund – i.e. the shortfall between the money coming in and the money due to be paid out. This is also known as unfunded liability.

Why governments fail financially

It is possible for a government to fail financially, and there are two main ways this can happen. The first is when it loses the ability to meet its obligations to repay its debt, potentially leading to a default. The second is when it fails to reassure the public that the value of its currency, or money itself, can still be trusted, potentially leading to hyperinflation. Fundamentally both causes are due to a loss of public trust. So, if a government cannot be trusted, it is more likely to fail.

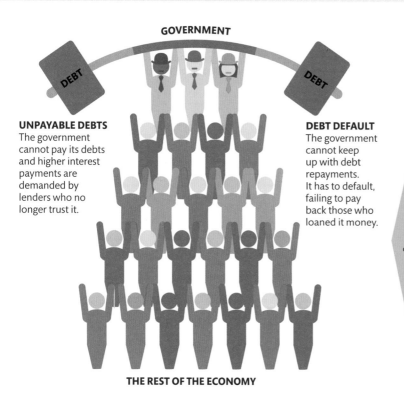

GOVERNMENT

UNPAYABLE DEBTS
The government cannot pay its debts and higher interest payments are demanded by lenders who no longer trust it.

DEBT DEFAULT
The government cannot keep up with debt repayments. It has to default, failing to pay back those who loaned it money.

THE REST OF THE ECONOMY

Uncontrollable debt and default

If a government has taken on excessive borrowing and cannot repay its creditors, it may cut spending and raise taxes, but if it cannot shift the burden, a default becomes inevitable. *See pp.146–147*

Loss of public trust and financial failure

When a government and the institutions of government lose trust through their own incompetence, corruption, or as a result of losing a war, there is a major crisis. To prevent this loss of trust from becoming disastrous a democracy may seek to remove its government.

A OUTCOME

GOVERNMENT TRUST

6

countries **have** never defaulted **on their** debt: New Zealand, Australia, Canada, Thailand, Denmark, **and the** US

THE IMPORTANCE OF TRUST

Gaining trust

Trust is critical to making money and governments work properly. It is also crucial for economic growth. If people do not believe a government's financial promises, it may lose control of the economy. Trust is hard to win, and usually comes from political stability over a period of time.

Losing trust

Governments can lose trust in many different ways. A weak government might decide to issue more money to meet the demands made on it, instead of raising taxes. A government unable to repay its own debts, especially those owed to other countries, may decide that defaulting on the debt is easier than trying to levy taxes to pay. In both cases, trust in the government and its money will be undermined.

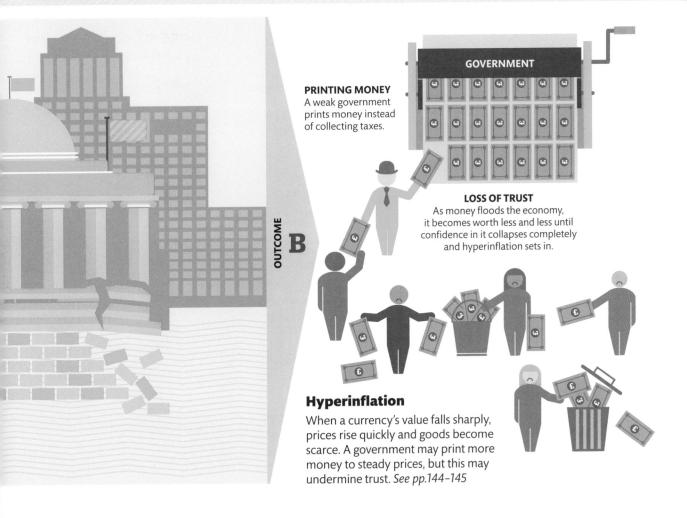

OUTCOME B

PRINTING MONEY
A weak government prints money instead of collecting taxes.

GOVERNMENT

LOSS OF TRUST
As money floods the economy, it becomes worth less and less until confidence in it collapses completely and hyperinflation sets in.

Hyperinflation

When a currency's value falls sharply, prices rise quickly and goods become scarce. A government may print more money to steady prices, but this may undermine trust. *See pp.144–145*

How governments fail: hyperinflation

If public confidence in a country's currency collapses, it can result in exceptionally high rates of inflation. These episodes of hyperinflation are comparatively rare, but always very serious.

How it works

Trust in the value of a currency is essential to maintain price stability in modern economies. Governments therefore seek to control money supply in order to prevent dramatic price fluctuations that could erode trust. But when governments are weak or not trusted, these controls can break down. A weak government, for example, may be unwilling to raise taxes to pay for public spending, printing money to pay for it instead. Prices can thus rise very rapidly as citizens refuse to believe that money has any value, and so they demand more of it in any sale. Governments can subsequently feel pressured to issue more and more money in order to keep the economy moving. When this happens, hyperinflation sets in, and it can be very hard for governments to regain control.

 Case study: Hyperinflation in Germany, 1921–24

Germany experienced an infamous period of hyperinflation after World War I.

COLLAPSE IN TRUST

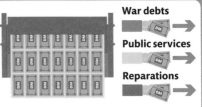

War debts

Public services

Reparations

1. Following the war, Germany's new government is unstable. It prints money to pay for war debts, reparations, and public services.

2. The German government starts using the money it prints to purchase foreign currency, causing a collapse in the value of the German mark.

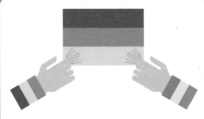

3. By 1922, Germany cannot pay its war reparations. France and Belgium occupy the Ruhr valley to enforce payment in goods instead of money.

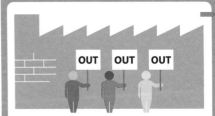

OUT OUT OUT

4. German workers in the Ruhr go on strike. The government prints more money to pay their wages.

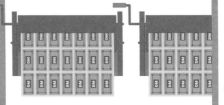

5. As the economy collapses, the German government continues to print money.

6. Domestic prices in Germany explode as confidence in the currency evaporates.

HYPERINFLATION

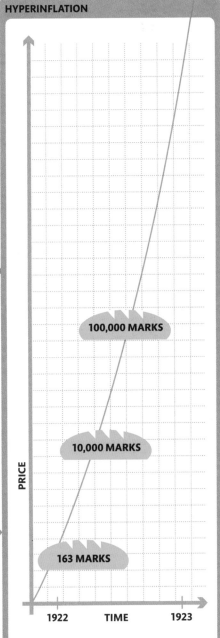

200,000,000,000 MARKS

100,000 MARKS

10,000 MARKS

163 MARKS

PRICE

1922 TIME 1923

7. Hyperinflation sets in and prices rise faster than people can spend their money. In 1922, a loaf of bread costs 163 marks – by November 1923 this has risen to 200,000,000,000 marks.

STOPPING HYPERINFLATION

Credibility

Because hyperinflation is based on expectations about the future, with people believing prices will carry on rising rapidly, it can also be halted rapidly (in theory). If the government can credibly commit to ending inflation (for example, by introducing a new currency with tight rules on issuing it), it can stop hyperinflation with limited costs. However, fulfilling that commitment can be challenging, particularly for weak governments.

Dictatorship

One controversial argument is that as hyperinflation results from weak governments, ending hyperinflation requires a strong government – perhaps even one that ends democracy. The economist Thomas Sargent has made this argument for central Europe in the 1920s, where a series of hyperinflationary episodes were halted by authoritarian governments.

460 septillion

the number of Hungarian pengö to a single US$ at the height of hyperinflation in July 1946

NEW GOVERNMENT

8. A new government is formed in November 1923, with a new president of the German central bank. The central bank stops paying government debts with printed money. A new currency, the Rentenmark, is introduced, replacing the near-worthless paper Mark. The Rentenmark is backed by mortgages on land, while the new central bank president promises to fix its exchange rate against the dollar. These measures restore public confidence in the currency. Some of Germany's war debts are written off and reparations reduced in 1924–25. The situation is stabilized.

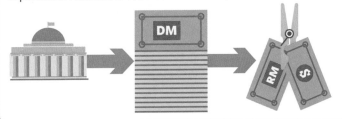

How governments fail: debt default

A government can find its debts spiralling out of control, if interest payments rise faster than it can raise taxes. Once this happens, the government is on the path to default.

How it works

Ideally, government borrowing should remain stable. Sometimes, however, even a well-run government can be hit by an unexpected and costly event, such as a currency crisis or a sharp recession. When this happens, the government may find itself borrowing increasing amounts to try to keep up with interest payments that are due on its existing debt.

To alleviate this pressure, a government may raise taxes and cut public spending to bring in money. In practice, a government may have to reduce public services or pay its employees with IOUs in lieu of cash. If these measures fail, a government may eventually be forced to default on the debt and admit that it cannot pay. Governments that do this will find it very difficult to borrow in the future, because trust in the country's economic stability will be low. However, countries that default on their debts do sometimes recover very rapidly afterwards.

INTEREST PAYMENTS

Those lending money to countries will charge more if they think the risk of a default is high, to compensate for that risk. The danger for any country with large amounts of debt is that a debt spiral can become a self-fulfilling prophecy. As lenders lose confidence and demand more in interest payments, the debt becomes more difficult to control, and default is more likely.

Argentina 1998–2001

The debt spiral in which Argentina found itself from 1998 until 2001 resulted in what was the largest default in history at that time (it has since been dwarfed by the 2012 "restructuring" of Greece's debt). Argentina owed a large amount of money, and was borrowing more from other countries and the International Monetary Fund (IMF), until a recession prevented it from repaying its debts fully and the country defaulted.

Borrowing increases

DEBT GROWS

IMF World Bank US

DEBT

Recession

1. Following a period of hyperinflation during the 1990s, Argentina attempts to implement IMF rules. It finds itself having to borrow substantially from official institutions such as the IMF, and from other countries such as the US.

6. The economic downturn in the country worsens.

5. Argentina's national government implements austerity measures in an attempt to cut costs.

€107 billion amount of Greek debt written off in 2012

7. Argentina's repayments are still too small to control rising levels of debt.

Borrowing increases

DEBT GROWS

8. Argentina fails to meet conditions set out by the IMF on deficit targets.

9. The IMF withdraws its economic support.

10. Argentina cannot repay its US$120 billion debt, and defaults.

3. Its repayments fail to bring the debt under control.

Argentina defaults

11. The value of the peso plummets.

2. Argentina borrows heavily from elsewhere in the world.

12. Argentinian unemployment reaches 20%.

DEBT

Borrowing increases

DEBT GROWS

13. A run on the banks leads to the government freezing deposits.

14. Civil unrest and rioting break out.

15. A period of political instability sets in.

4. The countries it has borrowed from lose faith in Argentina's ability to pay.

16. Agreements on repayments in 2002 help promote a boom.

Argentina enters a debt spiral

PERSONAL FINANCE

❯ Worth, wealth, and income ❯ Investments for income
❯ Wealth-building investments ❯ Managing investments
❯ Pensions and retirement ❯ Debt ❯ Money in the digital age

Worth, wealth, and income

Wealth is a measure of the value of the assets owned by an individual, group, or country. An individual's net worth is the value of any assets owned, minus any debt owed or personal liabilities. Income is earned through working and can also be gained from assets owned. Being aware of their net position can make it much easier for individuals to set financial goals, establish effective investment strategies, and achieve financial independence on or before retirement.

Planning for financial independence

To gain financial independence a person must have sufficient money to be able to pay their living expenses without work, for example after retirement. This can be achieved by saving and investing well to accumulate sufficient wealth to live on, or by generating a passive income that will continue paying out during retirement.

Assess situation
Investors calculate the value of assets such as cash, stocks, bonds, property, and retirement funds. Then subtract liabilities – loans, credit card debts, and mortgage. *See pp.152–153*

Set financial goals
Savers have to set a realistic age at which to retire. To do this they assess how much income they will need to maintain a good standard of living in retirement.

Increase savings from income
By converting a portion of income into savings, and ensuring their investments perform efficiently, savers stand a better chance of reaching their financial goals.
See pp.154–155

PROS AND CONS OF A FINANCIAL ADVISER

Pros

A financial adviser assesses their client's circumstances and identifies mortgage, pension, and investment products that best meet their financial goals. This is useful for people who do not have time to research markets. When a client feels an adviser has given them poor advice or potentially mis-sold a product, it is possible to take legal action.

Cons

Financial advisers have a limited role and do not advise on day-to-day money issues, such as finding the best savings rates or reducing household expenses, but this information can easily be found in newspapers or online. Financial advice can also be expensive – advisers will typically charge about one per cent of any assets managed.

52%
of pre-retirees in the US use a financial adviser

SHARES   BONDS   PENSION   HOUSE

Financial independence

DEBT   DEBT

Manage debt
Wise savers pay off loans and credit cards as quickly as possible and look for cheaper interest rates that can bring down the cost of borrowing and help reduce mortgage debt more quickly.
See pp.156–157

Use investment pay-outs
When investments produce additional income, individuals can use the funds to reduce any debt, as well as reinvesting to build up their assets. *See pp.160–161*

Financial independence
Effective investment over a lifetime builds up wealth or passive income. If it is successful, an individual can maintain a good standard of living without the need to work.

Calculating and analysing net worth

A person's wealth – or net worth – can be calculated by adding up all of the assets they own and subtracting from this total the amount of any debt that they owe.

Net worth statement

Individuals can calculate their net worth at any given time by subtracting their debts from their assets. They can then compare figures over months or years to track any changes.

ASSETS – DEBT = NET WORTH

Assets

Liquid assets

Easily accessible sources of cash

> Cash in hand
> Cash held in current account
> Cash value of life insurance
> Money market funds
> Certificates of deposit
> Short-term investments

Investment assets

Convertible to cash in the near or long term

> Term deposits held at the bank
> Securities, stocks, shares, or bonds
> Investment real estate
> Endowment policies
> Retirement funds

Debts

Short-term liabilities

Payable within the next 12 months

> Credit card interest and capital repayments
> Repayments on a personal or student loan
> Current monthly household bills – for example for utilities, communications, and insurance
> Unpaid personal income tax for the year

Long-term liabilities

Payable over more than 12 months

> Mortgage or rental payments
> Child support or alimony if separated or divorced
> A child's education through to university
> Payments to a pension fund
> A hire-purchase contract or lease for a car

How it works

The net worth figure tells financial institutions a lot about an individual's financial status. Over time, a person's net worth can fluctuate – for example, their total assets will grow if bank deposits earn interest, and their level of debt will increase if they take out a new mortgage. If a person's net worth increases, it means they are enjoying good financial health; if it decreases, the opposite is true.

Net worth is a more relevant indicator of financial health than income or wealth because it takes into account any debt that is owed.

US$30 million
liquid asset value of ultra-high net worth individuals

Personal assets

Can be sold for cash but may take time

❯ A home, which can be sold if downsizing
❯ Additional property such as a holiday home
❯ Art, jewellery, and other valuables
❯ Furniture, especially collectable pieces
❯ Vehicles (although they lose value quickly)

✔ NEED TO KNOW

❯ **High net worth individual (HNWI)**
A person with liquid assets that are worth over US$1 million.

❯ **Very high net worth individual (VHNWI)**
An individual with liquid assets that are worth at least US$5 million.

Net worth

This figure – assets minus debt – can be used by anyone to assess an individual's wealth at any point in time.

❯ If the figure is negative, then their debts are greater than assets and financial health is poor.

❯ If the figure is positive, their assets are greater than the value of their debts and their financial health is good.

❯ Financial advisers suggest that their clients calculate their net worth once a year.

Contingent liabilities

May be owed in the future

❯ Taxes such as capital gains
❯ A car or other loan guarantees for children who may not be able to keep up with repayments
❯ Damage claims such as lawsuits
❯ Solicitor fees for personal legal disputes

LIQUIDITY AND NET WORTH

Although net worth is a useful measure of current wealth, liquidity tells savers and investors how much cash they could access in an emergency. It is always worth keeping a proportion of investments in a form that can be easily converted into cash.

Income and wealth

Two of the key concepts of personal finance, income and wealth, represent different states of an individual's finances. Income is moving and often unstable, while wealth is mainly static and stable.

Income

Income is money that flows into a household. It is used to pay for housing, bills, food, and other essential needs as well as non-essentials such as holidays.

Turning income into wealth

Unless they inherit a large sum of money, or win it in a lottery, most people need to rely on creating wealth through savings. The method is simple but requires patience and discipline. The amount of money going out each week or month (outgoings) must be kept lower than the amount coming in (income) over the same period, and the difference should be saved or invested as soon as possible.

INCOME (AFTER TAX)

Earnings
Income includes any benefits or tax allowances as well as returns on investments.

OUTGOINGS

Costs
Household expenditure can be regulated via a budget, which will help pinpoint where savings can be made.

SALARY

RENTAL INCOME

INTEREST

SHARE DIVIDENDS

FOOD

HOUSING

TRANSPORT

CLOTHES

How it works

Wealth is the value of a person's assets, savings, and investments, while income is the money received regularly in return for work, from investments, or as a benefit or pension. Recognising the difference between the two concepts is key to both building and protecting wealth. Income that is closely managed and carefully invested can create wealth over time.

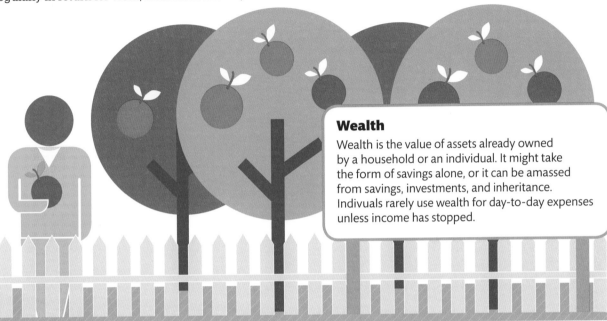

Wealth

Wealth is the value of assets already owned by a household or an individual. It might take the form of savings alone, or it can be amassed from savings, investments, and inheritance. Indivuals rarely use wealth for day-to-day expenses unless income has stopped.

WEALTH

Debts

Debt should be paid off as quickly as possible unless there are advantages in spreading repayments.

CREDIT CARD **LOANS**

MORTGAGE **EDUCATION**

Savings

The money left after costs and debt commitments are met is savings. This could be invested into assets.

INVESTED INTO

Assets

The most useful investments generate income in addition to increasing in value.

PROPERTY **SHARES**

ART **JEWELLERY**

Converting income into wealth

High earnings alone do not guarantee wealth. Keeping outgoings lower than income, accruing savings, and investing them wisely are key to long-term financial security.

How it works

There is no easy way to determine how much wealth is sufficient for retirement. It depends on the individual. High earners tend to have higher lifestyle expectations than those on lower incomes. They must therefore save more, and invest more, to generate the wealth they need to maintain their lifestyle during retirement.

The danger for this group is that high wages can lead to a false sense of affluence, resulting in big spending on lifestyle but little set aside in savings.

In order to start building wealth, individuals should save a proportion of their after-tax income regularly. Many financial advisers recommend setting a goal to save one-third of regular income.

When a high income fails to produce wealth

Even an individual earning a high salary is not guaranteed a secure retirement if they have poor saving habits. Setting aside a third of after-tax income might seem impossible, but even saving 10 per cent can create a decent stockpile of cash for investment over time.

High-income earners

Two senior managers at the same company earn identical salaries. However, they use their money differently, with contrasting results.

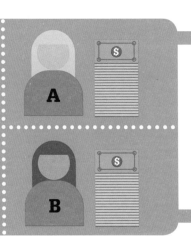

Spending levels

High-income earner **A** is accustomed to spending money on goods with little long-term value.

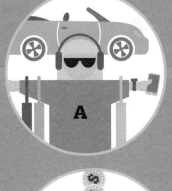

Earner **B** invests in a retirement fund and shares, and saves in a high-interest account.

70% of the richest Americans claim to be self-made

A PERSONAL BUDGET

There are many ways in which household spending can be curtailed in the pursuit of wealth – even the smallest changes can be significant when continued year after year, as any reduction in spending can be invested in savings. Setting and sticking to a budget will help meet savings goals. Other savings strategies include:

❭ **Setting financial goals**, such as buying a house or funding a masters' degree.

❭ **Drawing up a spending plan** for expenditures such as housing, food, transport, and debt repayments.

❭ **Monitoring budgets** weekly or monthly to keep track of spending.

❭ **Deciding on a percentage** of income to save each month, and setting up a direct debit for that amount to go straight into a savings account.

❭ **Finding cheaper accommodation**, or refinancing a mortgage to get a cheaper rate.

❭ **Comparing insurance rates** and switching to a cheaper insurer; reviewing deals from different energy suppliers to cut utility bills.

❭ **Shopping with a list** to eliminate impulse buys, and buying in bulk in order to take advantage of cheaper prices or sales.

Attitude to debt	Investment	Retirement

Attitude to debt

Because credit is easily available to high earners, **A** gets deep into debt.

Investment

Because her income is high, **A** doesn't feel the need to save for retirement.

Retirement

On retirement, **A** sees a dramatic drop in her income. Having no wealth to rely on, she spends her retirement in poverty.

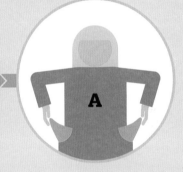

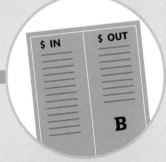

B ensures that her outgoings are always lower than her income.

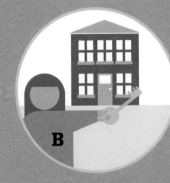

B uses some of her savings to invest in a house.

B enjoys comfortable retirement years.

Generating income

Earning sufficient income to ensure regular savings and investments is the basis of building wealth. The more sources of income the better, especially if some of those sources are passive, or unearned.

How it works

Wealth can be amassed in various ways, almost all of which rely on income. Inheriting money, property, or other assets is the fast track to wealth, but for anyone who can not rely on a large inheritance, savings and investments are the two principal strategies. Income can be earned in two main ways. The most common route is via active or earned income, such as wages, which usually involve a degree of exertion to generate.

Passive income includes rent from property and portfolio income, such as dividends from stocks and shares or interest from bonds. Regardless of the source of income, if an individual's earnings are not high enough to cover expenses and still have some left over, it becomes almost impossible to build wealth. With this in mind, the goal of building wealth must be underpinned by a strategy for generating enough income to allow saving.

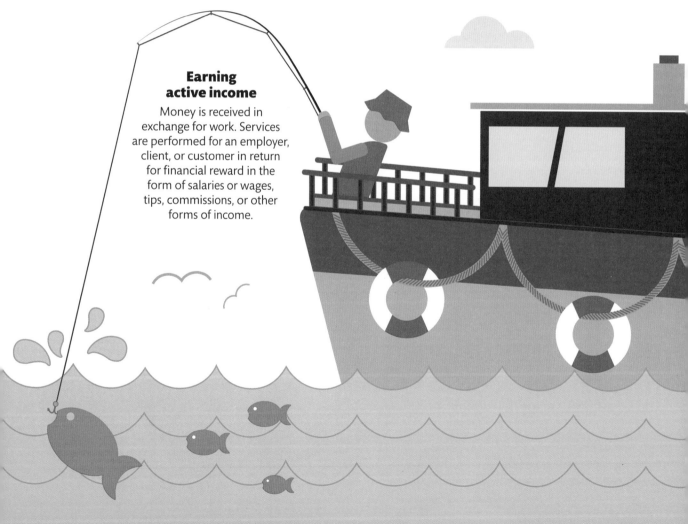

Earning active income

Money is received in exchange for work. Services are performed for an employer, client, or customer in return for financial reward in the form of salaries or wages, tips, commissions, or other forms of income.

EARNING PASSIVE INCOME

Savings accounts
can offer high returns,
but it is important to
know how easy it is
to access money.

**Rent from a house
or spare room**
can provide individuals
with a regular source
of funds.

Blogging on a
popular subject
can be monetized
in various ways.

Online market places,
car boot sales, and
auctions can raise
funds through selling
unwanted items.

Royalty payments
can be negotiated for
photography, writing,
or other creative work.

**Focus and market
research groups**
pay individuals to
trial new products.

✓ NEED TO KNOW

❭ **Portfolio income** Money earned
from interest, dividends, or capital
gains. This is recognized as a
separate type of income by tax
authorities in some countries, such
as the US.

❭ **Capital gain** The profit earned
from the sale of an asset, such as
a house or art, which has gone up
in value since it was first bought.

❭ **Unearned income** Passive income
from investments, pension funds,
alimony, interest, or rental property.

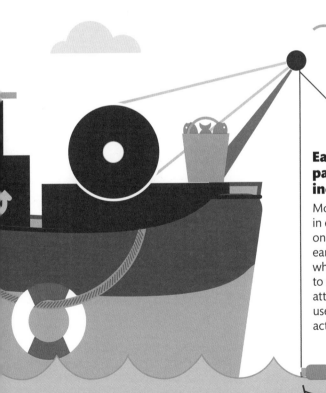

Earning passive income

Money is received
in exchange for little
ongoing effort. It is
earned from investments,
which require some work
to set up but then need less
attention. The term can also be
used to refer to money-making
activities outside employment.

Generating wealth

The billionaires who appear on annual lists of the world's wealthiest individuals may have built their empires in different ways, but almost all started with at least a little bit of cash to invest.

Building wealth

Most people begin by earning an income and saving a portion of it to build wealth, ensuring they have financial security in the future. Generating enough money for business ventures or investments goes hand in hand with creating wealth. Making small changes in lifestyle can limit spending and increase savings so that even people on the lowest incomes can take their first steps on the road to affluence.

2. Storing and saving

A strict household budget will reduce outgoings, which can then be reinvested.

❯ **Tracking spending** Monitoring money going out will highlight where costs can be cut.

❯ **Budgeting** Sticking to a plan makes it easier for individuals to see the path to personal wealth.

❯ **Building credit** High savings and low debt ensure a better credit rating, allowing options for future investment borrowing.

1. Earning income

Converting income to wealth is crucial. Working to earn an income, whether actively, passively, or a combination of the two, brings essential money into the household on a regular basis.

❯ **Active earnings** Saving can maximize money received and workers can relocate for a potentially higher income.

❯ **Passive income** Income can be boosted with investments, and by buying and selling possessions.

How it works

Building wealth requires discipline and a long-term strategy for optimum results. For most people wealth is amassed over time using funds saved from income, which are then invested to make even more money. It is a good idea to spread investments over a variety of financial instruments and, if a person is not confident initially, it is worth seeking professional guidance.

3. Investing wisely

Investing is a balancing act – the nearer a person is to retirement the less risk they can afford.

❯ **Factoring in retirement age**
Starting early gives savers greater flexibility.

❯ **Considering options** Cash savings, shares, property, and pensions offer differing returns.

❯ **Assessing the risk factors** It is important to balance the yield versus risk of each option.

4. Maintaining and managing wealth

Investors frequently reevaluate their portfolios to ensure they perform efficiently.

❯ **Monitoring investments**
Moving funds may mean better returns and lower fees.

❯ **Timing decisions** Global political and economic events affect when to sell or reinvest.

❯ **Making a will** A tax-efficient will ensures that wealth can be passed on.

"If you would be wealthy, think of saving as well as getting"

Benjamin Franklin, US polymath

DIFFERENT ROUTES TO BUILDING WEALTH

The aim of investing is to make money. There are various options to suit different lifestyles.

Traditional investment
Asset values fluctuate with economic changes, so many investors watch events closely to try to time their investments.

Property Residential property can provide capital growth or a steady rental income. Holiday homes generate less capital growth, but a potentially high income.

Business Ideas require little to no investment and there can be long-term potential. Investing in a start-up can result in big gains, but many fail so it can be risky.

Investments for income

The main aim of personal finance planning is to ensure that there is enough money to buy a larger house if an individual's family grows, to provide for children's education, and ultimately to have a healthy income in retirement. To achieve this individuals should invest in assets that will generate a stream of cash in the future. Many investors use a management service to look after their money in return for a percentage of the returns; others prefer to research and invest directly on their own.

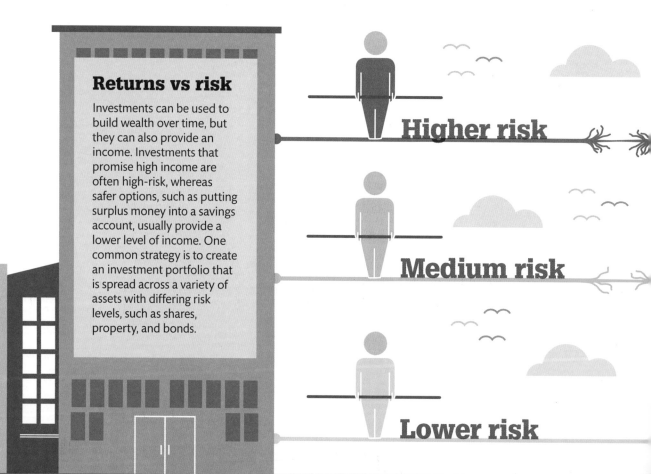

Returns vs risk

Investments can be used to build wealth over time, but they can also provide an income. Investments that promise high income are often high-risk, whereas safer options, such as putting surplus money into a savings account, usually provide a lower level of income. One common strategy is to create an investment portfolio that is spread across a variety of assets with differing risk levels, such as shares, property, and bonds.

Higher risk

Medium risk

Lower risk

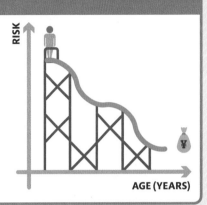

LIFESTYLING

This is an investment strategy that changes the ratio of different assets according to an individual's age. Moving money from higher-risk to lower-risk investments can be preset to happen automatically. For example, when young an investor may put 100 per cent of assets into high-risk investments such as futures. But more and more of their funds will transfer into safer, less risky investments such as government bonds as retirement nears.

RISK

AGE (YEARS)

"Risk comes from not knowing what you're doing."

Warren Buffet, US billionaire investor

Shares
Higher risk, potential for higher income

> **Ordinary** *See pp.182–183*
> **Preference** *See pp.164–165*
> **Options** *See pp.52–53*

> **Futures** *See pp.52–53*
> **Units in managed share funds** *See pp.168–169*

✓ NEED TO KNOW

> **Term deposits** A cash investment held at a bank or financial institution for a fixed term, usually between a month and a few years. Traditionally offer slightly higher interest rates than ordinary savings accounts.

> **Debentures** A long-term security issued by a company, yielding a fixed rate of interest. In the UK, debentures are secured against company assets; in the US they are unsecured.

Property
Medium risk, potential for steady income

> **Rent from residential, commercial, industrial**
> *See pp.170–171*

> **Profit from buying and selling**
> *See pp.176–179*

Interest-paying
Lower risk, potential for some income

> **Savings accounts**
> *See pp.166–167*
> **Term deposits**
> *See right*

> **Debentures** *See right*
> **Bonds** *See pp.166–167*

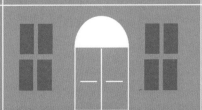

Dividends from shares

A dividend is a regular payment made to a company shareholder that is usually based on the amount of profit the company has made that year. Dividends provide a reliable stream of income for many investors.

How it works

Investors buy shares for two main reasons. The first is in anticipation of the share price going up in value, meaning that it can be sold for profit. The second is to earn an income from dividend payouts. For investors who rely on dividend income, it is important to choose shares in companies that prioritize generous dividend payments for shareholders, and to consider the type of shares bought, since not all shares guarantee a dividend. Investors may choose preference shares (*see opposite*) or rely on their research judgment to pick dividend-producing shares.

3% plus – the average dividend yield of the FTSE 100

Generous dividends likely

£ £ £ £ £ £ £

❯ **The amount** of the company's income that it pays as a dividend (dividend payout ratio) is steady.

£ £ £ £ £ £ £

❯ **The company's dividend** payouts have grown by more than 5% year on year.

£ £ £ £ £ £ £

❯ **The dividend yield** – the dividend price divided by the share price – is above 2%.

£ £ £ £ £ £ £

❯ **The company** has a comfortable profit barrier (enough to pay dividends without borrowing).

£ £ £ £ £ £ £

❯ **The company's additional** profit is sufficient to preserve its current dividend level.

What makes a company likely to pay dividends?

Investors can use several measures to work out which shares will provide the safest bet, with likely regular income now and in the future. Generally speaking, they will look for companies in good financial health with a history of steady dividend payouts over several years.

INVESTOR

Company A

❯ A history of paying decent cash dividends with no dramatic rises or falls in payout.

❯ Healthy cash reserves to fall back on.

Can a company afford the dividends it promises?

By comparing a company's profit with the amount it pays in dividends over several years, investors can judge if that company is a good long-term bet for providing a future income stream. Older, larger, and more established companies with steady earnings tend to pay healthy dividends, although their share value may not rise by much.

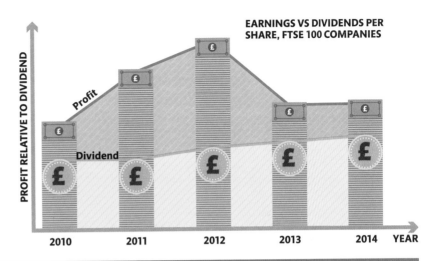

EARNINGS VS DIVIDENDS PER SHARE, FTSE 100 COMPANIES

PROFIT RELATIVE TO DIVIDEND

Profit

Dividend

2010   2011   2012   2013   2014   YEAR

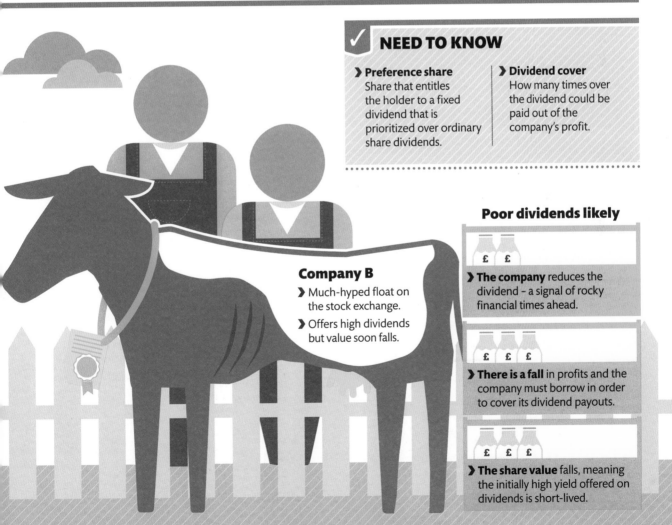

✓ NEED TO KNOW

> **Preference share**
Share that entitles the holder to a fixed dividend that is prioritized over ordinary share dividends.

> **Dividend cover**
How many times over the dividend could be paid out of the company's profit.

Company B
> Much-hyped float on the stock exchange.
> Offers high dividends but value soon falls.

Poor dividends likely

> **The company** reduces the dividend – a signal of rocky financial times ahead.

> **There is a fall** in profits and the company must borrow in order to cover its dividend payouts.

> **The share value** falls, meaning the initially high yield offered on dividends is short-lived.

Earning income from savings

Putting money into savings accounts and fixed-term deposits is low risk, making them safer options for wary investors. But investors also need to consider if their money is likely to "earn" enough income to live on.

Which savings or deposit account?

All investment products offer a trade-off between risk and return, and savings or deposit accounts are no exception. As a rule, such investments carry the least risk, but the downside is that they may not provide a very good return, which might be outpaced by inflation, and those savings-based products with the best return also tend to be the most risky.

INSTANT ACCESS SAVINGS ACCOUNTS
- Low return, low risk
- No minimum investment
- Cash can be withdrawn on demand

NOTICE SAVINGS ACCOUNTS
- Low to medium return, low risk
- May require minimum deposit
- Cash withdrawals must be arranged in advance

MINIMUM MONTHLY DEPOSIT ACCOUNTS
- Low to medium return, low risk
- Higher interest rates, but with restrictions
- Significant deposit needed to earn decent income

CERTIFICATES OF DEPOSIT
- Low to medium return, low risk
- Fixed interest rates
- Cash not instantly accessible as held for fixed term (from one month to five years)

How it works

Savings accounts and fixed-term deposits traditionally provide a guaranteed return with little of the risk associated with more volatile investment products such as shares or managed funds. However, when interest rates are low, it can be hard to find a savings or deposit product that offers high enough returns to provide a decent income. Many investors use fluctuating interest rates to their advantage, continually monitoring the latest offers to ensure their money is always earning the maximum interest possible. With a substantial deposit, even small changes in the interest rate can make a significant difference to earnings.

11% the gross saving rate of EU households in the last 10 years

MONEY MARKET DEPOSITS
> Medium to high return
> High risk, but some banks insure deposits
> High interest but high deposit and often limited term

TAX-FREE DEPOSITS
> Medium to high return
> Advantage of tax saved, which means earnings not depleted

FIXED-RATE BONDS
> Medium to high return
> Can be high risk, but some banks insure deposits
> High interest rates; some funds reinvest interest

PEER-TO-PEER LENDING
> Medium to high return
> Medium risk, but strong potential for gains
> Provides capital and interest payments

Investing in managed funds

Investors in managed funds do not have direct control over what happens to their money. Instead they rely on an investment manager to invest on their behalf.

How it works

When an investor puts money into a managed fund, their cash is pooled with money from other investors. An investment fund manager then invests the total amount in the fund in shares or other assets, such as bonds or property loans. As the funds earn interest, the interest money is paid out to the different investors relative to their original investment.

Investors can choose from either a single asset fund or a multi-sector fund, in which their money is invested across different assets. This has an advantage as poor performance by one asset will be balanced out by high returns from another *(see pp.188–189)*. Funds may be actively or passively managed. An actively managed fund tries to outperform the market, while a passive one aims to perform in line with the market at low cost.

The process

Investors who decide to invest in a managed fund need to make a series of decisions to ensure their investment is as profitable and safe as possible.

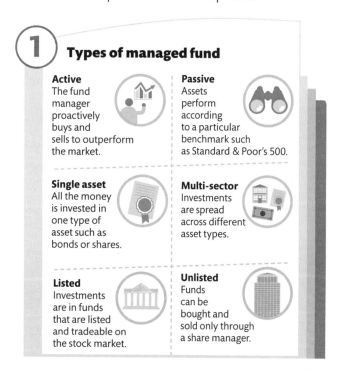

1 Types of managed fund

Active
The fund manager proactively buys and sells to outperform the market.

Passive
Assets perform according to a particular benchmark such as Standard & Poor's 500.

Single asset
All the money is invested in one type of asset such as bonds or shares.

Multi-sector
Investments are spread across different asset types.

Listed
Investments are in funds that are listed and tradeable on the stock market.

Unlisted
Funds can be bought and sold only through a share manager.

2 Choosing a fund

Risk Investors must decide how much of their investment they are prepared to risk losing.

Time frame The period of time over which the investment is made will affect the terms of the investment.

Product disclosure Before investing, investors research details of fees and penalties, insurance against loss, and performance guarantees.

Long-term performance Investors research the market to identify funds that consistently perform well.

RISK AND REWARD OF MANAGED FUND SECTORS

Generally, the more volatile the asset, the better the return. Spreading investments helps achieve high returns while minimizing risk.

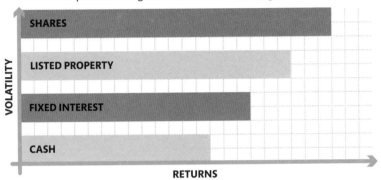

VOLATILITY

SHARES

LISTED PROPERTY

FIXED INTEREST

CASH

RETURNS

✓ NEED TO KNOW

❯ **Market index** A statistical measurement reflecting the performance of stocks, shares, and bonds in a single market.

❯ **Index arbitrage** An investment strategy of profiting from the price difference in buying and selling futures in the same stock index. *See pp. 64–65.*

❯ **Index fund** An investment fund consisting of stocks in one particular market index, such as Standard & Poor's 500 *(see below)*.

Indices to know

❯ **FTSE 100** Top 100 UK companies.

❯ **FTSE All-share** All companies on London stock exchange.

❯ **Dow Jones** Top 30 US companies.

❯ **Standard & Poor's 500** Top 500 US companies.

❯ **Wilshire 5000** Total US stocks.

❯ **MSCI EAFE** Equity markets in 21 European and Pacific countries.

③ Buying a fund

Registration Fund managers should be listed with the securities regulator.

Direct investment Funds can be bought and sold via online brokers.

Expert advice Advisors can suggest how much to spend and which units to buy.

Diversification By investing in different funds, potential risk can be reduced.

Fees Investors work hard to keep fees down, higher fees can mean lower returns.

Withdrawal rights There may be penalties for selling units in a fund early.

④ Managing a fund

Regular performance reports Figures received every month or quarter give updates on profits or losses.

Warning signs These might include the promise of high returns with little or no risk and should be investigated.

Statements Brokerage receipts, annual summaries, and other statements should all be filed.

Rental income from property

Potentially one of the most lucrative investments for generating income, property can also be risky because, unlike financial products such as bonds, it also generates expenses, and requires maintenance.

| **Rental income** | | **Landlord expenses** | ÷ |

High rental yield

£1,200 expenses

SOLD £200,000

RENT £14,400

An investor buys a house and becomes a landlord in an industrial town with a high population of seasonal workers. Demand for short-term rentals is strong.

In the first year, the investor-landlord has to repair the heating system, on top of meeting insurance costs and mortgage interest payments.

Low rental yield

£2,000 expenses

SOLD £500,000

RENT £17,000

An investor buys a house and becomes a landlord in a booming city. House prices are high, but people are only renting in the short term before they buy.

The investor-landlord has to pay for repainting. Their interest payments are high because the deposit amount was minimal and the loan amount is large.

How it works

Buying property to let has become a popular choice for investment in many parts of the world thanks to low interest rates on mortgages and comparatively high rents. However, landlords need to spend money on a regular basis on mortgage interest, insurance, agency fees, maintenance, and repairs, and may also need to spend time managing the property. There is also the risk that the landlord can lose out financially if their property remains empty for a long time, or if tenants default on their rental payments or cause any damage to the property. Landlords usually base the success of their investment on the value of the regular rental yield it produces.

Property cost **100** **Rental yield**

$$\frac{£14,400 - £1,200}{£200,000} \times 100$$

6.6%
RENTAL YIELD

After deducting expenses, the rental income as a percentage of the property cost – the yield – is high compared with the national average.

High rental yields can indicate:

> **The presence of large immigrant** or transient populations, who seek short-term housing while they take advantage of local opportunities, and are unwilling or unable to purchase property.

> **Rents are steady** and property prices have fallen – for example, in a booming town offering high wages, which attracts new residents who fuel local rental demand.

$$\frac{£17,000 - £2,000}{£500,000} \times 100$$

3%
RENTAL YIELD

After deducting expenses, the rental income as a percentage of the property cost – the yield – is relatively low compared with the national average.

Low rental yields can indicate:

> **Rents are steady** and property prices have risen – for example, when low interest rates fuel a property bubble, driving up the cost of houses relative to rent and income.

> **Rental demand has fallen**, so that rents have risen more slowly than property prices – for example, in a city with low unemployment when interest rates are low, encouraging renters to buy.

Life assurance

Although life assurance will not usually produce income for the policyholder until after their death, it will benefit their family, who can receive regular payments or a lump sum.

How it works

Although the two terms are sometimes used interchangeably, life assurance is different from life insurance. Assurance protects the holder against an inevitable event – their death – while insurance protects against the possibility that their death might happen within a set timeframe – for example, 50 years from the date the policy was purchased. So if a policyholder with 50-year life insurance dies before the term is up, their beneficiaries receive a payout. If, however, they die 51 years after the policy was taken out, there is no payout at all.

In contrast, a life assurance policy will pay out when the policyholder dies, whenever that happens, or provide a lump sum if the holder outlives the policy term.

SELLING A LIFE INSURANCE POLICY

> **Life settlement** The sale of a life insurance policy to a third party for more than its cash value, but less than its net death benefit. The buyer takes on the remaining premiums and gets a payout on the death of the original policyholder. People may sell a policy because they wish to purchase a different policy, or they cannot afford the premiums.

> **Viatical settlement** This is the same as a life settlement, only the policyholder sells because they have a terminal illness.

Life insurance

Decreasing term life
The payouts reduce over time, which means that the premiums are lower than for level-term insurance.

Family income benefit
This pays out an agreed monthly income from the date of the claim to the end of the term. Premiums are lower, but this type of policy would not clear a mortgage.

Life insurance
Also called term insurance, this covers the holder for a fixed period of time, with their estate receiving a payout if they die within the time period stated in the contract. Premiums are cheap but if the holder outlives the agreed term the estate will get nothing. Most mortgage agreements stipulate that the borrower must have life insurance.

Variable life
This is a permanent life insurance policy with an investment component. The policy has a cash value account – a tax-sheltered investment which is invested in sub-accounts.

Level-term life
This policy pays out a fixed lump sum if death occurs during the policy term. The sum does not change over time so the holder knows exactly what funds will be left in the event of their death.

Life assurance

Endowment

These are effectively investment schemes with life cover attached. They used to be popular with interest-only mortgage holders who used them to build up savings to repay their mortgage capital.

With profit

A with-profit whole-of-life policy includes an investment element, so that the payout on death is the sum assured, plus any investment profits allocated to the policy.

Over-50s

Designed for over-50s who have not already taken out any kind of life insurance or assurance, this guarantees a modest payout on death to cover funeral costs.

Both

Whole of life

This policy provides cover for the holder's entire lifetime with no set term, guaranteeing a lump sum at whatever age they die as long as premiums have been paid continuously from the start.

Life assurance

A life assurance policy promises the holder a payout – either when they die, or when the term of the policy comes to an end. It can also be used to pay any future inheritance tax. The fact that a payout is guaranteed inevitably means that monthly or annual premiums are higher for life assurance than for life insurance. It is an investment for the long term.

Maximum cover

This policy offers a high initial level of cover for a low premium, until a review. Premiums will then probably increase greatly to provide the same level of cover.

Universal

This gives flexible cover with a savings element which is invested to provide a cash value. Policyholders can use interest from their accumulated savings to help to pay the premiums over time.

Balanced cover

This has a premium set high enough by the provider so as to stay the same throughout the length of the policy. Some of the premium is invested to give additional cover over time.

Wealth-building investments

The purpose of investing is either to generate an income (to provide for retirement for example), or to build wealth, although the two functions often overlap. When an investment asset produces income – in the form of interest, dividends, rent, and so on – the money can be reinvested in order to build wealth, instead of being taken away as cash for living expenses. Other types of wealth-building investments do not produce income, but grow in value over time and can be sold for profit.

Building wealth through investments

Financial advisers agree that the best way to build wealth is by investing savings to make more, and by buying investments that will generate income and/or gain in value over time. To build wealth, investments need to match or outstrip the cost of living, so investors need to watch the markets closely and keep up to date with the economic news, especially changes in interest rates and inflation.

BUILD

MONITOR AND PRESERVE

EXPAND

CLIENT WEALTH

INVESTMENT PHASE

Income-producing investments and other investments that will grow in value over time provide the building blocks.

Close monitoring of investments and selling those that fail to perform, helps to maintain and enhance wealth.

Reinvesting income from investments that provide interest, rent, or dividends maximizes returns.

Investments that produce income

These investments produce income in the form of annual, quarterly, or monthly revenue. If this income is reinvested, rather than spent, then the asset's value will continue to grow, building greater wealth in the long term.

CASH IN BANK ACCOUNTS
Long-term accounts, which generally pay higher rates of interest, but may also have penalties for withdrawing cash early.

SUPERANNUATION
Purpose-designed to generate income at retirement, these schemes also often offer tax-saving incentives, adding to income potential.

MANAGED FUNDS
These funds carry higher risk than bank savings, but can produce greater income if their managers invest successfully.
See pp.184–185

7–9%
the average annual gain made by a **stock portfolio** since WWII

SHARES
Those shares that pay regular dividends and are likely to appreciate in the long term offer the best wealth-building potential. *See pp.182–183*

ANTIQUES
Investors must be confident that they can recognize a genuine article, and be willing to spend time scouring markets.

ART
Works by up-and-coming artists who are still early in their careers are good starting points for investment in art.

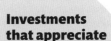

Investments that appreciate

These investments do not produce income, but their value can increase significantly over time.

PROPERTY
Property can appreciate in value and, in the case of rental property, generate a regular source of income too.
See pp.176–181

GEMS
Gemstones generally appreciate at the rate of inflation. Best bought as loose stones from a wholesaler, they are not easy to sell on quickly.

GOLD
This precious metal generally holds its value over time, but is best viewed as a long-term investment. Unlike gems, it is easy to sell on quickly.

Investing in property

There are various ways to make money from property, but each involves a lot of research and management, and also potential risk.

How it works

Unlike many other investments, such as buying shares or bonds, investors do not need to come up with the full sum to purchase a property, just enough for a deposit. Most lenders require around 25–30 percent of the total value, and a loan (mortgage) can be obtained to pay for the balance.

The aim of investing in property to build wealth is to buy when the value is low and sell for a profit, then use any profit to finance additional property purchases. There are several ways to do this. A person can buy and renovate a house then sell it for a profit, or buy in a cheap area and wait for the area to rise in value. Buying in a depressed market can reap rewards when conditions improve. Buying to let can generate an income that pays the mortgage and excess can also be used for a deposit for another investment property.

30%
the value lost on house prices in the US from 2004 to 2009

How to invest

Making money from property is a game of ups and downs that can entail short-term setbacks as well as gains on the road to the finish line. Success in the long run relies on the investor's strategy. There are several factors to consider: careful financial planning; good timing (to take advantage of rises and falls in the property market); thorough research of locations; appraisal of commercial versus residential investment options; and a clear understanding of economic indicators such as interest rates.

✓ NEED TO KNOW

> **Market value** The amount that a buyer would be willing to pay for a property (or other asset) at any given time.

> **Below market value (BMV)** The pricing of a property that is much lower than the average price of other similar type properties in the area (i.e. those priced at market value).

> **Buy-to-let (BTL) mortgage** A mortgage for investors who are buying a property with a view to renting it out for a period of time.

> **Buy-to-sell mortgage** A mortgage designed for investors who are buying property that will be sold shortly afterwards.

> **Capitalization rate** The rate of potential return on an investment property; the higher the better.

> **Operating expenses** The cost of the day-to-day administration of a property (or business).

> **Credit report** A detailed report on a person's credit history that includes a numerical credit rating, which indicates creditworthiness.

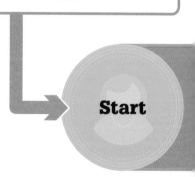

Start

Keep?   or   Sell?

When prices stagnate or increases are minimal, it is worth keeping a property until the market improves.

Whether investing long- or short-term, selling at the right time releases equity for further purchases.

Sell

Finish

HOUSE PRICES DROP

HOUSE PRICES PEAK

Reinvest

Maintain the property

Maintenance is essential to preserve the capital investment. Landlords must inspect properties on a regular basis and keep receipts as proof of work done as well as for tax purposes.

Buy

Buyers should compare prices, risks, and returns for a variety of properties – both flats and houses – and consider numbers of bedrooms.

Build a good team

A mortgage broker and solicitor are essential from the outset. In addition, it is important to find an accountant and a team of tradespeople – even a property manager can be useful.

Specialize in a type

It is a good plan to concentrate on one type of property, such as student accommodation.

SOLD

GOOD MORTGAGE BROKER HELPS FIND A SUITABLE MORTGAGE

Research

Undervalued areas with signs of growth, such as new shopping centres, can be a good investment.

Look at budget

Operating expenses and cost of mortgage repayments need to balance rental income and/or capital gain.

CAN'T AFFORD MORTGAGE REPAYMENTS

DEFAULT ON PAYMENTS – LENDER REPOSSESSES

Interest

Rises (and falls) in interest rates can affect cost of mortgage repayments.

INTEREST

Choose mortgage

Before beginning, a buyer must look at mortgage options, confirm their eligibility, and find out what they can borrow.

Save

The bigger the deposit the better the chance of a good mortgage offer with preferential interest rates.

INHERIT MONEY FOR INVESTMENT

Protect credit rating

A buyer should get a copy of their credit report – usually free online – and if necessary find out how to improve their rating.

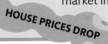

Buying and selling for profit

Knowing when to buy and sell is the key to amassing wealth through property. As with the financial markets, prices in the property market are cyclical, going up or down depending on the state of the economy. Factors such as interest rates and inflation, rate of GDP growth, employment, infrastructure, and immigration can all affect property prices. The trick to successful property investing is knowing how to assess the market and identify the right time to invest, the right type of investment, and the right time to sell.

The property cycle

Economics experts who have studied real-estate trends over more than a century have concluded that property prices rise and fall in distinct patterns, triggered by economic and social events and trends. A property boom is followed by a slowdown and a slump. Eventually the housing market recovers and begins to boom again.

COMMERCIAL VS RESIDENTIAL

Commercial property

As an investment, commercial property can offer much higher rental returns than residential property and longer leases, but capital growth is less likely. It can be harder to obtain a mortgage on a commercial property, but investment can also be made via commercial property funds.

Residential property

Investing in residential property generally offers a more predictable return than commercial property, both on rentals and resale, though location is key as always. Residential property can be valued more easily than commercial property, which can help when selling.

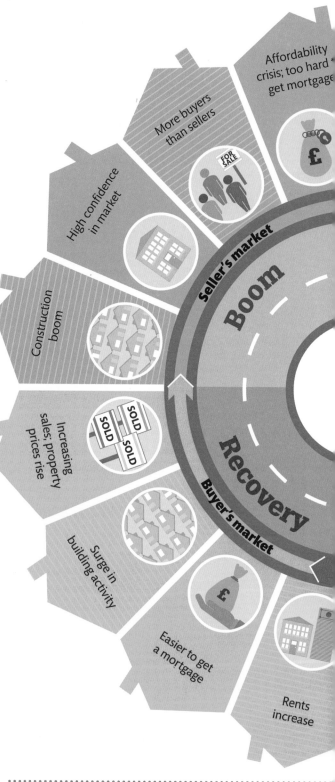

More buyers than sellers

Affordability crisis; too hard get mortgage

High confidence in market

Construction boom

Seller's market

Boom

Recovery

Buyer's market

Increasing sales; property prices rise

Surge in building activity

Easier to get a mortgage

Rents increase

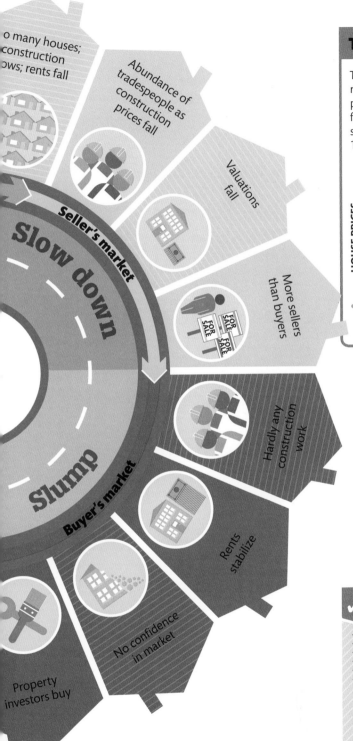

o many houses;
construction
ows; rents fall

Abundance of
tradespeople as
construction
prices fall

Valuations
fall

Seller's market

Slow down

More sellers
than buyers

Hardly any
construction
work

Slump

Buyer's market

Rents
stabilize

No confidence
in market

Property
investors buy

THE 18-YEAR REAL-ESTATE CYCLE

The idea that ups and downs in the real-estate market
run in an 18-year cycle is based on US studies into the
property market over the last two centuries by economic
forecaster Phillip J Anderson. He demonstrated that land
sales and property construction peak on average every
18 years – 14 years up and four years down.

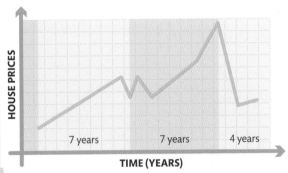

HOUSE PRICES

7 years   7 years   4 years

TIME (YEARS)

8.75%
annual rise in UK
house prices over
47 years between
1968 and 2015

✓ NEED TO KNOW

> **Appreciation** Rise in the value of a property over time.
> **Depreciation** Fall in the value of a property over time.
> **Capital gain** The increase in value of a property (or
> other asset) from its purchase price; this can be short
> term (under one year) or long term.
> **BRR** Buying, Refurbishing, and Refinancing strategy.

Home equity

The amount of equity in a home is a measure of a property's value. It is the realizable amount an owner could expect if, after taking account of debts against it, their property was sold.

How it works

The equity of a property is calculated by subtracting all of the outstanding debts relating to that property from its actual value. The amount of equity rises as the mortgage (loan) is paid off, and/or the property's value increases.

Financial institutions work out home equity as a loan-to-value (LTV) rate, which is arrived at by dividing any remaining loan balance by the current market value of the property. A low LTV (less than 80 per cent) is seen as lower risk for further lending.

✓ NEED TO KNOW

> **Collateral** A property or asset that a lender will take if a borrower fails to pay a loan.

> **Home equity loan** A loan that uses equity in a property as collateral.

> **Equity** A property's equity is equal to the current value of the property minus the outstanding loan amount.

US$11.9 trillion
US mortgage debt at the end of 2008

Loan
As the mortgage is paid off, loan-to-value decreases.

£

£

Positive equity

If the actual market value of a property is greater than the amount of debt owed on it in the form of a mortgage, then the property is said to be in positive equity.

Equity = house value – loan

£160,000 Loan

£40,000 Equity

House value = **£200,000**

£13,000 of loan paid over five years

£100,000 increase in house value

£147,000 Loan

£153,000 Equity

New house value = **£300,000** minus new loan value = **£147,000**

LOANS, VALUE, AND EQUITY

Equity fluctuates depending on the market value of a property and the amount of any mortgage held against it. If a house is bought for £500,000, with a loan of £400,000, the equity in it is £100,000. If after five years, the loan has been paid down to £300,000, but the value falls below £300,000, then the house is in negative equity as the loan is greater than the market value.

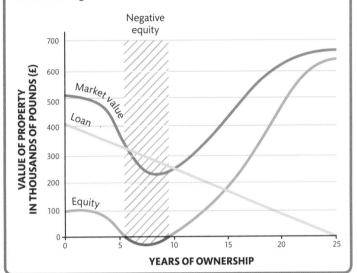

Equity

As the mortgage is paid off and/or the property's value increases, the level of equity goes up.

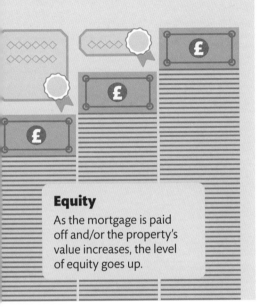

Negative equity

If the value of a property falls, generally as the result of a real-estate slump, to the point at which it is lower than the amount of mortgage loan owed on it, then the property is said to be in negative equity.

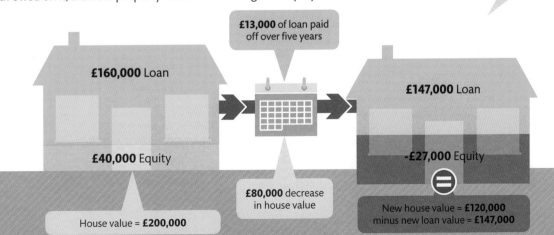

£160,000 Loan

£40,000 Equity

House value = **£200,000**

£13,000 of loan paid off over five years

£80,000 decrease in house value

£147,000 Loan

-£27,000 Equity

New house value = **£120,000** minus new loan value = **£147,000**

Shares

When individuals invest in shares, they are buying "a share" of a business, meaning that they have part ownership of that company. Shares can be bought and sold, and their price can go up or down.

How it works

Companies issue shares (or equities) to raise money. Investors buy shares in a business because they believe the company will do well and they want to share in its success.

It is not necessary for a company to be listed on the stock market for it to issue shares. Some start-ups raise money from a small number of outside investors, who are given a share of the company in return.

When a company wants to raise money more widely, it can apply to become publicly listed – or quoted – on a stock exchange, such as the London Stock Exchange. The company will need to go through an approval process in order to be listed. Once listed, the company's shares are described as "quoted" because their prices are quoted daily on the stock exchange. Trading in shares is executed by stockbrokers, who buy and sell shares on behalf of investors.

Shareholders are entitled to a say in the running of the business in which they own shares: for example, they can vote on directors' appointments and their pay packages.

How to buy shares

Investing in the stock market can be a good way for individuals to build their wealth. There are a number of ways in which shares can be bought and held.

Online share dealing platform

Low-cost online, discount, or execution-only stockbrokers allow investors to buy and sell shares simply, and usually without receiving any specific guidance or advice on investments.

Sharesave scheme

Some companies offer their employees the opportunity to purchase shares in the business. The shares might be offered at a discount to the market price, and are often paid for via deductions from employees' monthly salaries.

BULL AND BEAR MARKETS

Bull market

Several months or years of rising stock prices, along with high sales volumes and a generally strong economy. Investors are optimistic, and buy stocks expecting the price to keep rising.

Bear market

A general decline in the stock market over a period of time, with falling prices, stagnant sales volumes, and little optimism. This leads to a weak economy, falling business profits, and high unemployment.

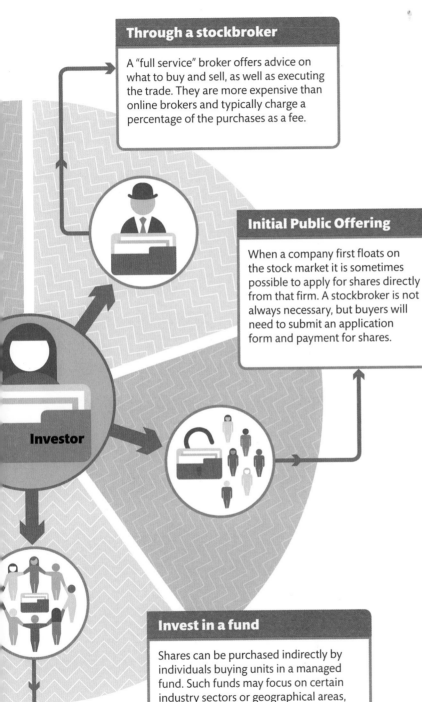

Through a stockbroker

A "full service" broker offers advice on what to buy and sell, as well as executing the trade. They are more expensive than online brokers and typically charge a percentage of the purchases as a fee.

Initial Public Offering

When a company first floats on the stock market it is sometimes possible to apply for shares directly from that firm. A stockbroker is not always necessary, but buyers will need to submit an application form and payment for shares.

Investor

Invest in a fund

Shares can be purchased indirectly by individuals buying units in a managed fund. Such funds may focus on certain industry sectors or geographical areas, and are often used as a way to diversify an investment portfolio or manage risk.

WHY SHARE PRICES MATTER

> **Investors focusing** on capital growth will only make a profit if the share price of their stock increases. They may also lose money if the share price falls.

> **A falling share price** can impact on the reputation of a company and its management, and also on its ability to borrow money.

> **Public traded companies** with a falling share price can become takeover targets for wealthy shareholders or rival companies.

> **The value of pension** savings pots linked to the stock market will fall if the underlying share prices fall. This is bad news for those nearing retirement.

> **When stock markets** in a country fall, foreign investors may remove money from that country altogether, reducing the value of its currency.

1987

marked the beginning of the longest US bull market to date, lasting 13 years

Managed funds

Inexperienced or time-poor individuals often opt to invest in a managed fund, where numerous people pool their money and invest in a variety of markets. The fund is managed by an expert.

How it works

Managed funds offer a simple way for investors to access a variety of investment markets. As well as the advantage of having the fund managed by investment professionals, investing via a fund is a straightforward way of diversifying investments.

In many cases only a small initial amount of money is required to get started and further investments can either be made by lump sum or regular (monthly) contributions. Managed funds are traditionally set up as "unit trusts", with each investor owning a number of units.

Unit trusts

When an individual invests in a managed fund, they are usually allocated a number of units based on the amount they invest and the current unit price. The unit price reflects the value of the fund's investments and rises, or falls, in line with those investments. Investors realise gains from managed funds by selling units.

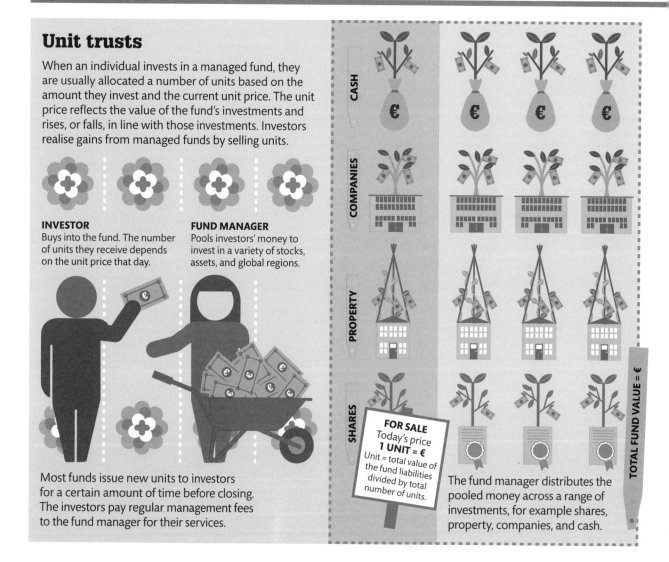

INVESTOR
Buys into the fund. The number of units they receive depends on the unit price that day.

FUND MANAGER
Pools investors' money to invest in a variety of stocks, assets, and global regions.

Most funds issue new units to investors for a certain amount of time before closing. The investors pay regular management fees to the fund manager for their services.

CASH

COMPANIES

PROPERTY

SHARES

FOR SALE
Today's price
1 UNIT = €
Unit = total value of the fund liabilities divided by total number of units.

TOTAL FUND VALUE = €

The fund manager distributes the pooled money across a range of investments, for example shares, property, companies, and cash.

MANAGED FUND STRATEGIES

Index funds

These funds aim to match the performance of a particular financial index, such as the FTSE 100.

Actively managed funds

These aim to deliver higher than average returns. Active managers analyse, research, and forecast markets to make investment decisions on which securities to buy and hold, or sell off.

Absolute return funds

These funds aim to deliver consistent returns regardless of whether the stock market rises or falls.

! WARNING

⟩ **The value of investments** will fluctuate depending on the stock market, which will cause fund prices to fluctuate as well.

⟩ **Fluctuations** mean that investors may not get back the original amount of capital invested.

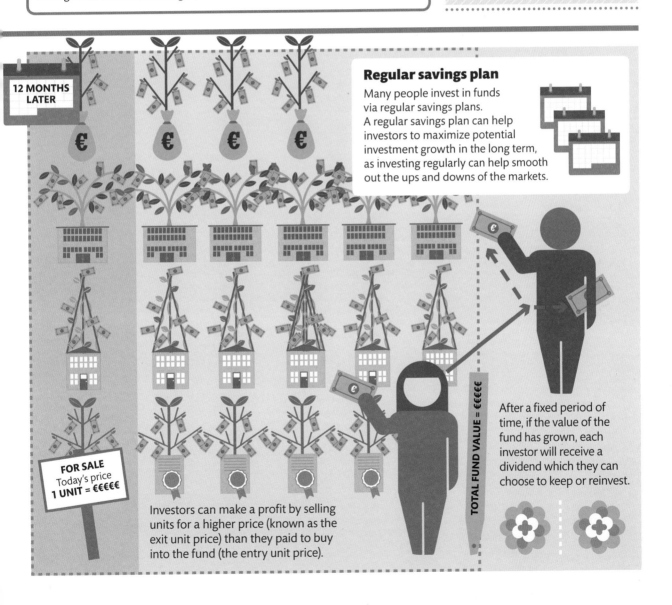

12 MONTHS LATER

Regular savings plan

Many people invest in funds via regular savings plans. A regular savings plan can help investors to maximize potential investment growth in the long term, as investing regularly can help smooth out the ups and downs of the markets.

FOR SALE
Today's price
1 UNIT = €€€€€

Investors can make a profit by selling units for a higher price (known as the exit unit price) than they paid to buy into the fund (the entry unit price).

TOTAL FUND VALUE = €€€€€

After a fixed period of time, if the value of the fund has grown, each investor will receive a dividend which they can choose to keep or reinvest.

Managing investments

Investments are something individuals buy or put money into in order to make a profit, or "return". There are different types of investments – known as asset classes – each of which offers a different type of return. Investors may receive interest (from cash or bonds), dividends (from shares), rent (from property), or capital gains when they sell an asset (the difference between the purchase and sale price). Investors can manage their own investments or pay someone else to do it.

Personal investment basics

Investing money for the first time is a big step, and it is essential to prepare well. Investing means taking a risk with money, and it is possible to lose some or all of the capital invested. Before deciding what to invest in, an individual must assess the state of their personal finances. They should pay off any outstanding debts and loans first, and maintain access to a source of cash in case of emergency.

Asset allocation

Asset classes are simply different categories of investments. The four main classes are cash, bonds (or fixed-interest securities), shares (or equities), and property (*see pp.188–189*).

CASH
Money held in savings accounts is both secure and accessible. However, returns are low and could be wiped out by inflation.

BONDS
Fixed-interest securities such as bonds and gilts provide regular income, and are generally a lower risk than investments such as shares.

SHARES
Buying shares means investing in a company and thereby owning a part of it. Shares may pay regular dividends or gain capital value.

PROPERTY
Residential housing and commercial units can provide a good rental income and high returns when sold, but property is relatively illiquid.

Asset diversification

Diversification means investing in different asset classes. It helps to spread risk and, by spreading money across assets, there is less potential to lose everything if things go wrong, compared to if money is chanelled into one class.

> "The most important thing about an investment philosophy is that you have one you can stick with"

Daniel Booth, US businessman

HOW TO INVEST

> **Take a DIY approach** This is an investment method in which an investor, without professional advice, builds and manages his or her own investment portfolio.
> **Consult a financial adviser** This is a professional who can give advice on which assets to buy, and when, based on goals and risk tolerance.
> **Buy from a fund supermarket or discount broker** These financial companies offer "execution-only" services, without advice, allowing individuals to buy and sell shares or funds.
> **Invest in a fund company** These investment firms spread risk by pooling investors' money and buying units in a fund that invests in a number of companies.

Dollar cost averaging

Also known as unit cost averaging, dollar (or pound) cost averaging is the practice of buying a fixed monetary amount of an investment gradually over time, rather than investing the desired total in one lump sum. This strategy can reduce the average cost per share of an investment as more units may be purchased when the price is low, and fewer when the price is high. *See pp.190–191*

> Dollar cost averaging is also known as "drip feeding" money.
> Using this approach means that investors don't have to monitor market movements and time their investments strategically.
> Most investment companies offer regular savings plans that allow investors to take advantage of dollar cost averaging, also enabling them to save a little at a time.

MONTH 4

MONTH 3

MONTH 2

MONTH 1

INVESTMENTS

Risk tolerance/risk-return trade off

In investment terms, risk is the possibility of losing some or all of the capital invested. An acceptable level of risk must be decided before investments are chosen. *See pp.192–193*

> All investments carry a degree of risk, but some have the potential to be much riskier than others.
> A financial adviser can help to build a portfolio to match an investor's risk tolerance.

The optimal portfolio

A portfolio in which the risk-reward combination yields the maximum returns possible is known as an optimal portfolio. Optimal portfolios differ between investors relative to their level of risk tolerance . *See pp.194–195*

Risk   Reward

> Portfolio "weight" is the percentage of a particular holding in a portfolio.
> Investors should reassess and rebalance their portfolios annually.

Asset allocation and diversification

To reduce the risk of their investment, investors often try to diversify their portfolio, spreading the risk they are exposed to by investing in different assets, sectors, or regions.

Strategic asset allocation

A defensive investor may choose to use strategic asset allocation. This involves investing in a combination of asset classes, taking into account the expected returns for each asset class, and therefore the overall expected return of the investment. In the illustration on the right, the expected returns of stocks are 10 per cent, so by allocating 20 per cent of the portfolio to stocks, the investor will expect them to contribute 2 per cent to the returns.

MARKET CAPITALIZATION

The total value of a company – its market capitalization – is equal to the total number of its shares multiplied by the price of one of those shares. For example, if a company had 100 shares and one share in that company was worth £50, its market capitalization would be £5,000 (100 x £50).

The investment industry refers to the size of market capitalization when it talks about large- (or "blue chip"), medium- and small-cap companies. Large caps are usually more stable but offer an investor limited growth opportunities. Medium and small caps can be riskier, but can grow quickly.

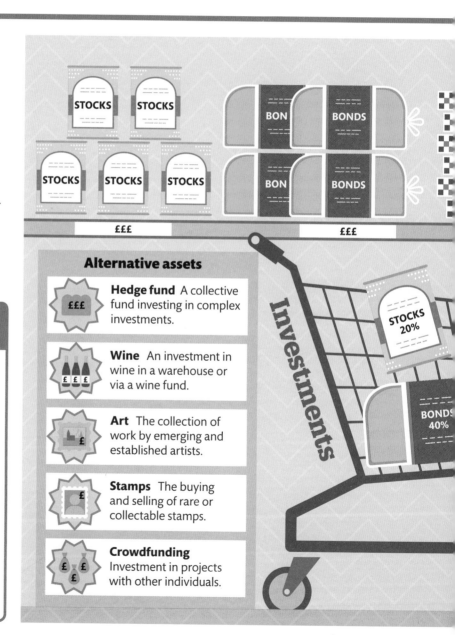

Alternative assets

Hedge fund A collective fund investing in complex investments.

Wine An investment in wine in a warehouse or via a wine fund.

Art The collection of work by emerging and established artists.

Stamps The buying and selling of rare or collectable stamps.

Crowdfunding Investment in projects with other individuals.

How it works

Asset classes are different categories of investment. Investors diversify by investing in different asset classes, or in different companies, industries, markets, regions, or countries, within an asset class. Another strategy, known as asset allocation, attempts to balance risk versus reward by setting the percentage of each asset class in an investment portfolio – stocks and shares, bonds, property, cash, and alternative assets – according to the investor's risk tolerance, goals, and investment time frame. The percentage of a particular holding in a portfolio is known as the "portfolio weighting". Diversification helps reduce the risk of each asset class in the portfolio.

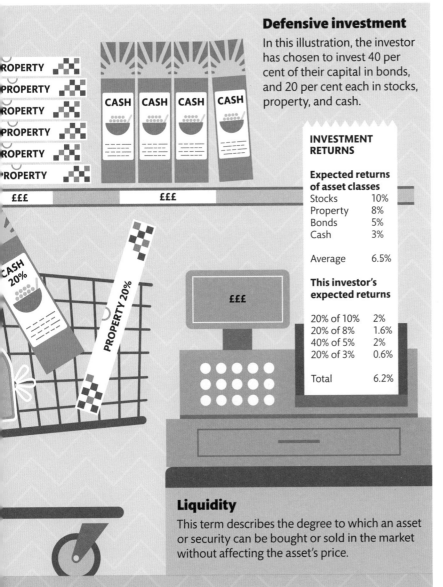

Defensive investment

In this illustration, the investor has chosen to invest 40 per cent of their capital in bonds, and 20 per cent each in stocks, property, and cash.

INVESTMENT RETURNS

Expected returns of asset classes

Stocks	10%
Property	8%
Bonds	5%
Cash	3%
Average	6.5%

This investor's expected returns

20% of 10%	2%
20% of 8%	1.6%
40% of 5%	2%
20% of 3%	0.6%
Total	6.2%

Liquidity

This term describes the degree to which an asset or security can be bought or sold in the market without affecting the asset's price.

> ## "Have a strategic asset allocation mix that assumes you don't know what the future holds."
> Ray Dalio, US businessman

ASSET ALLOCATION MODELS

> **Defensive** A small proportion of equities (stocks and shares) with the bulk of the capital invested in less volatile asset classes such as bonds and cash.

> **Income** Most of the investment is in bonds and alternative assets. This model is designed for income-seeking investors willing to take on a reasonable degree of risk.

> **Income and growth** Around half of the fund is in equities, with the remainder in bonds and alternative assets. This model focuses on a return composed of both capital growth and income.

> **Growth** Most of the investment is in equities, but some in bonds and alternative assets. This model aims for longer-term capital growth.

Dollar cost averaging

Dollar (or pound) cost averaging (DCA) is the practice of building up investment capital gradually over time, rather than investing an initial lump sum.

How it works

Catching the bottom of the market to get the best unit price is very difficult, and even the experts get it wrong sometimes. One way for investors to smooth out the market's highs and lows is to spread or drip-feed money into investments instead of buying in one go. This is known as dollar (or pound) cost averaging. For example, if US$100 a month is invested into a fund, this money will buy fewer fund units when the cost is high and more when the cost is low. The average cost per share over time is the average of highs and lows. As well as freeing investors from having to second-guess market movements, this approach encourages regular investing each month. DCA can be especially beneficial in a falling market, as more shares are bought so increasing the gains when the market rises.

Dollar cost averaging vs lump-sum investing

One key argument for regular drip-feed investing is the effect of dollar cost averaging. Dollar cost averaging allows savers to benefit from market volatility as by investing a small amount regularly, it allows them to buy units more cheaply on average.

Investor A

Lump sum investment

Investor A has a lump sum of US$1,400 to invest and is trying to "time the market". At the time of the investment, each share costs US$20 so the lump-sum investment buys 70 shares.

VS

Investor B

Dollar cost averaging

Investor B also has US$1,400 but decides to feed the money into the market at US$200 a month. This buys a varying number of shares each month.

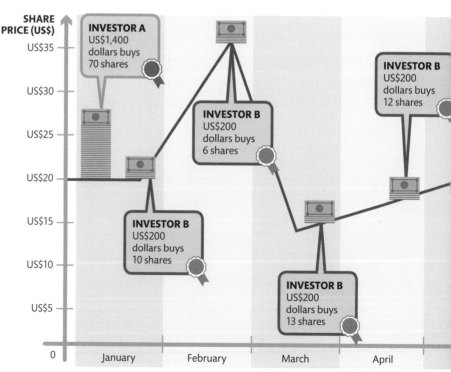

SHARE PRICE (US$)

INVESTOR A
US$1,400 dollars buys 70 shares

INVESTOR B
US$200 dollars buys 6 shares

INVESTOR B
US$200 dollars buys 12 shares

INVESTOR B
US$200 dollars buys 10 shares

INVESTOR B
US$200 dollars buys 13 shares

US$35
US$30
US$25
US$20
US$15
US$10
US$5
0

January   February   March   April

WHAT IS MARKET VOLATILITY?

Volatility is the degree of variation in a trading price over time. It is measured by looking at the standard deviation of returns – that is how spread out returns are from an average value. Lower volatility means a share's price does not fluctuate dramatically, but changes in value at a steady pace.

✓ NEED TO KNOW

❯ **Lump-sum investing** Although high returns are possible, putting large single sums into the market tends to require a more impulsive, or short-term approach, which may be counterproductive.

❯ **Market conditions** Dollar-cost averaging means investors do not have to study the details of market behaviour to maximise their returns.

❯ **Investments from income** By regularly investing directly from regular income, investors can keep cash on hand for other purposes or emergencies.

"The individual investor should act consistently as an investor and not as a speculator."

Benjamin Graham, 20th-century, British-born, US economist and investor

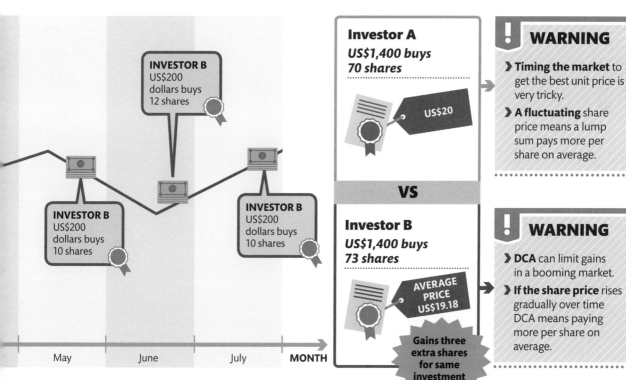

INVESTOR B
US$200 dollars buys 12 shares

INVESTOR B
US$200 dollars buys 10 shares

INVESTOR B
US$200 dollars buys 10 shares

May   June   July   **MONTH**

Investor A
US$1,400 buys 70 shares

US$20

VS

Investor B
US$1,400 buys 73 shares

AVERAGE PRICE US$19.18

Gains three extra shares for same investment

! WARNING

❯ **Timing the market** to get the best unit price is very tricky.

❯ **A fluctuating** share price means a lump sum pays more per share on average.

! WARNING

❯ **DCA** can limit gains in a booming market.

❯ **If the share price** rises gradually over time DCA means paying more per share on average.

Risk tolerance

Before investing, it is very important for investors to understand their personal risk tolerance – that is their ability to cope with large swings in the value of their portfolio over time.

How it works

To assess their tolerance to risk, investors should review worst case scenarios for different asset classes to see how much money they might lose in bad years, and gauge how comfortable they feel about such losses. Factors that affect an investor's risk tolerance include timescales, personal circumstances, and future earning capacity. In general, the longer the timescale the more risk an investor can take. Investors also need to assess how much money they can afford to lose without it affecting their lifestyle. Even for high-net-worth individuals with very large sums available as liquid assets, investing a small percentage of capital is wiser than investing a large one.

Investor types

Fund managers and financial advisers often provide risk-profile questionnaires to individual investors to help them determine which investments best suit them. The questionnaires examine an investor's tolerance to risk, time frame, objectives, and investment knowledge.

Conservative

Investors who are unwilling to take much risk and are happy to accept lower returns as a result might prefer a portfolio that has a significant proportion in cash or assets with guaranteed returns such as bonds.

5 KEY FACTORS THAT AFFECT RISK TOLERANCE

Investors need to consider these factors to choose investments that fit the risk–return trade-off they are comfortable with.

Time frame The period over which investment will be made. More risk may be taken over a longer time frame.

Risk capital The money available to invest or trade, which, if lost, should not affect an investor's lifestyle.

Investment goals Objectives such as funding for education or retirement.

Experience An investor's experience of past investments, and their understanding of assets and risk.

Risk attitude An investor's stance on losing his or her investment capital.

High risk

Investors who are willing to accept more risks for potentially higher returns might consider including emerging markets and alternative asset classes in their portfolios.

Balance

Investors who are happy to invest in more shares and property are likely to want only a small proportion of their capital in cash in fixed-interest accounts.

Cautious

Investors who are more willing to take some risk in return for a profit are likely to go for a mix of growth and defensive assets, and invest more in shares than in bonds.

✓ NEED TO KNOW

❯ **Capital risk** The possibility of losing the initial capital (money) invested. With more risky investments, capital could grow significantly but it could also be dramatically reduced.

❯ **Inflation risk** The threat of rising prices eroding the buying power of money. If the returns on investments do not match or beat inflation, they will effectively be losing value each year.

❯ **Interest risk** The possibility that a fixed-rate debt instrument, such as a bond, will decline in value as a result of a rise in interest rates. If new bonds are issued with a higher interest rate, the market price of existing bonds will decrease.

❯ **Negative interest** Currently tens of billions are invested in Europe at negative interest rates simply to provide low risk and security.

"The only strategy that is guaranteed to fail is not taking any risks."

Mark Zuckerberg, founder of Facebook

The optimal portfolio

A portfolio consists of a selection of different assets. The optimal portfolio achieves the ideal trade-off between potential risk and likely reward, depending on an investor's desired return and attitude to risk.

How it works

The optimal portfolio is a mathematical model that demonstrates that an investor will take on increased risk only if that risk is compensated by higher expected returns, and conversely, that an investor who wants higher expected returns must accept more risk.

The optimal portfolio reduces risk by selecting and balancing assets based on statistical techniques that quantify the amount of diversification between assets. A key feature of the optimal portfolio is that an asset's risk and return should not be assessed on its own, but by how it contributes to a portfolio's overall risk and return. The main objective of the optimal portfolio is to yield the highest return for a given risk or the lowest risk for a given return, these being investors' most common goals.

Efficient frontier

The efficient frontier is considered the optimum ratio between risk and reward – that is, the highest expected return for a defined level of risk, or the lowest risk for a given level of expected return. Portfolios that lie below the efficient frontier are sub-optimal, either because they do not provide enough return for that risk level, or because they have too high a level of risk for a defined rate of return. Asset correlation is a measure of the way investments move in relation to one another, and is important to the efficient frontier. A portfolio is better balanced if the prices of the securities in it move in different directions under similar circumstances, effectively balancing risk across the portfolio.

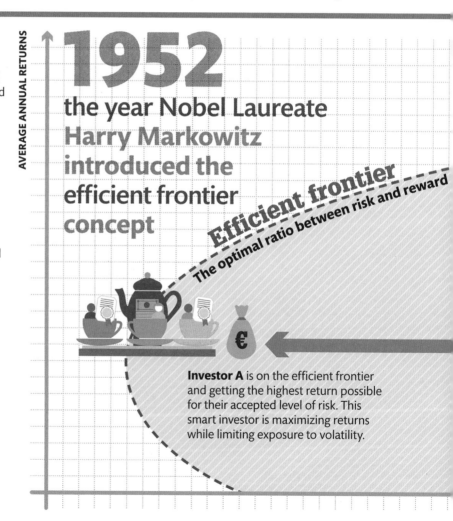

AVERAGE ANNUAL RETURNS

1952
the year Nobel Laureate Harry Markowitz introduced the efficient frontier concept

Efficient frontier
The optimal ratio between risk and reward

Investor A is on the efficient frontier and getting the highest return possible for their accepted level of risk. This smart investor is maximizing returns while limiting exposure to volatility.

REBALANCING A PORTFOLIO

The different assets in a portfolio will perform according to the market. Over time this will cause the percentage of each asset class in the portfolio, which was originally tailored to the investor's preferred level of risk exposure, to shift . If left unadjusted, the portfolio will either become too risky or too conservative. To keep a portfolio's risk profile reasonably close to an investor's level of risk tolerance, its investments should be reviewed regularly and rebalanced when necessary.

The goal of rebalancing is to move the asset allocation back in line with the original plan. This approach is one of the main dynamic strategies for asset allocation and is known as a constant-mix strategy.

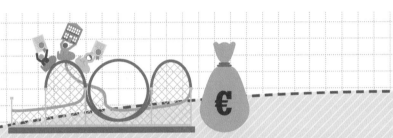

Investor C is also on the efficient frontier. C has a high-risk portfolio but is compensated by receiving higher returns.

The efficient frontier flattens out as it goes higher because there is a limit to the returns that investors can expect, so there is no advantage in taking more risk.

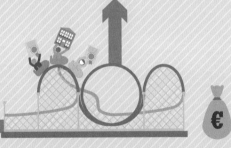

Investor B has a sub-optimal portfolio. If happy with the risk level, B should rebalance the portfolio closer to C's position to achieve higher returns. Alternatively, to lower the risk for the same rate of return, B should adjust the asset allocation closer to A's position.

RISK, MEASURED BY THE STANDARD DEVIATION OF ANNUAL RETURNS

✓ NEED TO KNOW

❭ **Weighting** The percentage of a portfolio consisting of particular assets. Calculated by dividing the current value of each asset by the total value of the portfolio.

❭ **Variance** The measure of how the returns of a set of securities in a portfolio fluctuate over time.

❭ **Standard deviation** A statistical measurement of the annual rate of return of an investment that gives an indication of the investment's historical volatility which can be used to gauge future expected volatility.

❭ **Expected return** The estimated value of an investment, including the change in price and any payments or dividends, calculated from a probability distribution curve of all of the possible rates of return.

❭ **Asset correlation** A statistic that measures the degree to which the values of two assets move in relation to each other. A positive correlation means that assets move in the same direction; a negative correlation means that they diverge.

Pensions and retirement

A pension scheme is a type of savings plan to help save money for retirement. Pensions enable workers to invest a proportion of their income regularly during their working life to give them an income when they retire. It is important for workers to think about making pension contributions when they are young, rather than when they are approaching retirement age. In many countries, pensions have certain specific tax benefits in comparison with other forms of savings.

Saving

Early investment

Jane, aged 25, wants to retire at 68 with a £15,000-a-year pension. She needs to save £165 a month. *See pp.198–199*

25

10% of monthly salary

WORKING LIFE

Later investment

Paul, aged 45, wants to retire at 68 with a £15,000-a-year pension. He needs to save £322 a month. *See pp.198–199*

45

15% of monthly salary

The changing age of retirement

In most countries there is a minimum age an individual must reach before they can access any of their private pensions – in the UK it is currently 55. This is different from the state pension age, when retirees begin to receive money from the government. The UK state pension age is expected to rise from 65 to 68 by the mid 2040s. People tend to retire earlier in mainland Europe – at present this is partly due to the fact that there tend to be fewer jobs for older people. *See pp.202–203*

Pension plan

State pension

Contributions are taken from taxpayers by the government. People who have contributed enough then receive a state pension at retirement age.

Tax contributions for a number of years

Company pension

Employees and employers make monthly payments into a fund managed by a pension company. They may also receive government tax relief.

Employee contributes a % of salary monthly

Company contributes an additional % to employee pension

Private pension

DIY pensions allow workers to choose their own investments and pension company. They may also be able to claim government tax relief.

Individual makes a monthly contribution

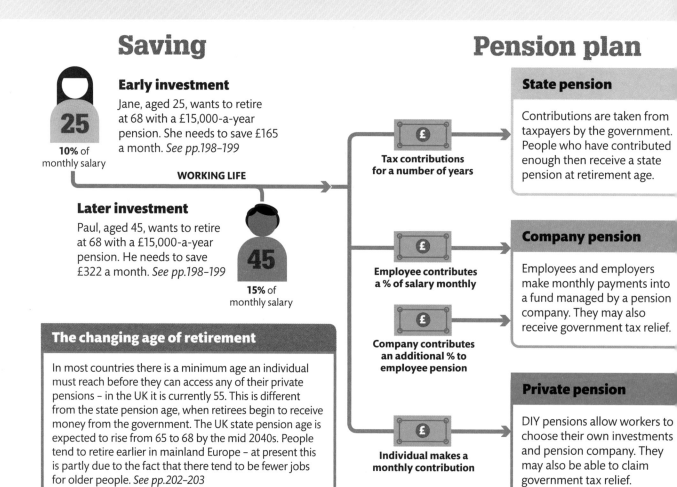

OPTIONS FOR ACCESSING YOUR PENSION

Different countries have different rules about how to access pension savings. In the UK there are three main options:

❯ **Option 1** Take 100 per cent of the pension as cash out to spend or invest. Only 25 per cent of a pension pot can be accessed tax-free – the rest will be taxed in the same way as any other earnings. There is a risk of running out of cash sooner or later.

❯ **Option 2** Buy an annuity. This is an insurance product that provides a fixed amount of cash every year for life. An annuity means the money won't run out, but the rate of income will be lower.

❯ **Option 3** Use income drawdown. This means withdrawing invested money as it is needed. There is the risk of running out of cash if too much money is withdrawn or the fund performs badly.

> "You can be young without money, but you can't be old without it."
>
> Tennessee Williams, US playwright

Retirement

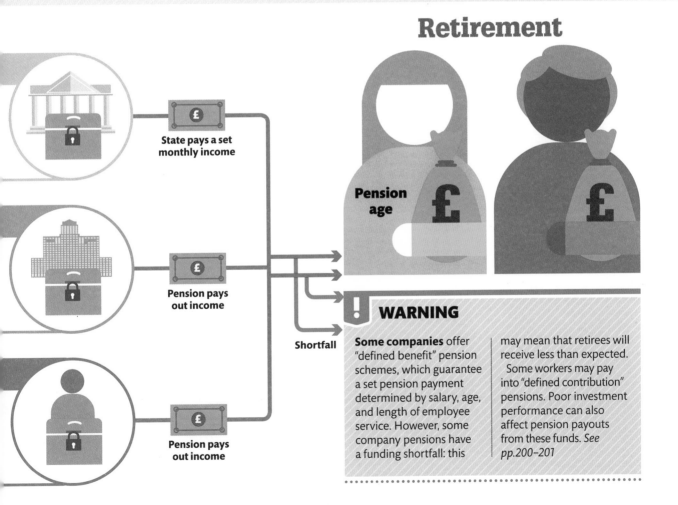

State pays a set monthly income

Pension age

Pension pays out income

Pension pays out income

Shortfall

⚠ WARNING

Some companies offer "defined benefit" pension schemes, which guarantee a set pension payment determined by salary, age, and length of employee service. However, some company pensions have a funding shortfall: this may mean that retirees will receive less than expected. Some workers may pay into "defined contribution" pensions. Poor investment performance can also affect pension payouts from these funds. *See pp.200–201*

Saving and investing for a pension

The amount of income a pension can provide in retirement depends on how much has been saved and how well the investments have performed.

How it works

Some countries pay retirees a state pension based on taxpayers' contributions. However, a state pension only provides enough money for a very basic standard of living, and so many countries encourage people to save money while they are working to provide them with additional income for a more comfortable retirement.

Saving into a private pension is the most common way of doing this. A pension is a long-term savings plan in which the money is invested in shares, bonds, or other types of asset with the aim of providing a return on the money invested. The more money saved while working, and the better the investments perform, the more money there will be to live on in retirement.

✓ NEED TO KNOW

- ❯ **State pension** Pension payout determined by the taxpayer's regular contributions.
- ❯ **Defined contribution** Pension payout determined by the amount paid in and the investment fund's performance.
- ❯ **Defined benefit** Pension payout from an employer determined by final or average salary.
- ❯ **SIPP** Self-invested personal pension; saver picks investments.

Early investment for maximum return

The earlier an individual starts to save for a pension, the better. Firstly, they will need to save a smaller amount each month to reach their desired sum for retirement. Secondly, some employers also contribute to their employees' pension savings, while some governments offer tax benefits on pension savings. Thirdly, investments will have longer to weather the ups and downs of the markets, so savers will benefit from more interest as it accrues over the years.

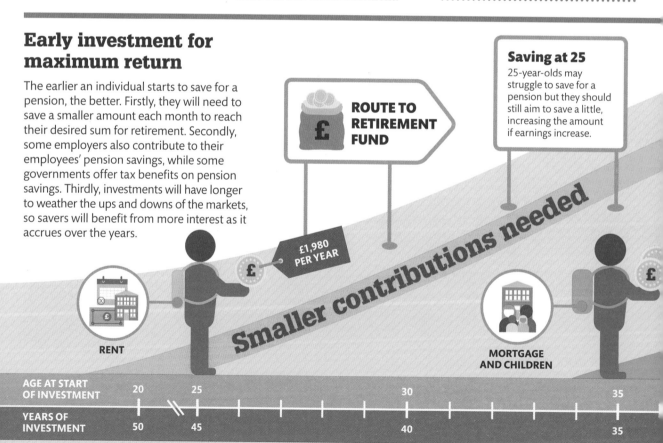

ROUTE TO RETIREMENT FUND

Saving at 25
25-year-olds may struggle to save for a pension but they should still aim to save a little, increasing the amount if earnings increase.

£1,980 PER YEAR

Smaller contributions needed

RENT

MORTGAGE AND CHILDREN

AGE AT START OF INVESTMENT	20	25	30	35
YEARS OF INVESTMENT	50	45	40	35

PENSION CONTRIBUTIONS

Calculations by a British consumer association reveal that to achieve an annual pension income of £15,000 by age 68, savers starting at age 25 need to save £165 a month. Starting at 35 would mean having to save £215 a month.

A professional financial adviser can calculate exactly how much an individual needs to save to meet their retirement goals, and offer advice on the different types of pensions and investments available.

50% of one's age is the percentage of salary to save for retirement when starting a pension.

RETIREMENT FUND

Saving at 50+

Savers aged over 50 may no longer be paying a mortgage but may still need to balance pension contributions with other financial burdens, such as paying their children's university fees or caring for elderly parents.

Very large contributions

£3,864 PER YEAR

£2,580 PER YEAR

Larger contributions needed

MORTGAGE AND CHILDREN

Very late starters will need to contribute large percentages of their salaries – 22.5% if aged 40 compared to 10% aged 20.

40   45   70
30   25   0

Defined benefit vs defined contribution

Company pension schemes that promise a fixed monthly pension are known as defined benefit schemes. These are risky for employers, who have to pay out regardless of how the pension investments perform. This "pension promise" has led to some pension funds having insufficient funds to meet their commitments due to poor financial results of the pension schemes. With defined contribution schemes, it is the employee who carries the investment risk. The success of both schemes hinges on the investments in the pension performing well, but if defined contribution funds lose money, an individual's pension pot may be smaller than expected when they retire.

Why pensions fail

It is important for individuals to take professional financial advice at various stages of their lives to ensure that their pension is on track to pay out the desired level of income. A financial adviser can provide guidance on how much to save, the best way to pay money into a pension fund, and any steps that can be taken to reduce the risk of a pension failing. In some cases it may be advisable for savers to increase their contributions or diversify their pension investments.

5. High inflation

Increases in the cost of living need to be reflected in the value of the pension pot to ensure it will provide adequate income in retirement.

3. Taxes

Pensions are usually taxed as income, so relevant taxes should be factored in when a pension is designed.

1. Business failure

Company pension funds can be lost if an employer goes bust and the money is not ring-fenced (financially separate from other assets and liabilities).

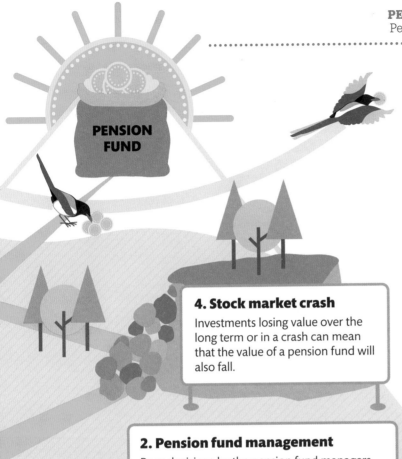

2030
the year by which one in six people will be aged 60+

AGEING POPULATION

The population is ageing in most countries. According to global averages, a child born in 1960 could have expected to live for 52 years, but if that child were born today, he or she could expect to live to the age of 69. By the middle of the century, average lifespan is likely to be higher still: well over 70. An ageing population has dramatic consequences for state pensions, as current workers' contributions are not invested by the state to pay for future pensions but are instead used to simply pay the pension benefits of current pensioners. As the population of pensioners continues to increase, the shortfall between tax income and pension payouts will increase.

PENSION FUND

4. Stock market crash

Investments losing value over the long term or in a crash can mean that the value of a pension fund will also fall.

2. Pension fund management

Poor decisions by the pension fund managers can lead to low returns, as with any investment.

Pension pathway

Converting pensions into income

On retirement, savers can invest the money from their pension to give themselves a fixed regular income, withdraw cash in one or more lump sums, or opt for a combination of both options.

How it works

There are two main options for turning pension savings into income. The first involves buying an insurance product that will provide a fixed sum as either a monthly or annual income for life. This is called an annuity, and may also be known as "steady payments" or "a retirement income stream".

The second option is to take out pension savings as cash, in one or more lump sums, with the rest of the money remaining invested. Withdrawing money and leaving some invested in this way is called income drawdown. Savers may combine an annuity with cash withdrawals.

Pension fund options

The options available to retirees will depend on the type of pension they have (defined benefit or defined contribution), the size of their pension pot, and the laws and tax rules of the country they live in.

PENSION POT AT RETIREMENT AGE

Cash lump sum

Some pension plans allow savers to take some or all of their pension fund as a cash lump sum on retirement. Retirees can then spend, invest, or save their pension money as they see fit. However there is the risk with this approach that, sooner or later, the money will run out, especially if they live a long life.

TAXMAN

Tax-free percentage

%

The way in which pension savings are taxed varies from country to country. For example, in the UK savers can take 25 per cent of the lump sum tax-free, either in one go or in a number of instalments. The remainder is taxed at the marginal rate (the rate on earnings in each income tax band) alongside other income.

TAXMAN

HOW TO CONSOLIDATE PENSIONS

Most people will have paid into different workplace pensions over the years as they move from employer to employer. As a result it can be hard to keep track of how each pension fund is being run, how much has been saved into it, and how it is currently performing. Consolidating pensions into one plan makes it easier for savers to keep track of their pension savings – and it may save money too, through a reduction in fees and administration costs. However, some older pension schemes have better benefits that may be lost if all pension plans are consolidated into a single pot.

WARNING

All pension schemes have very strict rules, so if a saver receives a letter, call, or email suggesting they break these rules penalty-free, they should be very suspicious. Fraudsters try to tempt savers into handing over their pension funds by talking about:

- ❯ A money-making investment or other business opportunity
- ❯ New ways to invest their pension money
- ❯ Accessing their pension money before retirement age

1891

the year the world's first old-age pension was introduced in Germany

Annuities

An annuity is an insurance product that offers a fixed monthly or annual income for life. Use of annuities varies from country to country. For example, about 80 per cent of pension funds are converted to annuities in Switzerland, but far fewer are in Australia. A rule change in the UK means that savers are no longer legally obliged to buy an annuity on retirement.

Income drawdown

Some pension plans offer the option of keeping money invested – and hopefully producing decent returns – with cash sums withdrawn as necessary. If too much cash is withdrawn, or the investments perform badly, however, then again there is a risk that the saver will run out of money.

Debt

This is an amount of money borrowed by one party from other parties. Borrowing is the way in which corporations and individuals make large purchases that would otherwise be unaffordable. They pay interest, a fee charged for the privilege of borrowing money, which is normally a percentage of the money borrowed. Banks and other financial institutions offer various different types of consumer debt products, ranging from bank overdrafts and credit cards to mortgages and loans.

Ways to borrow money

There are various institutions willing and able to lend individuals money, and each will offer a number of different financial products. Borrowers need to research the best options for their circumstances.

Loans

Personal loans allow individuals to borrow a lump sum of money that will be repaid at set intervals over a pre-agreed period of time. Loans can be secured or unsecured. *See pp.210–211*

❯ **Types of loan** There are many types such as car, student, debt consolidation, and payday loans.

❯ **Who offers loans** Banks, building societies, and other financial institutions all offer loans.

Credit cards

These allow a type of revolving credit that allows borrowers to make purchases without using their own money, which can be paid back monthly, or later for an additional fee. *See pp.218–219*

❯ **Instalment credit** The opposite of revolving credit – the money is paid back in instalments.

❯ **Dual-purpose cards** In some countries, banks issue cards with both debit and credit facilities.

Statement

TRANSACTIONS

DESCRIPTION

MORTGAGE

CREDIT CARD

CAR LOAN

SALARY

CASH

OVERDRAFT FEE

CURRENT TOTAL

CLOSING BALANCE

£1.496 trillion the debt owed by people in the UK

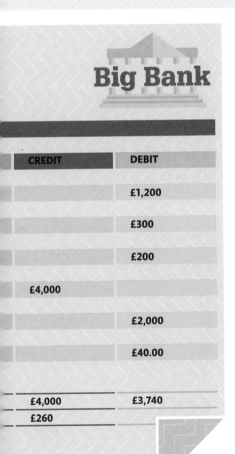

Big Bank

CREDIT	DEBIT
	£1,200
	£300
	£200
£4,000	
	£2,000
	£40.00
£4,000	£3,740
£260	

Mortgages

A mortgage is a longer-term loan used to purchase a property, which is secured against it. The lender can repossess the property if the mortgage is not repaid as agreed. *See pp.212–215*

❯ **Mortgage payments** These consist of the capital repayments – against the amount borrowed – plus the interest charged.

❯ **Loan-to-value (LTV)** This is the mortgage value as a percentage of the property's purchase price.

Credit unions

Credit unions are not-for-profit community organizations that provide savings, credit, and other financial services to their members. Borrowers need to be members of a credit union to be able to borrow money from it. *See pp.216–217*

❯ **Size and assets** Credit unions vary.

❯ **Ownership** Credit unions have no shareholders, only members.

Why people use debt

People use debt to buy things or make investments they could not normally afford. Borrowing to invest can yield larger returns than could be realised otherwise, but debts have to be repaid in full with interest.

How it works

Countries, companies, and individuals all use debt in order to function. Debt can be a useful method of spreading the cost of purchases, making investments, or managing finances. However, it is dangerous if it cannot be repaid. Taking out a mortgage to buy a property is an example of "good debt", as few people are able to buy a house outright.

There are plenty of examples of "bad debt" where people borrow money, often at high interest rates, to make arguably unnecessary purchases. Those who do so can find that simply paying the interest on their loans is more than they can manage. This can lead to taking out more loans just to pay off the interest, and the borrowers never make an indent into the capital borrowed in the first place.

Leverage

Leverage, or gearing, is the use of borrowed money to multiply gains (or losses). It is used on the stock market, by companies, as well as by individuals.

£50,000 TO INVEST

USING BORROWED MONEY

Leverage involves buying more of an asset by using borrowed funds, in the belief that the asset will appreciate in value by more than the cost of the loan. In this example, Buyer B buys 10 E-type Jaguars by splitting his £50,000 cash (equity) into ten £5,000 down-payments and borrowing the extra £450,000. This means the buyer is "highly geared" as there is a high proportion of debt to equity. This is risky as the £450,000 borrowed (plus any interest) will have to be repaid regardless of the sale prices of the cars.

CASH PURCHASE

Buyer A buys an E-type Jaguar

Buyer A pays seller the full £50,000

£50,000

A

£50,000

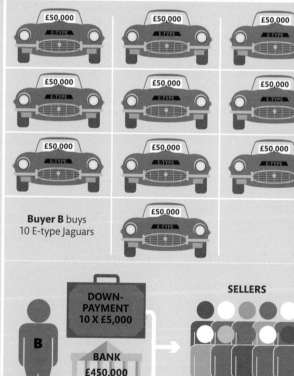

£50,000

£50,000

£50,000

£50,000

£50,000

£50,000

£50,000

£50,000

£50,000

£50,000

Buyer B buys 10 E-type Jaguars

SELLERS

B

DOWN-PAYMENT 10 X £5,000

BANK £450,000 BORROWED

£50,000 TO INVEST

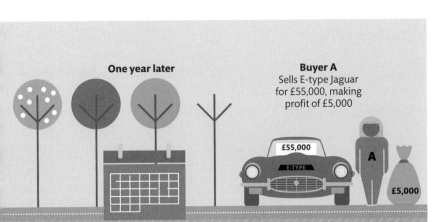

One year later

Buyer A
Sells E-type Jaguar for £55,000, making profit of £5,000

£55,000
E-TYPE
A
£5,000

265%
the ratio of household debt to household income in Denmark – the highest in the world

One year later

£55,000 (E-TYPE) ×12

CARS INCREASE IN VALUE
Buyer B makes a larger profit as the gains are multiplied when selling the cars at a profit of £5,000 each. His gross profit is £50,000; net profit can be calculated by deducting interest payments. However, there is also the possibility of losing more money if the cars lose value.

Buyer B makes a gross profit of £50,000

£50,000

INTEREST AND BANKRUPTCY

Interest
This is the cost paid to borrow money. It is expressed as a percentage of the capital borrowed. Various debt products have different interest rates. The rate might be fixed for a set period of time or be "variable", meaning it can change. It is very important for individuals to take interest costs into account when borrowing to invest.

Bankruptcy
This is a legal process that releases a person (or company) from almost all of their debts. People (and companies) can declare bankruptcy if they do not have a realistic chance of repaying their debts. Although it can be used for a fresh start, the financial consequence can be that it adversely affects a person's credit rating, and therefore their ability to borrow in the future.

Interest and compound interest

When money is saved it "earns" interest. Compound interest accrues if the investor re-invests it, as opposed to withdrawing the interest.

The snowball effect

If a snowball is rolled down a hill, it gets bigger and bigger as it gathers more snow. The rate at which the snowball grows also increases as it rolls down the hill because there is a greater surface area for the snow to stick to. So, given enough time, a tiny snowball can become a giant one. Compound interest has been described as a "snowball effect" as it works in much the same way, meaning that a small investment can provide bigger returns than an investment where the interest sum is paid out to the investor annually.

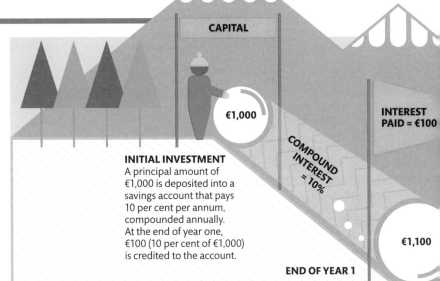

CAPITAL

€1,000

INITIAL INVESTMENT
A principal amount of €1,000 is deposited into a savings account that pays 10 per cent per annum, compounded annually. At the end of year one, €100 (10 per cent of €1,000) is credited to the account.

COMPOUND INTEREST = 10%

INTEREST PAID = €100

€1,100

END OF YEAR 1

INVESTMENT GROWS
The savings account now has €1,100, then earns €110 (10 per cent of €1,100) interest in the second year. By the end of year two the account has a balance of €1,210.

✓ NEED TO KNOW

> **Principal amount** The original capital sum invested or borrowed.

> **Compounding frequency** The number of times that interest is added to the principal amount in one year. For example, if interest is added monthly, the compounding frequency is 12.

> **Effective interest rate (EIR)** Also referred to as annual equivalent rate (AER). Takes into account the number of compounding periods within a specific period of time, so can be used to compare financial products with different compounding frequency.

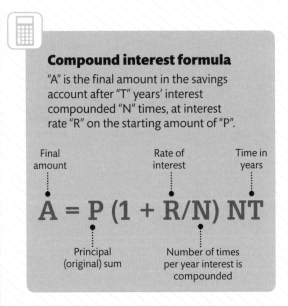

Compound interest formula

"A" is the final amount in the savings account after "T" years' interest compounded "N" times, at interest rate "R" on the starting amount of "P".

Final amount — Rate of interest — Time in years

$$A = P (1 + R/N)^{NT}$$

Principal (original) sum — Number of times per year interest is compounded

How it works

Interest is the cost of borrowing money, for example from a bank, and it is calculated as a percentage of the capital. When money is saved it is effectively being lent to the institution, which then pays interest to the investor, meaning that the capital "earns" interest.

With simple interest money is paid out to the investor each year. Compound interest is interest paid on reinvested simple interest, and works for both saving and borrowing. The interest from the first year is added to the initial sum, so in the second year interest is paid on the capital plus the interest accrued. In the third year it is paid on the capital plus the first two years' interest, and so on.

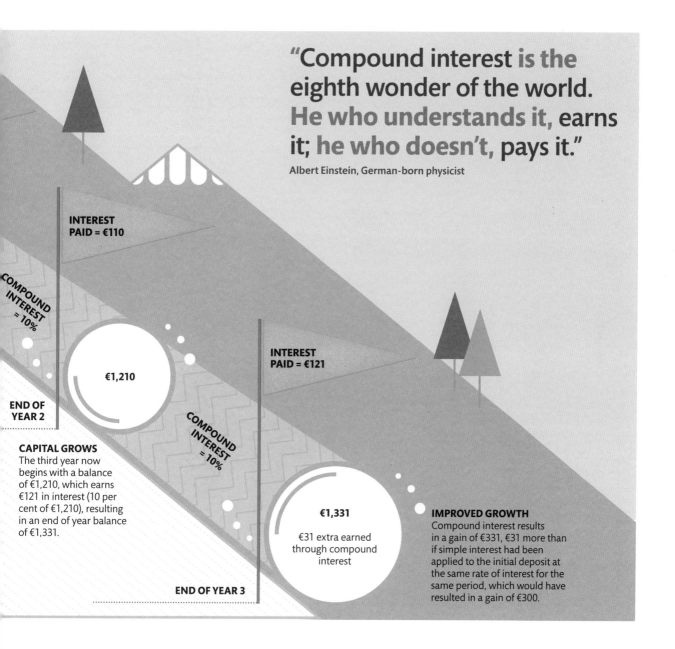

"Compound interest is the eighth wonder of the world. He who understands it, earns it; he who doesn't, pays it."

Albert Einstein, German-born physicist

INTEREST PAID = €110

COMPOUND INTEREST = 10%

€1,210

END OF YEAR 2

CAPITAL GROWS
The third year now begins with a balance of €1,210, which earns €121 in interest (10 per cent of €1,210), resulting in an end of year balance of €1,331.

INTEREST PAID = €121

COMPOUND INTEREST = 10%

€1,331

€31 extra earned through compound interest

END OF YEAR 3

IMPROVED GROWTH
Compound interest results in a gain of €331, €31 more than if simple interest had been applied to the initial deposit at the same rate of interest for the same period, which would have resulted in a gain of €300.

Loans

Loans offer a fixed sum of money to be repaid, plus interest, over a fixed period of time. Personal loans can be used at the borrower's discretion but some other types of loan have a defined purpose.

How it works

Loans allow individuals to borrow a lump sum to use in the short term, which they then repay in instalments at set intervals over an agreed longer-term period. For example, a person might borrow £10,000 to be repaid over five years. As well as repaying the capital, the borrower also pays interest on the loan. Periodic repayments are calculated so that the borrower repays some of the capital and some of the interest with each payment.

Loans can be used as a cheaper alternative to other borrowing facilities such as overdrafts and credit cards. If a loan is "secured" on an asset (such as a house), and the loan is not repaid on time, the lender is entitled to take the asset. Typically a secured loan is less expensive to the borrower than an unsecured loan. A mortgage is a type of secured loan used to buy a property without paying the entire value of the purchase up front.

Various institutions including banks, building societies, payday lenders, credit unions, supermarkets, and peer-to-peer lenders sell loans. Loan brokers may also offer loans from a range of different providers.

NEED TO KNOW

> **APR (Annual Percentage Rate)**
> The annual rate of interest payable (on loans), taking into account other charges.

> **AER (Annual Equivalent Rate)**
> Used for savings accounts, the AER takes into account how often interest is paid, as well as the impact of compound interest.

WARNING

Payday loans are designed to cover short-term financial shortfalls. The idea is that people repay the debt on their next payday. Customers typically pay about £25 to borrow £100 for 28 days – an equivalent APR of over 4,000 per cent. They are also charged fees for missed payments or to extend the loan.

5,583%

APR of payday loan company Wonga before new rules applied in 2014

CASE STUDY

Loan repayments

For loans with a fixed monthly repayment of principal plus interest, payments at first consist of mainly interest. This is because the interest paid each month is a percentage of the outstanding balance of the loan. As each payment also repays some of the principal, the outstanding balance (and therefore interest paid) decreases each month, while more of the payment goes to reducing the loan. Final payments consist of a larger proportion of principal to interest (as interest is paid on ever smaller outstanding balances).

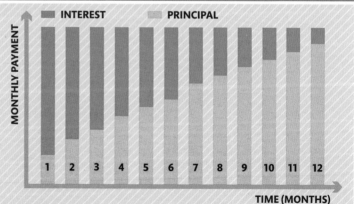

Loan agreement

Abank

A loan agreement is a formal document provided by the lender that sets out the terms and conditions of the loan.

This Loan Agreement ("Agreement") is made and will be effective on **04-04-17**.

BETWEEN	Lender: ("A Bank")	**AND**	Borrower: ("A Person")

TERMS AND CONDITIONS

1. PROMISE TO PAY

Within **60 months** from today, the Borrower promises to pay the Lender the sum of **€20,000** and interest and other charges stated below.

2. DETAILS OF LOAN

The Borrower agrees to repay the full amount of capital borrowed, plus fees and charges, the interest rates, the monetary amount of interest, and the total amount repayable.

Amount of loan:	€20,000.00
Other (such as arrangement fee):	€200.00
Amount financed:	€19,800.00
Total of payments:	€23,533.94
Annual rate:	6.8%

3. REPAYMENT

The Borrower will repay the amount of this note in **60** equal continuous monthly instalments of **€392.23** each on the **04** day of each month preliminary on the **04** day of April 2017, and ending on the **04** day of April 2022.

4. PREPAYMENT

The Borrower has the right to pay back the whole amount at any time, but a charge may be levied for early repayment: **€1,360.00**

5. LATE CHARGE

Any instalment not paid within **15** days of its due date shall be subject to a late charge of 4% of the payment: **€15.69**

6. DEFAULT

If for any reason the Borrower fails to make any payment on time, the Borrower shall be in default. The Lender can then demand immediate payment of the entire remaining unpaid balance of this loan without giving further notice.

Term of loan The length of time over which the loan will be repaid in regular instalments. This is normally expressed in months.

Amount The capital originally borrowed and advanced to the borrower. It is expressed in the currency of the loan, such as pounds, euros, or dollars.

Total amount repaid The total capital, interest, and fees paid by the borrower to the lender over the whole term.

APR The annual percentage rate: a calculation that takes into account the interest rate plus fees and charges such as arrangement fees.

Regular payments The periodic instalments in which the loan will be repaid, for example, weekly, monthly, or quarterly.

Early repayment charge An additional charge applied if the borrower redeem's (repays) the loan before the end of the term.

Late fees An additional charge applied if the borrower does not pay the instalment on the agreed date. The borrower continues to be charged until the original payment schedule is restored.

Default The failure to meet the legal conditions of a loan puts the borrower in default. A loan agreement sets out the consequences of a default.

Mortgages

A mortgage is a long-term loan, which enables the borrower to purchase property or land. A mortgage is made up of the amount borrowed – the principal – plus the interest charged on the loan.

How it works

The word mortgage is derived from an old French term used by English lawyers in the Middle Ages, literally meaning "death pledge", because the deal dies when the debt is paid or a payment fails. A mortgage is secured on the borrower's property, which means that a legal mechanism is put in place that allows the lender to take possession in the event that the borrower defaults on the loan or fails to abide by its terms. This is known as repossession or foreclosure. Most mortgage lenders require borrowers to put down a percentage of the property value as a deposit (or down payment) before they will be given a mortgage, and the bigger the deposit is, the less they will need to borrow.

Types of mortgage

Different countries have different types of mortgage, and different rules governing their issue. The amount that can be borrowed will depend on the property, individual circumstances, and prevailing economic conditions, but all loans will eventually need to be repaid with interest.

Repayment mortgage or annuity repayment mortgage

- This is the most common type of mortgage in the UK.
- The bank first checks the borrower's background to ensure they can afford the loan repayments.
- The borrower then puts down a deposit, and the bank lends them the remainder of the purchase price. For example, if the purchase price of a property is £300,000, the borrower may put down a 5% deposit (£15,000) and borrow the remaining £285,000 from the bank. This amount is known as the principal, or capital.
- The bank charges an interest rate on the principal, based on the type of mortgage and the base rate. Interest rates may be fixed for a period of time, or variable.
- The borrower pays back both the principal and the interest via monthly repayments. When they have repaid the total amount borrowed, plus the interest, they own the property outright.

Offset mortgage

- If a borrower has a savings account at the same bank as they have their mortgage, an offset mortgage will allow them to offset their savings against the amount they borrow.
- The result is that less interest is paid on the mortgage, meaning that the borrower will be able to pay their mortgage off more quickly.
- For example, if a borrower has a mortgage of £200,000 and savings of £30,000, an offset mortgage allows them to pay interest on only £170,000 of their loan.
- Not all banks offer borrowers offset mortgages, and interest rates may be higher than they are for other mortgage products.
- If a borrower only has a small amount of savings, the higher rates involved may mean it is not worth them seeking an offset mortgage.
- If a borrower has a large amount of savings, it may be better for them to consider using a portion of these savings to decrease the loan-to-value ratio (LTV) of their mortgage.

70% of EU citizens live in an owner-occupied home

Interest-only mortgage

❯ Interest-only mortgages allow borrowers to repay just the interest on the amount they have borrowed, and not the principal itself.

❯ The bank gives the borrower a mortgage, for example £240,000, and the borrower repays the interest on this amount via monthly repayments.

❯ The amount paid each month will be lower than for repayment mortgages, but borrowers will usually need to put down larger deposits, or demonstrate higher earnings, in order to be given an interest-only mortgage.

❯ At the end of the loan period, the borrower must repay the whole of the principal loan amount, in this case £240,000. If prices have increased a lot over the lifetime of the mortgage, due to inflation, then the amount owed will be smaller in relative terms. But if they do not have sufficient savings, the borrower may need to sell the property to repay the loan.

Reverse annuity mortgage

❯ This type of mortgage allows a homeowner to access the value of a property that they fully own.

❯ People who opt for a reverse annuity mortgage are usually elderly – in the UK, borrowers must be at least 55 years old to qualify for this type of mortgage, whereas in the US they must be at least 62.

❯ The bank lends the homeowner money against the value of their property (the equity) but there are usually high fees involved.

❯ The bank then pays this money to the homeowner, either in the form of monthly instalments or, occasionally, in the form of a one-off lump sum.

❯ When the homeowner dies, their property is sold in order to repay the loan amount.

❯ Any remaining money from the sale of the property, after the loan amount has been repaid, goes to the beneficiaries in the homeowner's will.

✓ NEED TO KNOW

❯ **Loan-to-value ratio (LTV)** Percentage of a property's value borrowed as a mortgage.

❯ **Security** Collateral for the loan; for mortgages, the property.

❯ **Remortgage** A different or additional loan taken out on a property.

❯ **Term** Years over which the mortgage is repaid.

❯ **Equity** Value of the property over the mortgage amount.

❯ **Negative equity** Value of the property being less than the mortgage amount.

❯ **Guarantor** A person who agrees to be responsible for meeting the mortgage repayments if the borrower fails to do so.

ISLAMIC MORTGAGES

Islamic law prohibits interest being charged on home loans. There are three types of Islamic mortgage that are sharia-compliant:

❯ **The bank purchases** a property on behalf of a buyer, and leases it to them. At the end of the lease term, ownership is transferred to the buyer/tenant.

❯ **A buyer purchases** a property jointly with the bank, and pays rent on the portion they do not own. They then buy shares in the remaining portion of the property, and as their share increases, their rent decreases.

❯ **The bank buys** a property and sells it on to a buyer, who makes fixed monthly repayments that amount to a higher price than the original purchase cost.

Mortgage rates

Banks offer a range of mortgages with different interest rates, each of which offers a different ratio of risk to affordability.

Fixed-rate mortgages offer the borrower fixed monthly payments for a set period of time. In the UK, fixed rates of two, three, or five years are common. The borrower either then remortgages to a new fixed-rate mortgage product or the original mortgage defaults to a variable rate. Fixed rates are not altered by changing interest rates or other economic conditions. This means the lender, not the borrower, carries the main interest rate risk.

Variable rates

Variable- or adjustable-rate mortgages have rates which can change during the mortgage term, sometimes tracking a market index such as the country's central bank base rate. Monthly mortgage payments will therefore increase or decrease following fluctuations in the base rate. This means the interest rate risk is carried by the borrower, who will need to be sure they can still afford the mortgage should the interest rate increase. The proportion of mortgages that are variable-rate varies from country to country.

Types of mortgage rates

Generally, the greater the guarantee of security for the borrower, the higher the fees involved. Some deals also lock borrowers in to a particular rate, offering less flexibility.

Fixed-rate mortgages

> The interest rate is set for a period or for the life of the loan, regardless of the base rate. This offers certainty, as borrowers pay a set monthly amount.

> These often come with higher arrangement fees, and payments will stay fixed even if the base rate falls.

8%

4%

BASE RATE

FIXED RATE AT 3%

Usually for 2–5 years

Standard variable rate (SVR) mortgages

> The lender can raise and lower interest rates, which may be influenced by the central bank's base rate, but can also be changed regardless of the base rate.

> These are usually cheaper than fixed-rate mortgages, but borrowers are vulnerable to interest rate rises.

8%

4%

SVR

BASE RATE

Indefinite time period

Why interest matters

Small variations in the interest rate can make a big difference to the total amount of interest paid over the mortgage term.

Mortgage deal 1

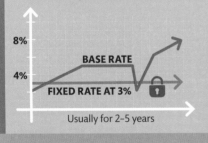

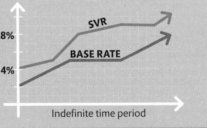

BANK

Loan
£200,000
over 25 years

3% interest

Jan

£948

Monthly repayments
to bank over 25 years

BANK

Total
repayment
= £284,400

Interest =
£84,400

2007

the year that defaults on US subprime loans became a crisis

SUBPRIME MORTGAGES AND CREDIT CRUNCH

The subprime mortgage crisis began in 2007, and led to fundamental changes in mortgage products and their regulation. In the US, mortgages had been sold to people without the income to repay them. When the housing bubble burst, this led to a wave of repossessions and bank losses. Mortgage-backed bonds lost value and several banks went bust.

❯ **Credit crunch** Banks and other lenders reduced the amount of credit available for mortgages and other loans.

❯ **Recession** The subprime crisis led to a recession or slowdown in several countries. As well as property repossessions, banks and other businesses collapsed.

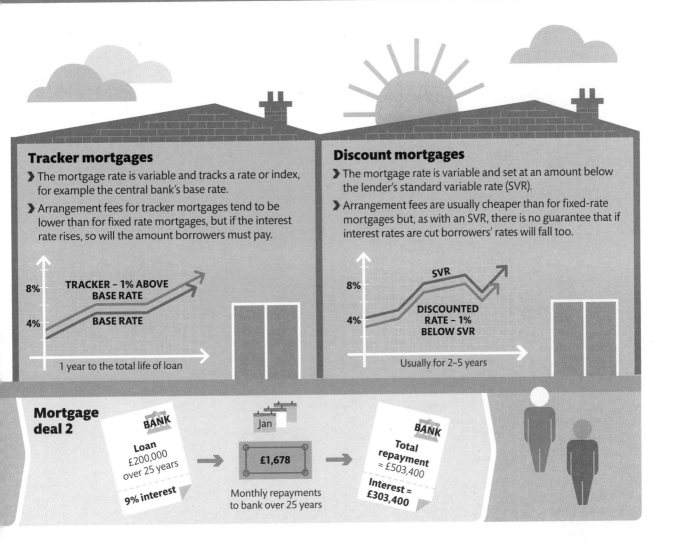

Tracker mortgages

❯ The mortgage rate is variable and tracks a rate or index, for example the central bank's base rate.

❯ Arrangement fees for tracker mortgages tend to be lower than for fixed rate mortgages, but if the interest rate rises, so will the amount borrowers must pay.

8%

TRACKER – 1% ABOVE BASE RATE

4%

BASE RATE

1 year to the total life of loan

Discount mortgages

❯ The mortgage rate is variable and set at an amount below the lender's standard variable rate (SVR).

❯ Arrangement fees are usually cheaper than for fixed-rate mortgages but, as with an SVR, there is no guarantee that if interest rates are cut borrowers' rates will fall too.

8%

SVR

4%

DISCOUNTED RATE – 1% BELOW SVR

Usually for 2–5 years

Mortgage deal 2

BANK

Loan
£200,000
over 25 years

9% interest

Jan

£1,678

Monthly repayments to bank over 25 years

BANK

Total repayment
= £503,400

Interest =
£303,400

Credit unions

Member-owned, non-profit financial organizations, credit unions provide savings, credit, and other financial services to their members.

How it works

Originating in Germany in the mid-19th century, credit unions are non-profit financial cooperatives set up by members, who share a "common bond", for their mutual benefit. The connection between members may, for example, be living in the same town, working in the same industry, or belonging to the same trade union or community group.

Traditionally very small organizations, today around 217 million people around the world are members of a credit union. Some of the larger unions have hundreds of thousands of members and assets worth several billion US dollars.

Credit unions are most prevalent in low-income areas and can be especially useful to those with lower credit scores who fail to qualify for high-street loans, or are charged higher rates on such loans because of their scores. Members also tend to benefit from paying fewer fees. Some unions require members to save with them before they can borrow money, as unions finance their loan portfolios by pooling their members' deposits, rather than relying on outside capital. Savings are however still covered up to set limits by government-backed compensation schemes in the event that the credit union ceases trading.

Not for profit

Credit unions are similar to mutual building societies in that they are owned by their members (customers), who each have one vote to elect a board of directors to run the organization. However, credit unions focus on community banking services that benefit members rather than on profit and returns to external shareholders. Surplus revenue is invested back in the credit union to provide personalized service, financial advice, better products, and rates that are as competitive as possible.

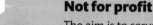

Not for profit
The aim is to serve members, not to make a profit. Any surplus revenue is re-invested in running the business.

Owned by members
Members elect a board of directors to run the business. Each member has one vote.

Community orientated
Members share a common link such as employment, religion, or the area where they live.

Personalized service
Staff are committed to helping members to improve their financial situation.

Financially inclusive
Customers are often from financially disadvantaged groups who fail to qualify for mainstream financial products.

Credit Union

57,000
number of credit unions in 105 countries around the world

For profit
The goal is to make money and maximize profit for owners and shareholders. The organization's own goals and interest are put before those of its customers.

Owned by private companies/shareholders
Banks are run by highly paid directors, and voting rights depend on the amount of stock owned.

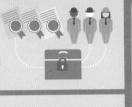

Business orientated
Banks develop and sell money-making products to return a profit to shareholders.

More online services
Run partly or completely online, banks offer little face-to-face or personalized service.

Focus on creditworthy customers
Customers who don't meet the bank's preferred credit profile are routinely rejected.

Bank

CREDIT UNION PRODUCTS

> **Loans** There are no hidden charges, and loans can often be repaid early without a penalty charge. Some loans also include life insurance.

> **Savings** Deposits are made available to members who need to borrow money. Returns on savings can be low and will be paid either by interest or by annual dividend. Some credit unions have maximum savings limits.

> **Current accounts** No credit checks are required, there is no monthly fee for the account, and no overdraft is available. Some accounts offer budgeting facilities and advice.

! WARNING

> **Loan rates and terms** may not be as competitive as those of market-leading products, but they are better than those of payday lenders.

> **Maximum loan amounts** are comparatively low. Approval is often conditional on having saved with the credit union.

> **As non-profit organizations**, credit unions often have limited capital to install ATMs in convenient locations or to invest in technology such as websites or online account access.

Credit cards

Issued by lenders such as banks or building societies, wallet-sized plastic credit cards function as flexible borrowing facilities which allow their holders to purchase goods or services on credit.

A credit card account allows an individual to make purchases on credit up to an agreed maximum limit. Users can spend as much as they want up to that limit without being charged – as long as they pay off the balance (accrued debt) in full by an agreed date each month. Interest is charged on any outstanding balance beyond this point, but users are obliged to meet only a minimum repayment (*see below*). The minimum amount may vary, but generally users pay a percentage of the remaining balance or a fixed minimum amount, whichever of the two is higher, plus the interest and any default charges.

There is not usually a deadline by which a credit card debt must be repaid in full – it is up to the users to make repayments as they see fit – but repaying only the credit card's minimum payment each month is one of the most expensive ways to manage credit card bills, as interest will build up on the unpaid amount.

Minimum repayments

Unlike loan and mortgage borrowers, credit card users can choose how much over and above the prescribed minimum repayment they repay each month. The minimum repayment is the lowest amount users must repay each month in order to avoid a fine. If they pay only the minimum amount each month, however, the remaining unpaid balance will continue to accrue interest, and the amount they owe will increase. This means that their debt will last for longer than it would do if they were to repay a larger, fixed amount each month, or if they paid off all of the monthly balance.

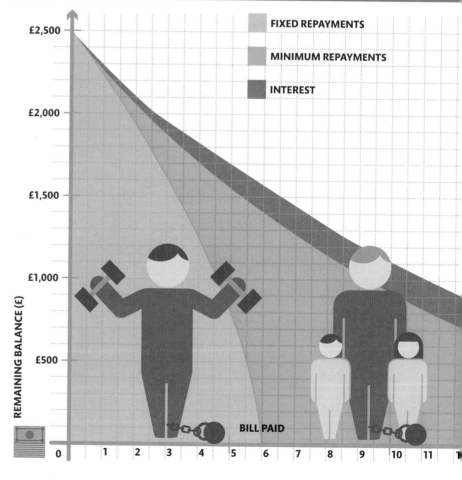

FIXED REPAYMENTS

MINIMUM REPAYMENTS

INTEREST

REMAINING BALANCE (£)

£2,500

£2,000

£1,500

£1,000

£500

BILL PAID

0 1 2 3 4 5 6 7 8 9 10 11

✓ NEED TO KNOW

> **Balance transfer** The transfer of all outstanding balances from one credit card to another.

> **Cash advance** The use of a credit card to withdraw cash from an ATM (automated teller machine). A credit card company normally charges more interest as well as additional fees when cards are used in this way.

> **Revolving credit** A line of credit that allows customers to use funds when they are needed. It is usually used for operating purposes and can fluctuate each month depending on the customer's cash flow needs.

> **Credit limit** The maximum amount an individual can borrow at any one time.

REVOLVING CREDIT

A credit card is a form of revolving credit. This is an arrangement that allows for a loan amount to be withdrawn, repaid, and then redrawn again any number of times. The borrower can withdraw funds up to a set limit.

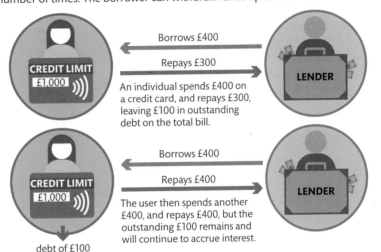

Borrows £400
Repays £300

An individual spends £400 on a credit card, and repays £300, leaving £100 in outstanding debt on the total bill.

debt of £100 accrues interest

Borrows £400
Repays £400

The user then spends another £400, and repays £400, but the outstanding £100 remains and will continue to accrue interest.

⚠ WARNING

Credit-card fraud involves using a credit card as a fraudulent source of funds in a transaction.

In the simplest form of the crime, the fraudster obtains an individual's credit card details and uses them over the phone or on the internet to make purchases in the cardholder's name.

At the other extreme, the fraudster may use the cardholder's details to assume his or her identity and open bank accounts, obtain credit cards, or organize loans and other lines of credit in the cardholder's name.

Credit-card users should always check their monthly statements carefully in order to determine whether there have been any fraudulent transactions.

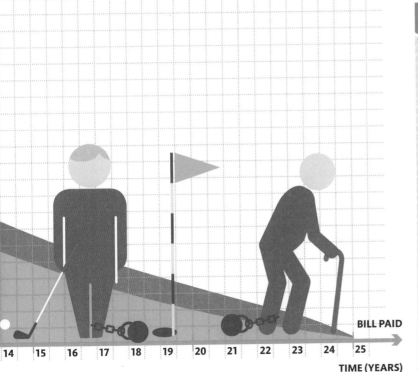

BILL PAID

14 15 16 17 18 19 20 21 22 23 24 25

TIME (YEARS)

Money in the digital age

In the same way that the internet revolutionized communication and made globalization possible, digital money, also known as cryptocurrency, promises to change the way people pay for goods and services. Digital money offers a single international "currency" that is not under the control of any financial institution. Instead of notes and coins being printed and minted by individual national banks, computers are used to generate units of digital money.

Breaking free

The money of the future, cryptocurrency, is a medium of financial exchange produced digitally by teams of experts known as "miners". These miners use specialized hardware to process secure transactions by solving the complex mathematical puzzles that encrypt the electronic currency. Cryptocurrencies can be traded between individuals, and are bought and sold through online exchanges. Cryptocurrencies can also be used for new methods of exchange such as peer-to-peer lending and crowdfunding.

26%
of Millennials
are expected to be using digital currencies by 2020

Traditional finance
Conventional money unique to a country or region. Also called fiat currency, from the Latin word *fiat* meaning "let it be done", a term used when making a government decree. Fiat currency is minted by the central banks of individual countries and its value is determined by supply and demand.

TIMELINE OF DIGITAL MONEY

Since the technology for digital money was perfected, many cryptocurrencies have been released – although Bitcoin remains the largest. Now even central banks have begun investigating the potential of digital money.

TIME (YEARS)

Bitcoin introduced
October 2008

First Bitcoin transaction
May 2010

Ripple launched
September 2013

Highest value of Bitcoin to date
29 November 2013

Mazacoin introduced
February 2014

Eretheum released
August 2015

Bank of England announces RSCoin
March 2016

Digital currency

Money that can be traded on exchanges directly between individuals using a computer or mobile device that is connected to the internet. Digital currency can also be bought and sold using conventional currencies. *See pp.222–225*

Crowdfunding

A way for individuals and groups to raise donations from donors over the internet, bypassing banks, charitable organizations, or government institutions. It is managed via an online intermediary who takes a percentage as a fee. *See pp.226–227*

Peer-to-peer lending

Loans arranged by online agencies who match would-be borrowers with lenders. Peer-to-peer lending is usually subject to fewer regulations than conventional lending. Borrowers are screened for risk, which is reflected in the interest rate they pay. *See pp.228-229*

Cryptocurrency

A form of encrypted digital currency, a cryptocurrency is created, regulated, and kept secure by a network of computers. Bitcoin was the first example of a cryptocurrency, but there are now many more available.

How it works

There are two main features of a cryptocurrency. The first is that it exists only in the form of virtual "coins". Instead of being generated by a national central bank, it is created digitally by teams of specialists known as "miners", who use dedicated computer hardware. Encrypted in constantly changing digital codes to reduce the risk of counterfeiting, cryptocurrency can be easily transferred online between individuals independently of financial or government institutions.

The second feature is that the total amount of a cryptocurrency is capped. Each "coin" created by a "miner" is listed on a virtual public ledger called a"blockchain". Every coin spent is registered on the same ledger, so that unlike currencies generated by central banks, once this cap is reached no more coins can be created. As a result, cryptocurrencies are considered less prone to the pressures of inflation and deflation resulting from political and economic changes that affect conventional currency.

Conventional currency and cryptocurrency

The appeal of a cryptocurrency is that it can be used to make direct financial transactions anywhere without requiring a bank account. Transactions are virtually anonymous, there is no central control from banks or governments, and fees are minimal. Cryptocurrencies differ from national currencies in many ways, such as how they are valued, generated, and controlled, to their storage and transfer.

! WARNING

> **Cryptocurrency balance is stored on a computer** If the currency holder's computer crashes and there is no back-up of the transactions, there is no proof of cryptocurrency funds held by that person.

> **Not many retailers accept cryptocurrency** In general, the more place that take it, the better, but some cryptocurrencies have specialist uses.

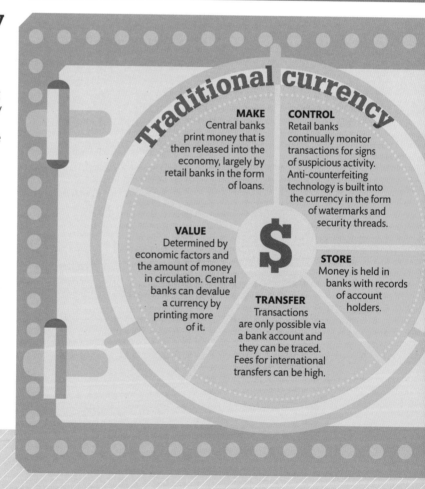

Traditional currency

MAKE
Central banks print money that is then released into the economy, largely by retail banks in the form of loans.

CONTROL
Retail banks continually monitor transactions for signs of suspicious activity. Anti-counterfeiting technology is built into the currency in the form of watermarks and security threads.

VALUE
Determined by economic factors and the amount of money in circulation. Central banks can devalue a currency by printing more of it.

STORE
Money is held in banks with records of account holders.

TRANSFER
Transactions are only possible via a bank account and they can be traced. Fees for international transfers can be high.

700+
number of cryptocurrencies available for trading

HOW TO VALUE CRYPTOCURRENCY

The total worth of all coins and their daily trading volume

A high total worth can indicate a high value per "coin", or it can simply mean that there are a lot of coins in circulation. The daily trading volume is an indicator of the number of coins that change hands in a day. It is best to review the two statistics together. A cryptocurrency that has a very substantial trading volume as well as a high market capitalization is likely to have a high value.

The means used to secure and verify transfers

Different cryptocurrencies have varying ways of verifying and securing transactions. The systems rely on complex mathematical problems, and their effectiveness is based on the time a transaction takes and its vulnerability to attack. Most currencies use one of two systems, Proof of Work (bitcoin) or Proof of Stake, or a combination of both, to ensure the best network security.

Cryptocurrency

MAKE
"Miners" create virtual "coins" using special hardware. The coins are then registered on an online public ledger.

CONTROL
Secure encryption is built in to the code of each virtual coin. Continually changing complex mathematical puzzles prevents counterfeiting.

VALUE
Cryptocurrencies become more valuable when they are easier to use, transaction time is faster and more secure, and the number of retailers using them rises.

STORE
Cryptocurrencies are held in the digital wallets of individuals. Records are kept on a virtual ledger.

TRANSFER
Anyone with online access can make transfers. Such transfers are virtually anonymous and their fees low or negligible.

Bitcoin

Cryptocurrencies such as Bitcoin are generated online. They can be transferred directly from one person to another across the internet, or bought with and sold for conventional currency.

How it works

Launched in 2009, Bitcoin was the first cryptocurrency and is still the most widely used. Unlike conventional currency, which is backed by the state, Bitcoin is based on cryptography, a system that creates mathematical codes to provide high levels of security. This makes it almost impossible for anyone to spend funds from another user's digital wallet, or to disrupt transactions, as each transaction needs to be verified by other users. This is done by users who transform transactions into pieces of unique digital code. The users who verify transactions in this way are rewarded with bitcoins. Coins can be traded on digital exchanges or by individuals.

A bitcoin transaction

Bitcoin users first set up a virtual "wallet". This acts like a highly secure online bank account for sending, receiving, and storing bitcoins. Wallets can be linked to a conventional bank account to transfer fiat money in exchange for bitcoins. When bitcoins are moved from one wallet to another, individuals in the Bitcoin network, called "miners", compete with one another to be the first to verify the transactions. Once verified, the funds will appear in the recipient's Bitcoin wallet. Buyers usually pay a small fee of about one per cent, which is distributed among the miners.

2. Mining for bitcoins

To prove that the transactions contained in the block are legitimate, and do not contain coins that have already been spent elsewhere, bitcoin miners use computer programs to solve the complex mathematical puzzles protecting the block. The first miner to do so is rewarded with new bitcoins – which is how new currency is issued – and the block joins the blockchain.

1. Buyer pays seller for item

A buyer pays a seller in bitcoins using an online transaction form, stating the wallet ID of the seller and the amount to send. The transaction becomes visible to the buyer, and to everyone on Bitcoin's network. It contains a secret code called a private key, showing which wallet it is from. It is grouped with other transactions from a set period into an encoded list called a "block".

MINERS

BITCOIN TRANSACTION

Buyer

3. Blockchains

The blockchain is a bit like a public ledger that can be viewed online. Each verified block is added to the previous one. As the "hash" or signature of each file is generated using part of the previous block's signature, it timestamps each transaction. This makes them very difficult to tamper with.

BITCOIN VALUE

The number of bitcoins that can ever be produced is limited to 21 million. This is intended to prevent a devaluation of the currency due to oversupply. In addition, as the number of bitcoins in circulation increases, the program will make verification more difficult, meaning the mining process will take longer, fewer coins will be produced, and the limited supply will ensure the value of the currency remains high.

Seller

10 MINUTES TO VERIFY

MINERS

4. Bitcoins arrive for use

Once bitcoins arrive in the seller's account, they can be used to make purchases through a retailer, sold through an exchange, or sold directly to an online buyer. In addition, by using websites such as LocalBitcoins.com and Meetup.com, users can make face-to-face transactions, bringing their digital wallets (on a mobile device) to make the trade.

WHY BITCOIN IS SO SECURE

As all transactions must be verified, it is difficult for attackers to tamper with the system. If there is an attempt to interfere with a transaction in the blockchain, it will change the resulting hash and invalidate all following blocks. However, as Bitcoin is so secure, it cannot be recovered if a password is lost or hardware is damaged.

Crowdfunding

Unlike conventional fundraising, crowdfunding allows anyone to raise money directly from potential donors – often online via social media. It works on the principle of asking many people to make a small contribution.

How it works

Most fundraising focuses either on charitable causes or on investment in a worthwhile or potentially lucrative venture. In the days before social networking, fundraising was typically organized through a third party such as a bank or a charity, through a subscription scheme, or by asking family and friends for financial help. Crowdfunding is an evolution of these methods that mostly takes place online instead of face to face.

Crowd advantage

Crowdfunding differs from conventional fundraising in that it cuts out the "middleman", ensuring that more of the donated money goes to the cause. It also enables anyone, regardless of their venture, to petition online for money, and it can reach a much wider audience than, say, enticing potential investors via a subscription scheme.

Screening process

Crowdfunding platforms screen applicants before they launch a campaign. As with banks, some platforms have stricter criteria than others.

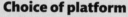

Choice of platform

Crowdfunding platforms usually offer templates, donation tallies, and automatic reminders. Some specialize in charity cases, others in investment projects.

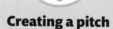

Creating a pitch

The pitch, designed to appeal to as many potential donors as possible, sets out the project or charitable cause to be funded, and usually stipulates a financial target.

Launching online

Digital marketing techniques help to target those most likely to contribute. Reward schemes offering pledgers a return on investment can help to maximize donations.

US$**2.6** billion

plus - the amount pledged on Kickstarter since its launch in April 2009

Online pledges

Most donations are made in the early part of a launch, but it is important to keep the campaign "live" with reminders, updates, and new posts.

FEES

Fees for crowdfunding platforms vary, but are typically around five per cent excluding any design charges or fees for payment processing. Some platforms offer an "all or nothing" structure, where the funds donated are returned to donors if the money raised falls short of the stated target.

Follow-up

When the campaign closes, the funds go to the host or are returned to the donors, depending on the agreement. The host might then prepare donors for the next venture.

Peer-to-peer lending

Also known as crowd-lending, peer-to-peer lending is a way to match savers looking for a return on their cash with borrowers or companies that require investment. A relatively new form of lending, it can offer good returns on savings.

How it works

Like a virtual dating agency for borrowers and lenders, peer-to-peer lending bypasses banks and other financial institutions by using a dedicated crowd-lending broker to vet potential borrowers and match them up with investors who are prepared to loan their spare cash.

The appeal for investor-lenders is higher rates of return than they would receive from banks – typically twice the rate. Borrowers, on the other hand, may benefit from lower rates on their loans (unless they are considered high risk.) The broker runs credit checks on borrowers and offers some protection by holding funds in trust to cover any bad debts. They also usually charge a fee to both borrower and lender. While P2P lending has boomed since the 2008 crash, it is relatively untested and unregulated, meaning that there are potential risks for lenders.

Using peer-to-peer lending

Any individual or business can register with a peer-to-peer lending company. Loan terms are usually between one and five years, and interest rates and fees vary. This is a typical scenario.

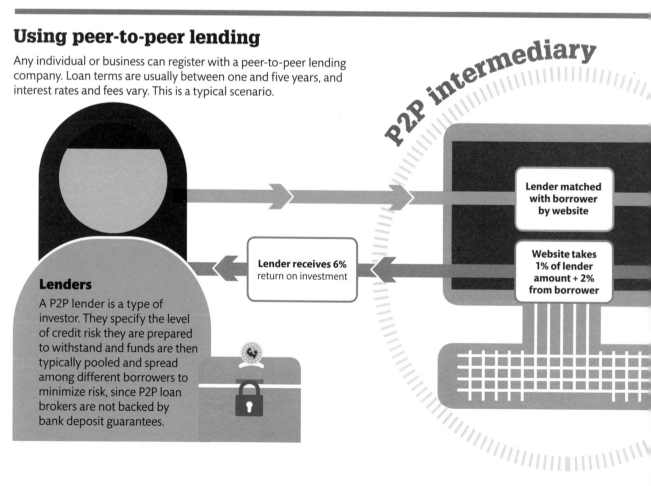

P2P intermediary

Lender matched with borrower by website

Website takes 1% of lender amount + 2% from borrower

Lender receives 6% return on investment

Lenders

A P2P lender is a type of investor. They specify the level of credit risk they are prepared to withstand and funds are then typically pooled and spread among different borrowers to minimize risk, since P2P loan brokers are not backed by bank deposit guarantees.

SPREADING YOUR RISK

Some lenders reduce their risk by actively managing their loans, providing a portion of what they are willing to lend to one borrower, and leaving other lenders to provide the rest.

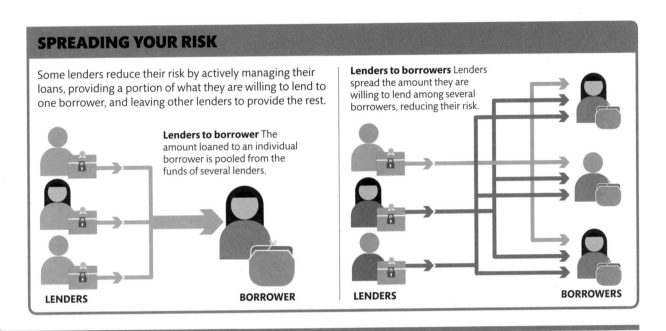

Lenders to borrower The amount loaned to an individual borrower is pooled from the funds of several lenders.

LENDERS

BORROWER

Lenders to borrowers Lenders spread the amount they are willing to lend among several borrowers, reducing their risk.

LENDERS

BORROWERS

US$1 trillion the forecasted value of global P2P lending by 2025

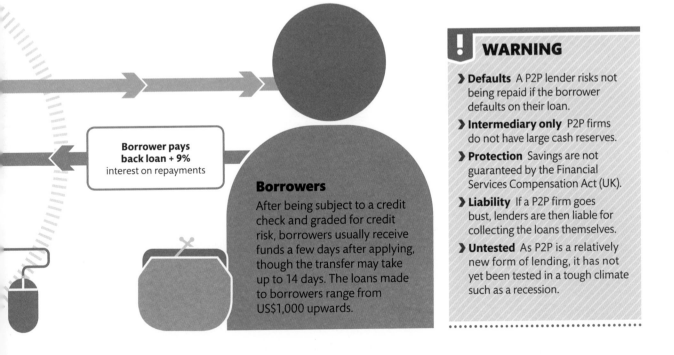

Borrower pays back loan + 9% interest on repayments

Borrowers

After being subject to a credit check and graded for credit risk, borrowers usually receive funds a few days after applying, though the transfer may take up to 14 days. The loans made to borrowers range from US$1,000 upwards.

WARNING

> **Defaults** A P2P lender risks not being repaid if the borrower defaults on their loan.

> **Intermediary only** P2P firms do not have large cash reserves.

> **Protection** Savings are not guaranteed by the Financial Services Compensation Act (UK).

> **Liability** If a P2P firm goes bust, lenders are then liable for collecting the loans themselves.

> **Untested** As P2P is a relatively new form of lending, it has not yet been tested in a tough climate such as a recession.

MONEY
IN THE UK

The London Stock Exchange and FTSE Index

One of the world's oldest stock exchanges, the London Stock Exchange (LSE) allows companies from around the world to raise money, increase their profile, and obtain a market valuation through a variety of routes.

London Stock Exchange

The centre of the UK financial world is the London Stock Exchange (LSE). It is ranked third in the world in terms of market capitalization – the value of the company shares traded on the exchange. It is also one of the most international stock markets, with companies from more than 60 countries represented.

Shares make up the bulk of selling activity, but the LSE also sells other types of securities such as bonds, derivatives, funds, warrants, commodities, and gilts (mainly UK government bonds).

Around 2,600 companies are listed with the LSE. These are split between two main sections: the Main Market for the largest companies, and the Alternative Investment Market (AIM) for small- to medium-sized companies. There are also specialized sections, which include the Professional Securities Market (PSM) and Specialist Market Fund (SMF). All of these sections operate as marketplaces. Buyers can purchase investments from companies or institutions that are raising money by selling a stake in their businesses (shares), or offering a return on a temporary debt purchase (debt securities such as bonds).

The total value of all the companies trading on the LSE is around £3 trillion. The top 100 companies account for close to 80 per cent of this amount. These are the well-established, top-performing blue-chip companies that trade on the Main Market, which is tracked by the FTSE, the Financial Times Stock Exchange 100 Index. The remaining companies trade on the secondary market, AIM, or on the PSM or SMF.

Owned by the London Stock Exchange Group, the LSE also offers access to the group's other trading platforms: the Borsa Italiana, Italy's main stock exchange in Milan; MTS, Europe's leading fixed-income market that trades mostly government bonds; and Turquoise, a pan-European multilateral trading facility that trades securities from 19 different European countries.

Main Market

Before it can be listed on the LSE's Main Market, a company must be valued at £700,000 or more. It must also provide at least three years' worth of audited accounting statements that have been prepared in accordance with International Financial Reporting Standards (IFRS).

The Main Market comprises a number of sections, each of which has its own requirements for listing and an index for tracking ups and downs in trading.

FTSE 100 The best-known index of the LSE is the Financial Times Stock Exchange (FTSE) 100 Index. Nicknamed the "Footsie", the index tracks the sale of shares from the top 100 blue-chip companies listed on the LSE including BP, Rio Tinto, Tesco, and RBS. It is recalculated every 15 seconds to indicate live trading volumes and track performance minute by minute. The companies in the top 100 are reviewed and adjusted every quarter to make room for new top performers.

FTSE 250 The FTSE 250 lists the LSE's 250 next most valuable companies (following the FTSE 100 companies), ranking them from 101 to 350.

FTSE 350 The FTSE 350 lists the top 350 companies in the UK, and is a combination of the FTSE 100 and the FTSE 250.

FTSE SmallCap The FTSE SmallCap companies (the next tier down from FTSE 350 companies) are ranked by their worth from 351 to 619. The name SmallCap alludes to the fact that these firms have smaller capitalization than those of the FTSE 350.

FTSE All-Share A combination of the FTSE 100, 250, and SmallCap, the FTSE All-Share Index gives a broader overview of how public companies on the LSE are performing.

FTSE Fledgling The FTSE Fledgling Index comprises around 200 companies that are smaller than those on the FTSE All-Share but still qualify for a listing on the Main Market.

Alternative Investment Market

The Alternative Investment Market (AIM) is designed for companies that issue shares and sell them on the LSE, but find it hard to meet the Main Market's strict regulations. In AIM Rules, for example, unlike in Main Market Rules, there are no requirements for companies to be of a minimum size or have an established trading record. This makes it possible for companies that are at an earlier stage of their business development to join the public markets.

Also referred to as the "junior market", AIM was launched in 1995 to give these smaller companies the opportunity to raise money from investors. There are around 1,450 companies listed on AIM, and they are divided into three categories:

FTSE AIM UK 50 Index The top 50 UK companies.

FTSE AIM 100 Index The top 100 companies.

FTSE AIM All-Share Index All the companies listed on AIM.

Regulation

Activities on the LSE are regulated by a branch of the Financial Services Authority (FSA) called the UK Listing Authority (UKLA). Any company that applies for listing on the LSE has to go through the UKLA for approval, and must meet certain eligibility criteria. Requirements differ depending on what type of listing a company wishes to have. The more elevated the listing – with the Main Market at the top – the more stringent the UKLA's eligibility review process.

HEDGE FUNDS

Hedge funds are an investment option that can offer potentially huge returns, although they are also high risk. A hedge fund puts money into a wide variety of financial products, including shares, bonds, and a more complex category of assets called derivatives – options, warrants, futures, and swaps, for example. Anything that the fund manager anticipates will turn a profit is a potential target, regardless of the current economic situation. There are few controls over the types of investments a hedge fund manager can make, which means they are high risk.

Where other types of investments try to outperform a particular index, such as the FTSE, hedge funds are designed with the aim of simply producing a profit. This means that investors rely solely on the skill of the hedge fund manager in deciding on an investment strategy and choosing the most lucrative mix of financial products. Fund manager fees are usually around 2 per cent, plus an additional 20 per cent performance fee.

Until recently, hedge funds were reserved for the super rich or financial institutions, since millions were required as the minimum spend. However, private investors in the UK with more modest budgets can now put their money into a "fund of funds", which pools money from numerous investors and spreads it across several hedge funds in order to minimize risk. In the UK, the marketing of these funds is restricted to protect small private investors, and there is little recourse if things go wrong, unless the manager is registered with the FCA.

Companies House and corporate accounting

Companies House, an agency sponsored by the Department for Business, Energy & Industrial Strategy, incorporates and dissolves limited companies, registers companies' information, and makes this available to the public.

Company registration

Any company that does business in the UK has legal obligations. If it has a physical place of business in the UK, whether it is an enterprise founded in the UK or is from overseas, one of its first obligations is to register with Companies House.

Overseas companies must register within one month of opening a place of business in the UK, but some types of overseas enterprises, such as partnerships, limited partnerships, or government agencies, cannot register in the UK.

In order to register, businesses must complete a registration form and pay a small standard fee. Some overseas businesses may also have to provide copies of their incorporation documents as well as their most recent set of accounts. Once registered, companies are expected to submit an annual tax return to Companies House. They must also submit quarterly statements and an annual return to Her Majesty's Revenue and Customs (HMRC), and pay corporation tax annually on profits up to £1.5 million, and in instalments on profits above £1.5 million.

Three types of enterprises must pay corporation tax on their profits: UK companies; overseas companies registered in the UK; and clubs, co-operatives, or other types of associations such as community groups or sporting clubs.

Partnerships do not register with Companies House and are not obliged to submit accounts to HMRC – other than the personal income tax returns of the individuals in the partnership.

UK Accounting Standards

Both Companies House and HMRC require financial statements to be prepared in a format that complies with official UK accounting standards, which means that specific items and types of calculations must be included in the accounts. The standards are issued by the Financial Reporting Council (FRC), and the UK Generally Accepted Accounting Practice (UK GAAP) is the body of regulations that have been established over time, stipulating how UK company accounts must be prepared and reported. It includes accounting standards as well as UK company law. The accounting framework is made up of six different standards, FRS 100–FRS 105, each of which sets out the reporting standards required for the different kinds of companies in the UK, for instance, as parent companies, unlisted companies, and insurers.

Company accounts need to be submitted to both HMRC and to Companies House at the end of the financial year. The accounting year begins on 1 June and finishes on 31 May, but these dates can differ in a company's first year since a company begins its first accounting period from the day it is incorporated, not the day it starts trading.

Companies do not have to use an accountant to prepare accounts, but directors are legally obliged to ensure that financial statements adhere to the guidelines issued by the FRC. Private companies are obliged to hold their accounting records for three years, whereas public companies must keep them for six years.

Fraud prevention

From 2017, the law on tax evasion will include the new corporate offence of failure to prevent the facilitation of tax evasion, both in the UK and overseas. This means that anyone who turns a blind eye to tax evasion for an employer, or who is in any way involved in the evasion process while acting for a corporation, is liable to be prosecuted. The law is aimed at anyone representing an organisation, such as an employee or accounting agent, as well as at individual taxpayers.

Intellectual property law

Companies doing business in the UK can apply to the Intellectual Property Office (IPO) to register intellectual property. Intellectual property includes trademarks such as product names; jingles and logos; registered designs (that is, the appearance of a product, including its packaging, pattern, and shape); and patents, which are applicable to inventions and products such as machines and medicines.

Copyright of written works, films, photography, music, web content, and sound recordings are automatically covered under UK law, as are design rights, which refer to the shape of objects and how their different parts are arranged together.

After the UK withdraws from the European Union, UK companies will still be able to register an EU trademark or a design, and UK businesses will still be able to apply to the European Patent Office for protection. Companies that have made an international patent application can apply to have this registered in the UK as well, so long as application is made within 31 months of the international application.

Corporation tax rates

The main rate of corporation tax was set at 20 per cent until 2016, but in the Budget of 2016, the government announced that the rate would change to 19 per cent for the tax years (beginning 1 April) of 2017, 2018, and 2019, and that on 1 April 2020, it would drop to 17 per cent. This rate applies to all companies except for those that profit from oil extraction or oil rights in the UK (known as ring-fence companies).

TAX SUBMISSION

The accounting year

Every year, limited companies must submit annual accounts to Companies House, and a company tax return to HMRC. For new companies, the first accounting year starts at the end of the first month of incorporation. This is called the Accounting Reference Date (ARD). The deadline for filing accounts is 21 months after the ARD for private companies, and 18 months after the ARD for public limited companies (plcs).

Deadlines for filing

Action	Deadline
Filing first accounts with Companies House	21 months after registration with Companies House
Filing annual accounts with Companies House	9 months after the company's financial year ends
Paying corporation tax, or informing HMRC that the limited company doesn't owe any corporation tax	9 months and 1 day after the company's accounting period for corporation tax ends
Filing a company tax return	12 months after the company's accounting period for corporation tax ends

The Bank of England and the UK economy

The Bank of England acts as a banker to the government, as well as to commercial banks. The Bank issues bank notes, sets the base interest rate, and regulates the banking system, influencing the UK's economy.

The UK's central bank

The Bank of England (BOE) was established in 1694, making it the second oldest central bank in the world after Sweden's Riksbank. Since June 1998, the Bank of England has been fully independent from the UK government. Following the 1997 election that brought Labour to power, the then chancellor Gordon Brown initiated the Bank of England Act 1998 to give the Bank of England operational independence over monetary policy.

The Bank serves as the banker for commercial banks in the UK and acts as a "lender of last resort". It also maintains the government's bank account: the Consolidated Fund.

Aside from acting as banker to the government, the Bank of England has three primary roles: issuing bank notes, setting the base interest rate, and regulating the banking system. In its first two roles, the Bank of England aims to maintain stable prices throughout the UK economy and confidence in the UK currency, known as the pound, or sterling. It makes vital decisions over both the supply of money and the base interest rate that is charged on loans to commercial banks, and which is payable on their deposits with the central bank. In turn, these functions contribute to movements in the exchange rate, pushing the sterling higher or lower against the currency of other countries. By manipulating the money supply, the Bank of England has the power to directly influence the economic course of the UK.

Foreign currency

The Bank of England is also responsible for managing gold reserves and foreign exchange for Her Majesty's Treasury (HMT). The UK's stock of foreign currency is held in a government account for HMT. The Bank of England acts as HMT's agent, buying and selling foreign currency, and investing some of it within limits set by HMT. These reserves can be used in part to guard against large fluctuations in the pound sterling. For example, in the 12 months leading up to the 2016 Brexit vote to leave the European Union, the Bank of England increased its foreign currency reserves by 34 per cent. Economists saw this move as a precautionary measure to protect sterling from being devalued too much in the uncertainty following the Brexit decision.

Banknote printing and security

In England, sterling notes are printed solely by the Bank of England, but in Scotland and Northern Ireland seven other banks have a licence to print local currency with permission from the Bank of England. Three are based in Scotland and four in Northern Ireland. The Bank of England issues banknotes in denominations of £50, £20, £10, and £5 for circulation in England and Wales. Scotland and Northern Ireland also issue £100 notes, but only Scotland issues a £1 note.

Banknotes issued by Northern Ireland and Scotland can be used anywhere in the UK, but only if the trader agrees to accept them. Likewise, banknotes issued by the Bank of England can be used outside England and Wales if both parties conducting the transaction are in agreement. In other words, Bank of England banknotes are only legal tender in England and Wales, while banknotes issued in Scotland and Northern Ireland are only legal tender in their respective regions.

Interest rates

Before making decisions about raising, dropping, or maintaining interest rates, the Bank of England assesses current economic data, such as the rate of unemployment, the growth of Gross Domestic Product (GDP), and inflation. The Bank also collects data from around the UK through its 12 agencies stationed in Scotland, Northern Ireland, Wales, and the regions of England. These agencies act as the bank's "eyes and ears", gathering information on business conditions across the United Kingdom.

Interest rate decisions are made by the Bank's Monetary Policy Committee (MPC), and these are announced on a monthly basis, always at 12 noon on a Thursday. The MPC also releases forecasts on inflation and growth in its Inflation Report, published four times a year, in February, May, August, and November. These projections form the basis for decisions concerning interest rate changes.

If the economy is sluggish, the Bank of England will lower interest rates to encourage spending and to stimulate the economy. If the economy is in danger of growing too rapidly, potentially resulting in higher inflation, the Bank of England will increase interest rates to make borrowing more expensive and dampen spending activity. As part of its decision-making, the Bank must also factor in the government's stated aim of limiting inflation to 2 per cent.

Quantitative easing

When officially lowering the interest rate is still not enough to stimulate growth in the economy, the Bank of England can implement a monetary policy called quantitative easing (QE) to further influence interest rates. In quantitave easing, the Bank creates new money electronically (rather than printing banknotes) and uses it to buy government bonds. This has the effect of raising the price of government bonds, which reduces the yield or interest rate payable to investors. Reduced interest rates encourage businesses to borrow more. They, in turn, spend more and employ more staff, thereby boosting the economy.

BANK OF ENGLAND ACTIVITY

Introduction of polymer notes

In September 2016, the Bank of England introduced a £5 polymer note, printed on thin plastic film, marking the beginning of the end for paper banknotes in the UK. The old paper £5 ceases to be legal tender on 5 May 2017. New £10 and £20 polymer notes are both due for release in England and Wales by 2020. The three Scottish issuing banks will also print their new notes on polymer. Because polymer has greater durability, as well as more resistance to moisture and dirt, notes will last up to two and a half times longer. They can also be printed with transparent windows in the design, which makes them more difficult to counterfeit.

After Brexit

To stimulate the economy in the wake of Brexit, the Bank of England took the unprecedented measure of launching a scheme to buy company bonds, as of 27 September 2016. With a budget of up to £10 billion, the corporate bond-buying programme is intended to drive down borrowing costs, encouraging businesses to invest, thereby boosting employment and economic growth.

The UK tax system

Responsibility for UK taxation is shared across three different bodies – the central government in Westminster, local government, and devolved national governments.

Role of government

Central government collects both direct taxes, such as income tax, and indirect taxes, such as VAT. Local governments collect business rates and council tax.

The devolved national governments of Scotland, Wales, and Northern Ireland have some powers to set their own tax rates, especially business rates and land tax. Scotland has the additional power to set land and buildings transaction tax and landfill tax, which are collected by Revenue Scotland. From 2018, Wales also has the power to set land transactions tax and landfill tax, with the Welsh Revenue Authority being set up to deal with these taxes. Only Scotland has its own rate of income tax, although this is collected by the central government. Northern Ireland is now free to set its own rate of corporation tax.

The central government, based in Westminster, provides funding to local councils and the devolved national governments, and also earns revenue through many streams. These are managed by two primary financial bodies, Her Majesty's Treasury (HMT) and Her Majesty's Revenue and Customs (HMRC). While HMT is responsible for overseeing the tax system, HMRC is responsible for collecting taxes nationwide and fairly administering the tax system.

HMRC was set up by the Treasury in 2005 as a non-ministerial government department, a merger between Inland Revenue, the government department responsible for the collection of direct taxes such as income tax, and Her Majesty's Customs and Excise, which collected indirect taxes such as VAT.

Revenue sources

HMRC now collects most of the tax that comes into UK government coffers. The majority of revenue comes in the form of direct taxes, which are applied to income, profits, and other proceeds such as inheritance tax. These are either deducted at source – for example, through the pay as you earn (PAYE) system, which deducts tax from an employee's salary every month – or are payable to HMRC, such as corporation tax. Income tax and National Insurance contributions are the main direct taxes (around 45 per cent). Other direct taxes include capital gains tax, inheritance tax, and corporation tax.

Income tax is by far the most important source of revenue for the government. Over the past decade the amount of revenue coming in from high-income taxpayers has increased, and the amount coming in from lower-income taxpayers has decreased, following changes in government policy. The personal allowance for lower-income taxpayers has increased, while the threshold for higher-income taxpayers has reduced. As a result, the number of higher rate taxpayers has increased by over one million.

Indirect tax revenue is also collected by HMRC. These taxes are paid by consumers when they purchase products and services. It is then the seller's responsibility to pay the tax to HMRC. VAT is the main indirect tax, making up around 18 per cent of government revenue. When added together with other indirect taxes, charges on goods and services comprise 28 per cent of revenue.

Council revenue

At a local level, councils rely primarily on council tax and business rates for their revenue. They are allowed to raise council tax by a limited amount – a limit that is set by the national government. Councils have the power to increase business rates in line with the Retail

Price Index (RPI), which measures changes in the price of a "shopping basket" of retail goods and services. This "basket" includes a wide range of items that consumers might regularly pay for such as food, gas bills, childminding fees, and football tickets.

The RPI is officially known as the RPIJ – the "J" refers to the way in which the index is calculated, according to a method known as Jevons. This index is calculated every year, and the government then uses it to assess other types of taxation such as tax allowances and state pensions. If the RPI increases, for example, the government will have to consider increasing pension payments to compensate for the higher cost of living.

Tax collection

HMRC's tax collection powers have significantly increased since 2005. It now has the power to obtain contact information for defaulting taxpayers through a third party. It can also petition the courts to put a company into liquidation, and request security against the possibility of future bad debts if a company has previously failed to meet its tax obligations.

Since 6 April 2016, HMRC has been able to recover debts directly from a taxpayer's account, provided that the debt is more than £1,000 and that HMRC leaves a minimum of £5,000 in the debtor's account. HMRC can only do this if they have first followed a strict protocol that includes a face-to-face meeting with the taxpayer, discussion of manageable repayment options, and offering support to debtors who are considered to be "vulnerable".

TAX REVENUE

UK tax revenues

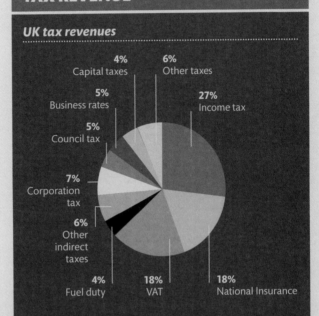

- **4%** Capital taxes
- **6%** Other taxes
- **5%** Business rates
- **27%** Income tax
- **5%** Council tax
- **7%** Corporation tax
- **6%** Other indirect taxes
- **4%** Fuel duty
- **18%** VAT
- **18%** National Insurance

The vast majority of tax revenue comes from income tax and National Insurance contributions, while tax from corporations and other business tax is small by comparison.

The tax gap

Every year a substantial proportion of the tax that is payable to HMRC is not collected. For example, the tax gap for 2013–2014 was around £34 billion, or 6.4 per cent of the total tax bill, according to HMRC statistics. This is 2 per cent less than the tax bill for 2005–2006; the decrease is mainly due to new measures giving HMRC more power and resources to decrease tax evasion, and encourage individuals and businesses to declare accurately and pay voluntarily. Government figures show that in 2014–2015 HMRC collected £517.7 billion in tax revenue, including £26.6 billion that would have been otherwise lost due to evasion.

National Insurance and indirect taxes

In the UK, government pension schemes are funded by National Insurance contributions. Revenue is also collected through charges on products as VAT, duties on certain items, and other indirect taxes.

Revenue from National Insurance

Money the government receives in National Insurance (NI) contributions is used exclusively for paying out state pensions. Essentially, this year's NI revenue pays for this year's pension requirements. NI contributions go directly into a dedicated fund and are kept separate from any other tax revenue. Unlike some other nations, such as the USA, United Arab Emirates, and Norway, the UK does not have a sovereign wealth fund, which is a state-owned investment fund that can be used for pensions, amongst other things. This means that the UK government does not buy shares or invest money on behalf of the nation. For example, the government could have invested earnings from tax on North Sea oil during the 1970s and 1980s, buying government bonds and substantially increasing its fund. However, this money was instead used to fund tax cuts and public spending, and the UK's current budget deficit makes it unlikely that a sovereign wealth fund could be established now.

Although there is no sovereign wealth fund, the UK government does invest NI contributions in its Call Notice Deposit Account, which is managed by the Debt Management Office. The money is placed in an overnight account and held on loan to earn interest at the going rate. The amount in the account is adjusted day by day so that the government can take funds out when they are needed for pension payments. There are no restrictions on withdrawals of the funds, and as a consequence, the interest that is earned is low, contributing only a small additional amount to the NI fund.

Since the 1990s, the NI pool has been in surplus – that is, more money has been coming in from NI payments than going out in the form of pension payments. However, the surplus has begun to dwindle because there has been a fall in earnings growth. The financial crisis of 2007–2008 triggered a decline in real wages of more than 10 per cent in the nine years up to 2016. Figures for "real" wages are adjusted for inflation so that they accurately measure spending power – the amount of goods and services that can be bought with an average monthly pay packet. Until real wages begin to recover, the NI surplus will continue to diminish, as employers and workers are paying in less money. Some government predictions forecast that if this trend persists, the fund will be exhausted by 2035–36. Partly in response to this challenge, the government introduced a New State Pension in 2016 and is now gradually increasing the age of retirement. For anyone retiring after 2021 there will be a flat rate of pension between £145 and £155 per week. To be eligible, the pensioner must have paid NI contributions for 35 years. Rises in the state pension are calculated according to a "triple lock", with the payment rising by the same rate as inflation, average earnings, or 2.5 per cent, whichever is the highest.

VAT

Value Added Tax (VAT) makes up around 18 per cent of government revenue, vying with National Insurance contributions as the second largest component after income tax. VAT is paid on all sales in the UK. It is the responsibility of vendors to pay VAT they have received to the government, minus any VAT they have paid. Businesses must register for VAT if turnover is more than £83,000 in a 12-month period.

The standard rate of VAT is 20 per cent, which is added to the majority of goods and services. This rate has been in place since January 2011, increased from

17.5 per cent. A reduced rate of 5 per cent is applied to some products, including children's car seats, sanitary products, and domestic gas and electricity.

A huge variety of items are rated zero, including basic foods; books, newspapers, and magazines; children's clothing and shoes; energy-saving measures installed in homes; and public transport fares.

Within VAT regulations, there are a few quirks. Cold take-away food is zero-rated, for example, but any take-away food that is sold hot and eaten while hot, such as pies, toasted sandwiches, pizza, and soup, is rated at the standard 20 per cent. Potato crisps are standard-rated, but maize and corn snacks, such as tortilla chips, are zero-rated. In a famous court ruling in 1991, McVitie's Jaffa Cakes were deemed to be cakes, which are zero-rated for VAT, rather than chocolate-covered biscuits, which are taxed at the standard rate.

Other indirect taxes

A raft of other indirect taxes contribute to revenues, such as fuel duty, duties on tobacco and alcohol, stamp duty and land tax, capital gains tax, inheritance tax, customs duty, landfill tax, betting and gambling tax, and insurance premium tax (IPT), which is applied to purchases of insurance policies and increased from 6 per cent to 10 per cent in 2017.

Additional smaller taxes have been introduced since 2010, in part to compensate for reduced revenue from corporation tax, as the rate is set to fall from a previous rate of 20 per cent to 17 per cent by 2020–2021. In 2011, a new bank levy came into effect, penalizing large banks for excessive liabilities on their balance sheets. A surcharge on bank profits was introduced in 2016, meaning that banks pay an additional 8 per cent on top of corporation tax on their profits, and are now a larger source of revenue than before. Other new taxes have social aims as well as generating revenue. For example, a soft drinks levy will not only generate revenue but also tackle the health risks associated with high sugar intake.

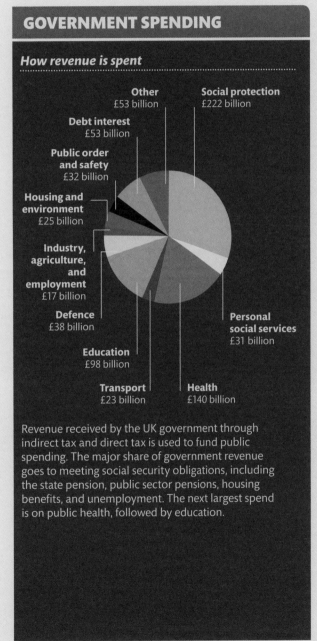

GOVERNMENT SPENDING

How revenue is spent

Other
£53 billion

Social protection
£222 billion

Debt interest
£53 billion

Public order
and safety
£32 billion

Housing and
environment
£25 billion

Industry,
agriculture,
and
employment
£17 billion

Defence
£38 billion

Personal
social services
£31 billion

Education
£98 billion

Transport
£23 billion

Health
£140 billion

Revenue received by the UK government through indirect tax and direct tax is used to fund public spending. The major share of government revenue goes to meeting social security obligations, including the state pension, public sector pensions, housing benefits, and unemployment. The next largest spend is on public health, followed by education.

Personal tax

Any UK resident who pays into a savings account, buys shares, or invests in other financial products is subject to tax on income from these activities. Exemptions are made for some groups, such as low earners and minors.

Tax on savings

In April 2016, a new Personal Savings Allowance was put in place, meaning that account holders earn some tax-free income from interest on their savings. Prior to April 2016, building societies and banks deducted the tax at source, and paid the interest net; interest is now paid gross, without any tax deducted.

If your total taxable income is £17,000 you will not pay any tax on savings income. Above that, basic-rate taxpayers can earn £1,000. Higher-rate taxpayers can earn £500, while additional-rate taxpayers, the highest band, have no Personal Savings Allowance and must pay tax on their interest. Income earned from tax-free accounts, such as Individual Savings Accounts (ISAs) and some National Savings and Investment accounts, do not count towards the allowance.

Different rules apply to children's accounts and foreign accounts. Although interest is usually tax-free on children's accounts, if the child's account earns over £100 in interest from money paid in by a parent, the parent will have to pay tax on the interest, if it exceeds their personal allowance. An exception to this rule is if the interest is earned on money given by grandparents, relatives, or friends, or on money in a Junior Individual Savings Account (ISA) or Child Trust Fund.

Money saved in a Junior ISA account is tax free up to a limit of £4,080. In the case of a cash ISA, there is no tax on interest earned. For an ISA invested in stocks and shares, there is no tax payable on any dividends or capital growth. These types of accounts are available to anyone under the age of 18 living in the UK. Junior ISAs have now replaced Child Trust Funds. The Child Trust Funds scheme is now closed, and no further accounts can be opened, but existing ones still benefit from tax-free savings of up to £4,080.

Tax breaks on investments

Income earned from investments is treated like any other income, with the exception of Individual Savings Accounts (ISAs), in which an amount of £15,240 can be saved, tax free, in any single tax year. This money can be deposited into one of three types of ISAs: cash, stocks and shares, or innovative finance. Investors can put it all into one type of ISA or split the total tax-free allowance across two or three types of ISAs. As with Junior ISAs, there is no tax to pay on interest earned in a cash ISA, nor on dividends or capital growth from stocks and shares, or an innovative finance ISA.

Innovative finance ISAs include relatively new types of investments, such as peer-to-peer loans. Other alternative investments are also accompanied by tax breaks. Investors in forestry land, for example, will pay no income tax, capital gains tax, or inheritance tax if they hold on to the forest for a minimum of two years.

Inheritance tax

In the 2015 Budget, the UK Chancellor announced changes to inheritance tax (IHT) that effectively increase the threshold for both single people and married couples (see box). From April 2020, next-of-kin who inherit property will only have to pay inheritance tax if the property is worth more than £500,000. If inheriting from a married couple or from civil partners, this figure increases to £1 million.

The main change to the tax is the introduction of a family home allowance worth £175,000 per person, which, added to the existing allowance of £375,000, makes up the new £500,000 threshold. Once the threshold is exceeded, an IHT rate of 40 per cent is applied. This can be reduced to 36 per cent if 10 per cent or more of the estate's net value is willed to charity. Any tax owing is paid directly from the estate to HMRC by the executor of the will.

As an incentive to those with large houses and grown children that have left home, the government offers an inheritance tax credit to property owners who sell and trade down to smaller properties, as long as the bulk of their estate is left to their descendants. If the deceased passes on the family home to a spouse, no inheritance tax is due. A seven-year rule applies to any gifts of more than £3,000 per year given to direct descendants. If the deceased dies within seven years of making the gift, a sliding tax rate applies based on the number of years that have passed since the gift was made.

Tax on digital currencies

The UK government is still developing a full policy on the regulation of bitcoin and other digital currencies. Up until March 2014, VAT of 20 per cent was applied to bitcoin purchases, but it is now treated as personal money, like any other currency. That means that no VAT is payable when bitcoin is exchanged for sterling or other currencies. However, if goods or services are being provided, with payment made in bitcoin, VAT is applied as usual, if the provider is VAT registered.

Profit and loss on any capital gains made from buying and selling bitcoin is taxable like any other capital gain. Income earned in bitcoin is taxed at the usual rates for income and corporation tax.

Several online cryptocurrency exchanges operate from the UK, offering a virtual marketplace for buying and selling bitcoin. Bitcoin can be bought or sold with sterling or other key currencies, and some exchanges allow the purchase of digital currency with a debit or credit card. Bitcoin is traded on virtual exchanges, as well as some international stock exchanges, which means investors can treat it as they would any other currency, buying bitcoin in sterling, for example, and exchanging it later when the value of bitcoin is up against the pound.

INHERITANCE TAX (IHT) RATES

Changes in inheritance tax thresholds take effect from April 2020. Different rates will apply to single people and married couples or civil partners.

Single person

Value of other assets	Value of family home	Value of the estate	IHT liability as of April 2020
£175,000	£175,000	£350,000	Nil
£200,000	£300,000	£500,000	Nil
£250,000	£400,000	£600,000	£60,000
£400,000	£600,000	£1,000,000	£200,00
£750,000	£750,000	£1,500,000	£400,000
£1,000,000	£1,000,000	£2,000,000	£600,000

Married couple

Value of other assets	Value of family home	Value of the estate	IHT liability as of April 2020
£175,000	£175,000	£350,000	Nil
£200,000	£300,000	£500,000	Nil
£250,000	£400,000	£650,000	Nil
£400,000	£600,000	£1,000,000	Nil
£750,000	£750,000	£1,500,000	£200,000
£1,000,000	£1,000,000	£2,000,000	£400,000

Mortgages and credit cards

The UK's mortgage and credit card markets are among the most developed in the world. A huge range of mortgages are available to the prospective house buyer, and more credit cards are in use in the UK than anywhere in Europe.

Mortgages

The UK has one of the most diverse mortgage markets in the world, with a wider range of products than in most countries. Around 300 lenders comprise banks, building societies, specialized mortgage organizations, insurance companies, and pension funds.

There are three types of mortgages in the UK. A fixed rate mortgage is the most popular, as the interest is set at the same level for two, three, five, or even 10 years, allowing borrowers to plan their repayments. A tracker rate mortgage is fixed to the base rate set by the Bank of England, while a variable rate can change at the discretion of the mortgage's lender.

The Mortgage Market Review

A borrower's eligibility for a mortgage is currently determined by the Mortgage Market Review rules introduced by the Financial Conduct Authority (FCA) in April 2014. This has made it more difficult to be approved by a lender. The lender now takes into account not only the applicant's declared income, but also their outgoings – what remains after their regular monthly expenditure, verified by their bank statements. Lenders also have to consider whether the prospective borrower will be able to meet repayments if interest rates rise, typically calculating potential increases at a rate of between 6 per cent and 7 per cent.

Mortgage trends

The 25-year mortgage, once the housing market's mainstay, is now rivalled by the 30-year mortgage, according to data from the Office of National Statistics. From 2006 to 2015, the 25-year mortgage's share of the entire UK market fell from 42.2 per cent to 21.5 per cent. Meanwhile, over the same period, the 30-year mortgage grew in market share from 7.2 per cent to 19.1 per cent. This longer-term mortgage makes the monthly repayments more affordable, especially for first-time buyers. In fact, almost a third of first-time buyers now opt for a term of 35 years.

Minimum deposits for mortgages start at 5 per cent, but most buyers aim for a higher deposit, as this gives access to better lending rates with lower repayments. In the UK, the average deposit as a proportion of the loan is now around 30 per cent, or just over £70,000.

Buy-to-let

The introduction of buy-to-let mortgages in the late 1990s stimulated huge growth in the number of investor landlords who bought multiple properties, vying with first-time buyers for properties in areas of urban growth and driving up prices. In 2015, buy-to-let accounted for 9 per cent of all property purchases in the UK. To dampen investor enthusiasm in favour of first-time buyers, the government introduced higher stamp duty on buy-to-let properties. Most buy-to-let mortgages require a minimum deposit of 25 per cent.

Incentive schemes

The government's Help to Buy mortgage scheme, which helped first-time buyers obtain a bigger deposit, closed at the end of 2016. Other measures were put in place, aimed at stimulating a housing market in which the level of house prices relative to earnings has been high, making it especially hard for first-time buyers to get onto the property ladder. Under the Right to Buy scheme, council and housing association tenants living in their homes for a minimum of three years may be eligible to buy them, with discounts of up to £103,900 in Greater London and £77,900 outside London.

First-time buyers in the private sector can open a Help to Buy ISA account to build up a deposit. For every £1 saved into the account, the government will boost it by 25 per cent, up to a maximum of £3,000. In England, the government's Starter Homes initiative aims to help first-time buyers under 40 years of age to purchase a new home, offering a minimum discount of 20 per cent off the market price. Under the scheme, the maximum cost of a new home outside London will be £250,000, with an upper limit of £450,000 inside London.

Credit card regulations

The UK has the most developed credit card market in Europe, with more credit cards in use and more transactions per person than anywhere else in the European region. There are more than 60 million credit cards in circulation in the UK, tied to 51 million accounts. Around 42 per cent of credit card accounts have balances that are accruing zero per cent interest, since the balances are paid off every month. Interest on accounts that are not paid in full is calculated in one of two ways: "average daily balance" or "daily balance". Both methods arrive at the same result by calculating interest owing on a daily basis, based on the day to day balance showing on the credit card.

Credit card companies usually charge interest on credit cards as soon as a purchase is made. However, as long as the balance is paid in full each month, most cards offer an interest-free period – the time between the purchase date and statement date, and/or the time between the statement date and payment due date.

The Consumer Credit Act 1974 governs credit cards in the UK. This legislation offers several safeguards for consumers, including a five-day cooling off period. Section 75 of the Act gives consumers protection for card purchases between £100 and £30,000 in the case of a breach of contract or misrepresentation by the seller. If the consumer cannot get a refund from the retailer, then the law holds the credit card company liable and they must then issue the refund.

STAMP DUTY

Regional stamp duty charges

Stamp Duty Land Tax (SDLT) is payable on purchases of land or property in England, Wales, and Northern Ireland. The tax applies to purchases above £125,000 for residential property and land, and £150,000 for non-residential land and property. Different rates apply to second property purchases or buy-to-let.

Tax on residential property purchases in England, Wales, and Northern Ireland

Property or lease premium or transfer value	SDLT rate
Up to £125,000	0%
The next £125,000 (from £125,001 to £250,000)	2%
The next £675,000 (from £250,001 to £925,000)	5%
The next £575,000 (from £925,001 to £1.5 million)	10%
The remaining amount (portion above £1.5 million)	12%

In Scotland, the equivalent of SDLT is Land and Buildings Transaction Tax (LBTT), which came into effect from 1 April 2015. The rate percentages are the same as for the rest of the UK, but the band thresholds are different.

Tax on residential property purchases, Scotland

Purchase price	LBTT rate
Up to £145,000	0%
Above £145,000 to £250,000	2%
Above £250,000 to £325,000	5%
Above £325,000 to £750,000	10%
Over £750,000	12%

Pensions

The UK government offers a pension to UK citizens who have made sufficient contributions towards their National Insurance during their working lives. Private pension options are available, sometimes augmented by employers.

The new state pension

A new UK pension system was introduced in April 2016 – the New State Pension with a maximum weekly payout of £155.65. This only applies to those who reached retirement age on or after 6 April 2016. Existing retirees were not affected and continue to receive the old state pension, comprising a basic payment of £119.30, plus an average of £40 for those who paid into the Second State Pension (also known as the State Earnings Related Pension, or SERPS).

To receive the minimum level of New State Pension, pensioners will need to have paid National Insurance contributions for 10 years. In order to receive the full state pension of £155.65, contributors will need to have paid in for 35 years. Those who have not paid in for this length of time will receive a pro rata amount based on the number of years they have paid in, as long as they meet the 10-year minimum requirement. This figure is calculated by multiplying the number of years that contributions were made by £4.45 (£155.65 divided by 35 years).

National Insurance

National Insurance contributions are payable when earnings exceed £155 a week. Income tax and National Insurance contributions are automatically deducted and paid to HMRC by employers, but the self-employed are responsible for paying in their own. Any gaps in National Insurance can be topped up in order to meet the minimum requirement, and those who have been unable to work due to illness, disability, unemployment, or being a carer, can apply for National Insurance credits. Usually a six-year time limit is imposed for top-ups to any tax year. For example, the deadline for top-ups for the tax year 2015–2016 is 2022.

The 2016 changes to the state pension also affect the age of retirement, and the options for accessing pension pots once retirees are eligible. Women reach retirement age later than previously. In 2018, the pension age for women will be 65, in line with the retirement age for men. By 2020, the retirement age for both sexes will rise to 66, and then to 67 by 2028.

When it comes to private pensions, including employer schemes, retirees will have more flexibility as to what money can be spent on. Until April 2015, retirees could take their pension pot as a lump sum and use it to buy an annuity – a life insurance company is given the pension and pays out a regular monthly income. Under new rules, that pension pot can be used for a lump sum withdrawal instead of spent on an annuity. The downside of an annuity is that when a retiree dies, the annuity dies with them; the upside is guaranteed income for life. On the other hand, a lump sum drawdown allows retirees to leave some money behind for loved ones after their deaths, and the rest of the money can be used for investment or pleasure.

Private pensions

The government encourages workers to pay into a private pension fund by offering tax incentives. Contributions to private pension schemes are usually tax-free up to a certain limit (*see box*) and this applies to most schemes. In the UK there are two main private pension categories: workplace pensions, where employers pay in as part of the employee's salary package, and private pensions that employees pay into, which may be offered via the workplace.

In private pension schemes, a contract is made directly with the insurance provider, whereas with a workplace pension the employer sets up the insurance contract and pays in on the employee's behalf. If the employee leaves their job they can transfer the accrued funds to a new scheme, or continue paying in to the workplace scheme, even though they are no longer an employee at the company.

Stakeholder pensions were introduced in 2001 as a simpler, more affordable personal pension option. Aimed at low-income earners in particular, these pensions must adhere to a set of government guidelines. These include capping charges at 1.5 per cent a year for the first 10 years.

SIPPs

One of the most popular types of personal pensions is the Self-Invested Personal Pension (SIPP). SIPPs offer more investment opportunities than most personal pensions, though charges are often higher. Contributors can build their own investment portfolio by investing in a wide range of assets, including listed shares of UK and overseas companies, unlisted shares, collective investments such as unit trusts, investments and trusts, insurance bonds, and real estate (but not residential property).

Once the SIPP is up and running the pension holder can monitor investment assets and make changes to them depending on their performance. SIPP providers differ in their choice of assets; those offering the fullest array of options within HMRC guidelines are generally managed through a financial adviser.

Retirement annuity contracts and buyout policies

Retirement annuity contracts and buyout policies are older types of pension funds no longer open to new investors. Providers are obliged to pay out a minimum guaranteed sum. Buyout policies were introduced in the early 1980s, but later phased out on 6 April 1988 when personal pensions were introduced. Retirement annuities were launched in 1970, but also wound down in 1988 when personal pensions came onto the market.

TAX RELIEF AND LIVING ABROAD

Tax breaks on private pensions

Tax relief is given on contributions to private pension schemes. Contributors must ensure, however, that their scheme is registered with HMRC, as it will otherwise not be eligible for tax relief. In addition, the pension provider must invest according to HMRC's rules. Personal pension schemes must be registered with the Financial Conduct Authority (FCA) and stakeholder pensions with the Pensions Regulator. A private pension can usually be drawn on between the age of 60 and 65, depending on the provider. From the age of 55, up to 25 per cent of the total fund may be withdrawn as a tax-free lump sum.

Contributions to private pensions are tax free for:
• up to 100 per cent of your earnings per year
• up to £40,000 per year
• up to £1 million over your lifetime

Tax allowances can be topped up with unused allowance from the previous three tax years. However, if money is withdrawn from the pension pot, the full tax allowance will be lost – usually dropping from £40,000 to £10,000. There are no restrictions on the number of pension funds that may be paid into, but the tax relief thresholds apply to the total contributions made to all funds.

Retiring abroad

UK citizens living overseas can claim a pension within four months of retirement age, provided they have paid in the requisite National Insurance contributions. The pension can be paid into an overseas bank account or a UK account. Retirees to the European Economic Area, Gibraltar, Switzerland, or a country with reciprocal social security rights, will have a pension that continues to be index linked, so it keeps pace with inflation. Retirees in countries that do not have reciprocal pension rights will have their payments frozen at the rate they were when they initially left the UK.

Index

Page numbers in **bold** refer to main entries.

24-hour-maturity money market funds 87

A

absolute return funds 185
accountability **112–13**
Accounting Reference Date (ARD) 235
accounting standards, UK 234
accounting year 235
accounts payable 39
accounts receivable 39
active income 158, 160
actively managed funds 168, 185
AER (Annual Equivalent Rate) 208, 210
ageing population 201
ageing schedule 39
alcohol, tax on 126, 241
Alternative Investment Market (AIM) 232,
   233
amortization **32–3**
analysis, market 62–3
Anderson, Philip J 179
angel investors 41
annual reports 44
annuities 197, 202, **203**, 246, 247
annuity repayment mortgages 212
antiques 175
APR (Annual Percentage Rate) 208, 210, 211
arbitrage **64–5**
Argentina, debt default 146–7
Asia, global data analysis 63
assets
  allocation and diversification 186, **188–9**
  asset classes 186, 189
  asset correlation 194, 195
  balance sheets 44–5
  bank 88, 89
  and capital expenditure 30
  depreciation of 27, 29, **32–3**, 206
  intangible 32, 33
  investment for income 162–3
  and managed funds 168
  and net worth 152–3
  personal 152–3
  purchasing vs leasing 33
  risk and return 194–5
  sale of 37
  and wealth 155
auditors 112

B

balance of payments **136–7**
balance sheets
  banks 88, 89
  corporate 34, 44–5
balance transfer 219
Bank of England 19, 125, 221, **236–7**
bank reserves 86, **90–91**
banknotes 13, 236, 237
bankruptcy 39, 41, 207
banks
  assets and liabilities 88, 89
  central **100–103**
  charges 29, 73
  commercial and mortgage **72–3**
  compared to credit unions 217
  deposits 57
  in a depression 95
  increasing money circulation 88–9
  investment banks **74–5**
  loans 37, 88, 89
  making and losing money 75
  and money market 56–7
  runs on 72
  surcharge on profits 241
  traditional 83
Barings Bank 53
barter 12, **14–15**, 16
base rate 100–103, 120–23, 236
bear markets 182
below market value (BMV) 176, 179
Bernanke, Ben 99
bid-offer spread 69, 76
bitcoin 19, 221, 222, **224–5**, 243
blockchains 222, 225
blogging 159
bonds
  central banks and 102–3
  fixed-rate 167
  government 108
  interest from 158
  investing in 47, **50–51**, 54, 80, 186
borrowing
  and capital spending 131
  companies 42–3
  cost of 121, 206
  government 96, 104, 105, **108–9**, 131, 142
  loans 210–11
  money market 56–7

mortgages 212–15
  peer-to-peer lending 228–9
  restrictions on 98
  ways to borrow money 204–5
Borsa Italiana 232
Börse Frankfurt (FWB) 55
bottom line 29
Brexit 59, 71, 235, 236, 237
broad money 96, 97
brokers/brokerage 54, 60, 61, 71, **76–7**
  investment banks 74
  peer-to-peer lending 228
Brown, Gordon 236
budget
  annual government 112
  budget balance 97
  budget constraint **104–5**
  budget deficit 104, 128
  personal **157**, 160
Buffett, Warren 31, 163
building societies 83
bull markets 182, 183
business rates 238–9
businesses
  corporate accounting **26–45**
  expansion 42–3
  investment in 39, 161
  registration 234
  VAT 240
buy-to-let (BTL) mortgages 176, 244
buy-to-sell mortgages 176
Buying, Refurbishing, and Refinancing
  strategy (BRR) 179
buyout policies 247

C

Call Notice Deposit Account 240
capital 36
capital account (BOP) 136, 137
capital expenditure 30, 37, 130–31
capital flight 138
capital gain 47, 159, 177, 179, 186
capital gains tax 241
capital gearing 40–41
capital reserves 72, 73, 98
capital risk 192, 193
capitalizing vs expensing 27, **30–31**
cash 186
  advances 219
  in bank accounts 174

conversion 38, 39
lump sums (pensions) 197, 202
cash flow 26, **36–9**
gap 39
management of 38–9
positive and negative 38–9
central banks **100–103**, 112
Bank of England **236–7**
and banking reserves 90
and base rate 120, 122–3, 236
case for independent 99
and money supply 98, 99
and negative interest rate 123
support for commercial banks 88
transparency and accountability 113
certificate of deposit 57, 165
Child Trust Funds 242
children
cost of 152, 153, 162, 198, 199
savings accounts 242
China, economic slowdown 71
claims, insurance 79
Classical School 23
coinage 12, 16–19
"coins", virtual 222, 223
collateral 180
commercial banks 71, **72–3**
and central banks 100–103, 113, 121, 124
interest rates 121
lending 98
loans 88, 89
negative interest rates 123
reserve rates 90
commercial loan providers 82
commercial paper 57
commercial property 178
commodities 54
commodity-backed currency 87
Companies House **234**, 235
company finance
bonds 50–51, 237
cash flow 36–9
corporate accounting **26–45**, **234–5**
depreciation, amortization and depletion
32–3
derivatives 52–3
expensing vs capitalizing 30–31
financial reporting 44–5
gearing ratio and risk 40–41
how companies use debt 42–3
and investment banks 74–5
issuing shares 182, 183
large-, medium- and small-cap 188
and money market 56–7
net income 28–9
pensions 196–7, 200

share dividends 164–5
shares 48–9
smoothing earnings 34–5
tax submissions 235
United Kingdom **232–5**
comparative advantage 21
competitors 62
compound interest 208–9
Consolidated Fund 236
Consumer Credit Act (1974) 245
Consumer Price Index (CPI) 120
consumption expenditure 114
consumption, government 97
contingent liabilities 153
contractionary policy 93
copyright 235
corporate advisory division (investment
banks) 74, 75
corporate finance see company finance
corporation tax 37, 126, 234, **235**, 238, 241
cost of living 132
cost-push inflation 132–3
costs
as assets 30–31
property 170–71
council revenue 238–9
council tax 238
coupons 50, 51
credit access 103
credit cards 18, 155, 204, **218–19**
charges 73
debt 207
fraud 219
UK 245
credit checks 82
credit crunch 92, 215
credit guidance 102, 103
credit limit 219
credit money 88
credit rating 160, 177, **205**, 207, 216
credit report 176
credit unions 83, 205
creditors 41, 43
cross-selling 73
crowdfunding 83, 188, 220, 221, **226–7**
cryptocurrency 220, **222–5**, 243
currency 46
central banks 100
in circulation 86, 99
commodity-backed 87
confidence in value of 97
digital 220, 221
fiat 87, 220
foreign exchange and trading 58–9
international currency fluctuations 138–9
representative 87

reserve 139
traditional 222
UK 236
UK stock of foreign 236
currency pairs 59
currency values 55
current accounts
balance of payments 136, 137
commercial banks 72, 73
credit unions 217
non-bank financial institutions 83
customs duty 241
cuts, vs spending 128

Dalio, Ray 189
day trading **68–9**
dealers 61
debasement 18
debentures 163
debit cards 88, 204
debt **204–19**
attitude to 157
credit cards 218–19
credit unions 216–17
finance 41
and gearing ratio 40–41
government default 142–3, 146–7
government repayment 97, 108, 109
how companies use 42–3
interest and compound interest 208–9
internal and external 111
loans 210–11
managing personal 151, 157
mortgages 212–15
and net worth 152–3
public debt 110–11
spirals 146–7
taxpayers' 239
ways to borrow money 204–5
and wealth 155
why we use debt 206–7
default 51, 109, 110, 111, 142, **146–7**, 211
deficit
government 104, 109, 110, 128
pension funds 141
defined benefit pension schemes 197, 198,
200
defined contribution pension schemes 198,
200
deleverage 41
demand-pull inflation 132, 134–5
demographics 141
Department for Business, Energy &

Industrial Strategy 234
depletion **32–3**
deposit (property) 176, 244
deposit accounts 56, 87, 166–7
deposit liabilities 90
depreciation 27, 29, **32–3**
depression **94–5**
derivatives 47, **52–3**
designs, registered 235
digital money 13, 18, **220–29**
 bitcoin 224–5
 crowdfunding 226–7
 cryptocurrency 222–3
 peer-to-peer lending 228–9
 tax on 243
dilution 41
direct taxes 106, 135, 238
discount brokers 76, 187
discount mortgages 215
disposable income 114
diversification 80, 169, 188–9
dividends
 commercial banks 72, 73
 dividend cover 165
 investment banks 75
 managed funds 185
 shareholders' funds 45
 shares 36, 38, 42, 43, 46, 48, 49, 68, 81,
  154, 158, 159, **164–5**, 174, 175, 186
dollar (pound) cost averaging 187, **190–91**
domestic expenditure 115
donations 37
double entry bookkeeping 88, **89**
Dow Jones 169
drip-feeding money 187, 190

E

early repayment charges 211
earnings 154, 156
 inflating 29
 per share 28, 29
 reported 31, 34
 volatile 34
economic indicators 114, **116–17**
economic policy 118–19
economic variables 119
economics, modern **20–21**
education
 costs 152, 155, 162, 199
 government investment in 131
effective demand 134, 135
effective tax rate 126
efficient frontier 194–5
Einstein, Albert 209

elderly parents 199
endowments 173
energy
 cost of 132
 government investment in 130
Enron 35
entry unit price 185
equipment 37
equities 80
 over investment in 141
equity
 finance 40
 home **180–81**
 property 213
Eretheum 221
Euro 19
Euronext 55
European Central Bank 100
European Patent Office 235
European Union, retirement in 247
excess (insurance) 79
excess reserves 90
exchange rates
 central banks and 100
 and inflation 133
 international currency fluctuations 138–9
excise duty 107
exit unit price 185
expansionary policy 93
expected return 195
expenses
 as assets 30–31
 corporate 27, 29
 property 170–71
expensing vs capitalizing 27, **30–31**
exports 115, 135
external debts 111

F

face value 50, 51
factors 39
fiat currency 87, 220
financial account (BOP) 136, 137
financial advisors 151, 187, 199, 200
Financial Conduct Authority 83, 244
financial institutions **70–83**
 brokerages 76–7
 commercial and mortgage banks 72–3
 insurance risk and regulation 78–9
 investment banks 74–5
 investment companies 80–81
 non-bank financial institutions 82–3
financial instruments **46–53**
 bonds 50–51

derivatives 52–3
 shares 48–9
financial markets **54–69**
 arbitrage 64–5
 day trading 68–9
 foreign exchange and trading 58–9
 manipulating the stock market 66–7
 the money market 56–7
 predicting market changes 62–3
 primary and secondary markets 60–61
financial reporting **44–5**
Financial Reporting Council (FRC) 234
Financial Services Authority (FSA) 233
financial statements 35
financing cash flow 39
first-time buyers 244–5
fiscal policy 112
Fisher, Irving 22
fixed rate bonds 167
fixed-rate mortgages 214, 244
flotation 36, 48, 60, 61, 165
focus groups 159
foreign balance 115
foreign exchange and trading **58–9**, 236
foreign reserves 139
forex markets 58–9
fourth markets 61
fractional reserves 90–91
fraud
 credit card 219
 pension 203
 prevention 234–5
Friedman, Milton 23, 118, 133
FTSE 100 76, 165, 169, 187, **232**
FTSE 350 232
FTSE All-share 169, 233
FTSE Fledgling 233
FTSE SmallCap 232–3
fund companies 187
fund managers 80–81, 169, 184
fund supermarkets 187
fundamental analysis 62, 63
funding level, pensions 141
fundraising 226
funds
 investment 47
 managed **168–9**
futures 52, 54, 163

G

gambling tax 241
Garfield, James 86
gearing ratio 27, **40–41**
Germany, hyperinflation 144–5

gilts 50
global data analysis 63
global financial crisis 35, 75, 82, 92,
    128, 215
global payment networks 204
goals, setting financial 150
gold reserves 236
Gold Standard 18, 95
Google 47
government bonds 50, 102–3, 108
government repurchase agreements 87
government-backed (fiat) currency 87
governments
    borrowing 108–9
    financial failure **142–7**
    loss of trust 142–3
    and money 98–9
    providing for the future 130–31
    raising money 105
    spending 96, 97, 115, **128–9**, 135, **241**
    see also public finance
Graham, Benjamin 191
grants 37
Great Depression (1929–41) **94–5**
Greece, economic crisis 71, 127, 146, 147
Gresham, Sir Thomas/Gresham's Law 19
grey economy 126, 127
Gross Domestic Product (GDP) 93, 94, 116,
    138, 139, 237
Gross National Income (GNI) 115
growth 116
guarantees 75
guarantors 213

H

Hamilton, Alexander 109
Hayek, Friedrich 23
hedge funds 56, 61, 65, 75, 188, **233**
hedging 52, 63
Help to Buy mortgage scheme 244
high gearing 40–41
high net worth individual (HNWI) 153
High-Frequency Traders (HFT) 64, 65
HMRC (Her Majesty's Revenue and
    Customs) 234, **238–9**, 246, 247
HMT (Her Majesty's Treasury) 236,
    238
home equity **180–81**
home equity loan 180
Hong Kong Stock Exchange (SEHK) 55
household expenditure 154
hyperinflation 97, 142, 143, **144–5**

I

illiquidity 54, 60
imports 115
income
    from managed funds 168–9
    from pensions 202–3
    from savings 150, 166–7
    from share dividends 164–5
    generating **158–9**
    investments for **162–73**, 174
    national 114–15
    personal 150
    rental income from property 170–71
    and wealth **154–7**, 160, 161
income drawdown 197, 202, **203**
income tax 106, 126, 238
independence, financial 150–51
index arbitrage 169
index funds 169, 185
indirect taxes 106, 107, 133, 135, 238,
    240–41
Individual Savings Accounts (ISAs) 242, 245
industrial organization 13
industries, subsidised 128
inflation 13, 18, 102, **132–5**
    and debt 110, 111
    as economic indicator 116
    and exchange rate 138, 139
    government targets 120
    hyperinflation 97, 142, 143, **144–5**
    inflation risk 193
    inflation targeting 100, 119
    and interest rates 121, 122
    and pensions 200
    and quantitative easing 125
    rate of 100
    UK 237
    and unemployment 118–19
infrastructure spending 128
inheritance tax 173, 238, 241, **242–3**
Initial Public Offering (IPO) 48, 60, 61, 75,
    183
insolvency by overtrading 38
instalment credit 204
instant access savings 86, 166
insurance
    against loss 46, 47
    costs 31, 157
    insurance companies 70
    life 172
    property 170
    risk and regulation **78–9**
insurance premium tax (IPT) 241
intellectual property law **235**

inter-bank lending rate 57, 121
interest
    and compound interest **208–9**
    on credit cards 218–19, 245
    from managed funds 168
    on government debt 108, 110
    as income 154, 159
    on investments 174, 186
    on loans 43, 210–11
interest cover ratio 41
interest rates **120–23**
    central banks and 98, 100–103, 113,
        120–21, 124, 236–7
    commercial banks 29, 72–3
    and debt 206, 207
    and exchange rates 138, 139
    fluctuating 122, 167
    and government borrowing 108–9, 114
    impact of changing 122–3
    and inflation 121
    mortgages 72, 177, 214–15
    profitable 72
    and quantitative easing 124, 125
    raising/cutting 119, 122–3, 135
    and risk of default 146
    spread 102
interest risk 193
interest-only mortgages 213
interim reports 62
internal debts 111
international agreements 107
International Monetary Fund (IMF) 146, 147
Internet 220
investing cash flow 39
investment
    bonds 50–51
    in business 36, 161
    company funding 42–3
    day trading 68–9
    derivatives 52–3
    dollar cost averaging 190–91
    earning income from savings 166–7
    financial instruments 46–7
    fluctuating values 185
    forex 58–9
    from income 191
    goals 192
    government 97, 114
    income-generating 151, **162–73**
    investment companies 80–81
    managed funds 168–9, 184–5
    managing 161, **186–203**
    money market 56–7
    and pensions 198–201
    predicting the stock market 62–3
    in property **176–9**

rental property 170–71
returns 189
risk tolerance 192–3
shares 48–9, 54, 60–61, 164–5, 182–3
and state pensions 140–41
tax breaks on 242
and wealth 154, 155, 157, 159, 161
wealth-building **174–85**
investment assets 152
investment banks 71, **74–5**
investment companies **80–81**
investment forums 67
investment funds 80
investor types 192–3
"invisible hand" 20–21
IOUs **14–15**, 16
Islamic mortgages 213

J

Japan Stock Exchange (JPX) 55
jewellery, investing in 155
joint-stock companies 19
Junior ISAs 242
junk bonds 51

K

Keynes, John Maynard 22–3

L

Laffer, Arthur/Laffer curve 127
laissez-faire 20, 21
land tax 238, 241
landfill tax 238, 241
landlords 170–71
late fees 211
latent demand 134
leasing, assets 33
legal tender 236
Lehman Brothers 35, 71
lender of last resort 100, 236
leverage 59, 206
liabilities
  balance sheets 44–5, 141
  bank 88, 89
  personal 152–3
Libor 57, 67
life assurance **172–3**
life insurance **172**
life settlement 172
lifecycle ("debt phase") 43
lifestyle 156, 192

lifestyling **163**
liquid assets 152
liquid shares 68–9, 76
liquidity 38, 61, 76, 189
  liquidity trap 95
  and net worth 153
listed (shares) 48, 168
living abroad, tax relief **247**
living standards 98, 117, 150, 151, 198
loan-to-value (LTV) rate 180, 205, 213
loans
  bank 88, 89
  brokers 210
  corporate 41, 47
  cost of 122, 123
  credit unions 216, 217
  and debt 155, 204, 210–11
  government 47
  interest on 72, 73
  loan agreements 211
  money market and 56–7
  and property value and equity 181
  repayments 36, 37, 210
  secured 121
  types of 204
  unsecured 121
  see also mortgages
London Stock Exchange (LSE) 55, 61, 65, 182, **232–3**
Long-Term Capital Management (LTCM) 65
long-term liabilities 152
low gearing 40–41
lump sum investment 190, 191
lump sum, pension 246

M

macroeconomics 13
Madoff, Bernie 35
Main Market (LSE) 232–3
maintenance, property 170, 171, 177
managed funds 174, 183, **184–5**
  investing in 163, **168–9**
margin call 59
margin trading 69
marginal tax rate 126
market capitalization 188
market changes, predicting **62–3**
market conditions 190, 191
market data 69
market equilibrium 20–21
market index 169
market makers 61
market power 134
market research groups 159

market value 50, 51, 176, 181
Marx, Karl 22
Mazacoin 221
mercantilism 20, **21**
mergers and acquisitions 75
microeconomics 13
miners 220, 222, 223, 224
minimum monthly deposit accounts 166
minimum repayments 218
Monetary Policy Committee (MPC) 237
money
  artefacts of 16–19
  barter, IOUs and 14–15
  characteristics of 16
  in circulation 88–9, 123
  creation of new 124
  in the digital age **220–29**
  economic theories of 22–3
  economics of 18–19
  evolution of **12–23**
  hoarding 95
  inflation and velocity of 134
  printing 96, **97**, 104, 105, 143, 236
  purchasing power 132
  value of 15, 16, 17
money market **56–7**
money market deposits 167
money market funds 57
money supply 13, **86–95**
  banking reserves 90–91
  central banks and 98, 100, 102–3, 236
  government and 98–9
  increasing money circulation 88–9
  recession and the money supply 92–3
  recession to depression 94–5
MONIAC 114, 115
mortgage banks **72–3**
Mortgage Market Review 244
mortgages 155, 157, 198, 199, 205, **212–15**
  buy-to-let 176
  buy-to-sell 176
  choosing 177
  and home equity 180–81
  interest rates 122
  Islamic 213
  mortgage rates 214–15
  sub-prime 92, 215
  types of 212–13
  UK 244–5
MSCI EAFE 169
MTS 232
multi-sector funds 168
multiplier effect 91

N

narrow money 86
the Nasdaq 61
national income 115
National Insurance (NI) 106, 140, **240–41**, 246
natural resources 32–3, 136
negative cash flow 39
negative equity 181, 213
negative interest 193
negative interest rate policy (NIRP) 123
negative net worth 153
net income 26, **28–9**, 106
net worth 150, **152–3**
New State Pension 240, 246
New York Stock Exchange (NYSE) 49, 55, 60, 61, 64
nominal rate 121
nominal values 133
non-bank financial institutions 70, **82–3**
not-for-profit organizations 205, 216, 217
notice savings accounts 72, 87, 166

O

offset mortgages 213
online brokers 76
online market places 159, 182
open market operations 98, 100, 103
operating cash flow 39
operating expenses (property) 176
optimal portfolios 187, **194–5**
options 52, 54, 163
ordinary shares 163
outgoings 154–5, 156, 157
over 24-hour-maturity money market funds 87
overdrafts 37, 73
overheads 36
overleverage 41

P

partnerships 234
passive income 158, **159**, 160
passively managed funds 168
patents 235
pawnbrokers 83
payday loans 210
PAYE system (pay as you earn) 238
payroll tax 37
peer-to-peer lending 82, 166, 167, 220, 221, **228–9**
pension contributions 199

pensions **196–203**
    consolidating 203
    converting into income 202–3
    pension funds 61, 201
    saving and investing for 198–201
    and share prices 183
    UK 246–7
    see also private pensions; state pensions
personal finance **148–229**
    debt 204–19
    income-generating investments 162–73
    managing investments 186–95
    money in the digital age 220–29
    pensions and retirement 196–203
    United Kingdom 242–7
    wealth-building investments 174–85
    worth, wealthy and income 150–61
personal loans 204
Personal Savings Allowance 242
Phillips, Bill 114
Pigou, Arthur/Pigouvian tax 126
pledges, online 227
portfolios
    asset allocation and diversification 188–9
    brokers' fees for managing 76
    diversified 80
    investment 47, 79, 162
    optimal 187, **194–5**
    portfolio income 159
    portfolio weighting 187, 189, 195
    rebalancing 175, 195
positive cash flow 38
positive equity 180
positive net worth 153
preference shares 163, 165
premiums, insurance 78, 79
prices
    hyperinflation 144–5
    inflation 116, 132–5
    and market equilibrium 20–21
    price data 63
    price stability 100, 120
    property 135
primary markets **60–61**
private investment 131
private pensions 196–7, 198
    tax breaks on 247
    UK 246–7
privatization 131
Professional Securities Market (PSM) 232
profit
    downturn in 34
    margins 72
    reported 34
    and share dividends 165
    steady increase in 35

profit and loss accounts 34, 35
profiting 55
Proof of Stake 223
Proof of Work 223
property
    buying and selling for profit 178
    commercial vs residential 178
    home equity 180–81
    incentive schemes 244–5
    investment in 161, **176–9**
    mortgages **212–15**
    prices 135
    property cycle 178–9
    property market 80, 176, 178
    rental income 155, 163, **170–71**, 186
    and wealth-building 175
protectionism **21**
provision, making 34
public companies 60, 183
public debt **110–11**
public finance
    attempting control **114–41**
    managing state finance **96–113**
    money supply **86–95**
    United Kingdom **236–41**
    why governments fail financially **142–7**
public services 104–5
public trust, loss of 142–3, 144

Q

quantitative easing (QE) 98, 114, **124–5**, 237
quoted shares 48, 182

R

raw materials, cost of 132, 133
real profit 28
real rate 121
real values 133
real-estate cycle, 18-year 179
real-time trading 77
recession 146, 215
    and depression **94–5**
    and money supply **92–3**
regulation
    banks 82, 83, 92
    credit cards 245
    insurance industry 79
    London Stock Exchange 233
    mortgage products 215
    peer-to-peer lending 221
remortgage 213
rental income 154, 158, 159, 163, **170–71**, 174, 186

repairs, property 170, 171
repayment mortgages 212
representative currency 87
reserve currency 139
reserve rates 100–103
reserve ratio 90, 98, 102
reserves, banking **90–91**, 124–5
residential property 178
retirement 156, 157, **196–203**
  abroad 247
  age of 161, 196, 246
  managing state pensions 140–41
  planning for financial independence
    150–51
  see also pensions; state pensions
retirement annuity contracts 247
returns
  on assets 88, 113, 188, 189, 198
  credit unions 217
  crowdfunding 227
  government 130, 131
  on investment 40, 47, 51, 79, 81, 130, 131,
    141, 154, 161, 162, 174, 186, 198
  managed funds 168, 169, 185
  optimal portfolios 194–5
  peer-to-peer lending 228
  pensions 201, 203
  on property 176, 177, 178
  savings and deposit accounts 159, 162,
    163
  snowball effect 208
  standard deviation of 191
  vs risk 166, 187, 192–3, 194
  see also yield
revenue
  analysis 62
  government 96, 115
  and net income 28
  and taxation 106
reverse annuity mortgages 212
revolving credit 204, 219
Ricardo, David 21
Right to Buy scheme 244
Riksbank (Sweden) 103, 236
Ripple 221
risk
  balancing with rewards 187, 189, 194–5
  control 46
  gearing ratio and 40–41
  insurance 78–9
  investments 47, 162–3, 186
  and managed funds 168, 169
  peer-to-peer lending 229
  risk tolerance 187, **192–3**
rogue traders 55, **66–7**
Roosevelt, Franklin D 95

Royal Mint 19
royalty payments 159
RPI (Retail Price Index) 238–9
RSCoin 221
Russian financial crisis 65

S

safeguarding 228
salaries and wages 13, 31, 36, 117, 154, 156,
  158
  cost of 132, 133
sales predictions 38
sales revenue 36
sales tax 37
Sargent, Thomas 145
savings
  credit unions 216, 217
  earning income from 162, 163, **166–7**
  from income 150, 154, 155
  interest rates 121, 123
  and investing for a pension **198–201**
  regular savings plans 185
  savings accounts 72, 73, 159, 162–3
  savings bonds 50, 51
  savings rates 72
  tax on 242
  and wealth 154, 155, 156, 157, 160, 161
scalping 69
scandals
  accounting 35
  Libor 67
scientific research 128, 131
Second State Pension 246
secondary markets 60, **61**, 68, 102
secured loans 121, 204, 210
securities 51, 60, 76, 80, 101
seed capital 43
Shanghai Stock Exchange (SSE) 55
shareholders
  London Stock Exchange 232
  payments to 36, 48, 49
  say in running of companies 182
shares
  arbitrage 64–5
  as assets 155
  brokerage 76–7
  buying 54
  day trading 68–9
  dividends from **164–5**
  earnings per share 28
  as financial instruments 46, **48–9**
  and gearing ratio 40
  guarantees 75
  high risk investment 163

  how to buy 182–3
  investment in **182–3**, 186
  issuing 42
  liquid 68–9, 76
  manipulating prices 66–7
  predicting market changes 62–3
  primary and secondary markets 60–61
  repurchases 36
  stock exchange 54–5
  unsold 61
  and wealth-building 175
  why share prices matter 183
sharesave schemes 182
Shenzhen Stock Exchange (SZSE) 55
shopping 157
short selling 66
short-term liabilities 152
Simmel, Georg 17
single asset funds 168
SIPPs (Self-Invested Personal Pension) 198,
  247
slump 34
Smith, Adam 14, 20–21
smoothing earnings 26, **34–5**
social housing 131
soft drinks, tax on 126–7, 241
specialist lenders 83
Specialist Market Fund (SMF) 232
speculation 52, 53
spending
  government 96, 97, 115, **128–9**, 135
  increasing/cutting 119
  personal 156–7
  vs cuts 128
  and wealth 156, 160
spread (forex) 59
stakeholder pensions 247
stamp duty 241, **245**
Standard & Poor's 500 169
standard deviation 195
standard of living 98, 117, 150, 151, 198
standard variable rate (SVR) mortgages 214
start-ups 43
Starter Homes initiative 245
State Earnings Related Pension (Serps) 246
state finance, managing **96–113**
  accountability 112–13
  budget constraint 104–5
  the central bank 100–103
  government borrowing 108–9
  governments and money 98–9
  how tax works 106–7
  public debt 110–11
state pensions 198, 201
  managing **140–41**
  National Insurance contributions 240, 246

New State Pension 240, 246
and retirement 196–7
UK 246
statements, company 44–5
stock exchanges 48–9, **54–5**
London Stock Exchange **232–3**
stock liquidity 67
stock market
crashes 201
financial markets **54–5**
manipulating **66–7**
predicting **62–3**
shares **48–9**, 182, 183
stockbrokers 182, 183
stocks 48
see also shares
stop loss 59
strategic asset allocation 188
sub-prime mortgages 92, 215
subsidies, government 128
superannuation 163, 174
suppliers, payment of 37
supply and demand 13, 134
surplus 110

tax-free deposits 167
taxation 96, **106–7**
and behaviour 106, 126
and cash flow 37
corporation tax 235
council tax 238
and government funds/debt 104–5, 108,
109, 110, 114, 128
increasing/cutting 118, 133, 135
indirect taxes 241
level of **126–7**
living abroad 247
and money supply 98
optimum level of 127
and pensions 197, 200, 202, 247
personal tax 242–3
and state pensions 140
tax collection 239
tax evasion and avoidance 107, 126, 127,
234–5, 239
tax gap 239
tax havens 107
tax rate 107
tax refunds 37
tax relief 126
tax returns 107
tax submissions 235
UK tax system **238–9**

unintended effects of 127
VAT 240–41
technical analysis 62, 63
term deposits 163
term insurance 172
Tesco 29
third markets 61
"tickers" 54
tobacco, tax on 106, 126, 241
Toronto Stock Exchange (TSE) 55
tracker mortgages 215, 244
trade, and money 12, 14–15
trademarks 235
traders 62
trading volumes 63
transatlantic trades 64–5
transparency 113
transport
cost of 132
government investment in 130
traveller's cheques 86
treasury bills 57
trust, public 142–3, 144
Turquoise 232

UK Generally Accepted Accounting
Practices (UK GAAP) 234
UK Listing Authority (UKLA) 233
underwriting 75
unearned income 159
unemployment 13, 93, 117
in a depression 94
and exchange rate 138, 139
and inflation 118–19
and interest rates 122, 123
unit trusts 184
United Kingdom
company finance **232–5**
personal finance **242–7**
public finance **236–41**
units (managed funds) 169, 184, 185
unlisted funds 168
unsecured loans 121, 204
US Bureau of Labor Statistics 117
US dollar 19
utilities, government investment in 130
utility costs 31, 36

variable-rate mortgages 214, 244
variance 195
VAT 37, 106, 107, 238, **240–41**

vault cash 90
velocity of money 134
venture capital 43
viatical settlement 172
volatility 34, 52, 53, 80, 169, 190, 191

wages *see* salaries and wages
Wall Street Crash (1929) 94
wallets, digital 223, 224
Warren, Elizabeth 141
wartime, government debt in 111
wealth **150–61**
calculating and analysing net worth 152–3
generating 160–61
and income 154–9
and managed funds 184–5
and property 176–81
and shares 182–3
wealth-building investments **174–85**
worth, wealth and income 150–51
wear and tear 32, 33
weighting 195
Welch, Jack 35
welfare spending 128
wills 161
Wilshire 5000 169
windfalls 37
WorldCom 35
worldwide markets 71
worth, net 150, 152–3

yield
bonds 50, 51
dividend 164
rental property 170–71
see also returns

Acknowledgments

Dorling Kindersley would like to thank Alexandra Beeden for proofreading, Emma Wicks for design assistance, Phil Gamble for icon design, and Helen Peters for indexing.

Sources of statistics and facts:

Jacket: blogs.spectator.co.uk/2016/09/paper-5-polymer-origins-banknote/; en.wikipedia.org/wiki/List_of_circulating_currencies; www.worldbank.org/en/topic/poverty/overview; en.wikipedia.org/wiki/Crowdfunding; en.wikipedia.org/wiki/1891; money.howstuffworks.com/currency6.htm; en.wikipedia.org/wiki/European_debt_crisis; www.bbc.co.uk/news/business-18944097; www.ilo.org/global/research/global-reports/global-wage-report/2014/lang--en/index.htm; en.wikipedia.org/wiki/Rai_stones; www.worldbank.org/en/news/press-release/2015/04/15/massive-drop-in-number-of-unbanked-says-new-report; manchesterinvestments.com/portfolio-compass-january-20-2016/; www.imf.org/external/pubs/ft/fandd/2014/09/kose.htm

p.13: money.visualcapitalist.com/; **p.19:** www.royalmint.com/bullion/products/gold-sovereign; **p.27:** www.moodys.com/research/Moodys-US-non-financial-corporates-cash-pile-increases-to-168--PR_349330; **p.29:** www.apple.com/uk/pr/library/2016/01/26Apple-Reports-Record-First-Quarter-Results.html; **p.33:** www.theaa.com/motoring_advice/car-buyers-guide/cbg_depreciation.html; **p.39:** www.modestmoney.com/cash-flow-problems-small-business-startups-tackle/9820; **p.41:** www.tutor2u.net/business/reference/gearing-ratio; **p.47:** www.cnbc.com/2015/07/17/googles-one-day-rally-is-the-biggest-in-history.html; **p.49:** www.thetradenews.com/Regions/Asia/Tokyo-needs-foreigners-to-revitalise-volumes/; **p.51:** www.tradingeconomics.com/germany/government-bond-yield; **p.53:** www.prmia.org/sites/default/files/references/Baring_Brothers_Short_version_April_2009.pdf; **p.59:** www.wsj.com/articles/pound-drops-to-31-year-low-against-dollar-on-brexit-concerns-1475566159; **p.60:** www.forbes.com/

sites/ryanmac/2014/09/22/alibaba-claims-title-for-largest-global-ipo-ever-with-extra-share-sales/#7e4c5c887c26; **p.65:** www.dbresearch.com/PROD/DBR_INTERNET_EN-PROD/PROD0000000000406105/High-frequency_trading%3A_Reaching_the_limits.pdf; **p.71:** www.investopedia.com/articles/economics/09/lehman-brothers-collapse.asp#ixzz4M7KQIMTg; **p.72:** www.federalreserve.gov/monetarypolicy/reservereq.htm; **p.76:** www.tdameritrade.com/about-us.page; **p.81:** www.morganstanley.com/im/emailers/media/pdf/liq_sol_updt_012013_rule_2a-7.pdf; **p.83:** www.ey.com/Publication/vwLUAssets/ey-global-consumer-banking-survey/$FILE/ey-global-consumer-banking-survey.pdf; **p.88:** positivemoney.org/how-money-works/how-banks-create-money/; **p.93:** As estimated by former Bank of England Governor Mervyn King, www.telegraph.co.uk/finance/recession/7077442/Recession-Facts-and-figures.html; **p.95:** www.nber.org/chapters/c2258.pdf; **p.97:** www.usgovernmentspending.com/; **p.100:** www.ecb.europa.eu/home/html/index.en.html; **p.103:** www.riksbank.se/en/The-Riksbank/History/Important-date/1590-1668/; **p.105:** www.worldbank.org/en/country/libya/overview; **p.107:** www.forbes.com/sites/frederickallen/2012/07/23/super-rich-hide-21-trillion-offshore-study-says/#386b08de73d3; **p.110:** www.nationaldebtclocks.org/debtclock/unitedstates; **p.115:** fred.stlouisfed.org/series/MKTGNIJPA646NWDB; **p.117:** www.bls.gov/k12/history_timeline.htm; **p.123:** www.tradingeconomics.com/argentina/inflation-cpi; **p.125:** www.aei.org/publication/since-2009-feds-qe-purchases-transferred-almost-half-trillion-dollars-treasury-isnt-gigantic-wealth-transfer/; **p.127:** www.economist.com/news/finance-and-economics/21623742-getting-greeks-pay-more-tax-not-just-hard-risky-treasures; **p.135:** www.federalreserve.gov/faqs/economy_14400.htm; **p.139:** www.dailyfx.com/forex/education/trading_tips/daily_trading_lesson/2014; **p.143:** *This Time It's Different: Eight Centuries of Financial Folly* – Preface Reinhart, Carmen and Rogoff, Kenneth University of Maryland, College Park, Department of Economics, Harvard University

2009; **p.145:** www.globalfinancialdata.com/gfdblog/?p=2382; **p.147:** en.wikipedia.org/wiki/European_debt_crisis; **p.151:** www.forbes.com/sites/jamiehopkins/2014/08/28/not-enough-people-have-financial-advisers-and-new-research-shows-they-should/#4e7ad5fd7648; **p.153:** en.wikipedia.org/wiki/Ultra_high-net-worth_individual; **p.157:** www.forbes.com/sites/afontevecchia/2014/10/02/the-new-forbes-400-self-made-score-from-silver-spooners-to-boostrappers/#2cf326c97d40; **p.164:** siblisresearch.com/data/ftse-all-total-return-dividend/; **p.167:** www.tradingeconomics.com/european-union/personal-savings; **p.175:** manchesterinvestments.com/portfolio-compass-january-20-2016/; **p.176:** en.wikipedia.org/wiki/Subprime_mortgage_crisis; **p.179:** www.thisismoney.co.uk/money/mortgageshome/article-3452615/SIMON-LAMBERT-house-prices-double-15-years.html; **p.180:** www.mybudget360.com/negative-equity-nation-for-1-out-of-5-homeowners-the-psychology-of-the-10-million-american-homeowners-with-zero-equity/; **p.183:** money.cnn.com/2016/04/29/investing/stocks-2nd-longest-bull-market-ever/; **p.194:** en.wikipedia.org/wiki/Efficient_frontier; **p.199:** www.moneysavingexpert.com/savings/discount-pensions; **p.201:** www.un.org/en/development/desa/population/publications/pdf/ageing/WPA2015_Report.pdf; **p.203:** en.wikipedia.org/wiki/1891; **p.205:** themoneycharity.org.uk/money-statistics/; **p.207:** uk.businessinsider.com/eurostat-data-on-household-debt-2016-3; **p.210:** www.theguardian.com/business/2014/dec/16/wonga-cuts-cost-borrowing-interest-rate; **p.213:** ec.europa.eu/eurostat/statistics-explained/index.php/People_in_the_EU_%E2%80%93_statistics_on_housing_conditions#Ownership:_tenure_status; **p.214:** news.bbc.co.uk/1/hi/business/7073131.stm; **p.217:** www.woccu.org/; **p.220:** thefinancialbrand.com/45284/banking-mobile-payments-bitcoin-research/; **p.223:** en.wikipedia.org/wiki/List_of_cryptocurrencies; **p.227:** www.kickstarter.com/about; **p.229:** www.statista.com/statistics/325902/global-p2p-lending/

10·3·17

BETTWS